Kant and the Problem of Nothingness

Bloomsbury Studies in Modern German Philosophy

Series Editors:
Courtney D. Fugate, American University of Beirut, Lebanon
Anne Pollok, University of South Carolina, USA

Editorial Board:
Desmond Hogan (Princeton University, USA)
Ursula Goldenbaum (Emory University, USA)
Robert Clewis (Gwynedd Mercy University, USA)
Paul Guyer (Brown University, USA)
Brandon Look (University of Kentucky, USA)
Eric Watkins (University of California, San Diego, USA)
Corey W. Dyck (University of Western Ontario, Canada)
Stefanie Buchenau (University of Paris, France)
Paola Rumore (University of Turin, Italy)
Heiner Klemme (Martin-Luther-Universität Halle-Wittenberg, Germany)

Central and previously overlooked ideas and thinkers from the German Enlightenment Era are showcased in this series. Expanding research into areas that have been neglected particularly in English-language scholarship, it covers the work of lesser-known authors, previously untranslated texts, and issues that have suffered an undeserved life on the margins of current philosophical-historical discussion about 18th-century German thought.

By opening itself to a broad range of subjects and placing the role of women during this period centre-stage, the series not only advances our understanding about the German Enlightenment and its connection with the pan-European debates, but also contributes to debates about the reception of Newtonian science and the impact of Leibnizian, Kantian and Wolffian philosophies.

Featuring edited collections and single-authored works, and overseen by an esteemed Editorial Board, the goal is to enrich current debates in the history of philosophy and to correct common misconceptions.

Titles in the series include:

Tetens's Writings on Method, Language, and Anthropology, edited by Courtney D. Fugate, Curtis Sommerlatte and Scott Stapleford

Kant's Rational Religion and the Radical Enlightenment, by Anna Tomaszewska

The Human Vocation in German Philosophy, edited by Anne Pollok and Courtney D. Fugate

The Philosophy of Friedrich Heinrich Jacobi, by Birgit Sandkaulen

Hope and the Kantian Legacy, edited by Katerina Mihaylova and Anna Ezekiel

Kant and the Problem of Nothingness

A Latin American Study and Critique

Ernesto Mayz Vallenilla
Translated by Addison Ellis

BLOOMSBURY ACADEMIC
LONDON • NEW YORK • OXFORD • NEW DELHI • SYDNEY

BLOOMSBURY ACADEMIC
Bloomsbury Publishing Plc, 50 Bedford Square, London, WC1B 3DP, UK
Bloomsbury Publishing Inc, 1385 Broadway, New York, NY 10018, USA
Bloomsbury Publishing Ireland, 29 Earlsfort Terrace, Dublin 2, D02 AY28, Ireland

BLOOMSBURY, BLOOMSBURY ACADEMIC and the Diana logo
are trademarks of Bloomsbury Publishing Plc

First published in 1965 in Spain as El Problema de la Nada en Kant
by Editorial Revista de Occidente

First published in Great Britain 2024
This paperback edition published 2025

Copyright © Estate of Ernesto Mayz Vallenilla, 2024

English language translation © Addison Ellis 2024

Addison Ellis has asserted his right under the Copyright, Designs and
Patents Act, 1988, to be identified as Translator of this work.

For legal purposes the Acknowledgments on p. xliii constitute
an extension of this copyright page.

Cover image: Several Circles, 1926. Found in the collection of © Solomon R. Guggenheim
Foundation, New York. (Photo by Fine Art Images/Heritage Images/Getty Images).

All rights reserved. No part of this publication may be: i) reproduced or transmitted in
any form, electronic or mechanical, including photocopying, recording or by means
of any information storage or retrieval system without prior permission in writing from
the publishers; or ii) used or reproduced in any way for the training, development or operation
of artificial intelligence (AI) technologies, including generative AI technologies. The rights
holders expressly reserve this publication from the text and data mining exception as per
Article 4(3) of the Digital Single Market Directive (EU) 2019/790.

Bloomsbury Publishing Inc does not have any control over, or responsibility for,
any third-party websites referred to or in this book. All internet addresses given
in this book were correct at the time of going to press. The author and publisher
regret any inconvenience caused if addresses have changed or sites have
ceased to exist, but can accept no responsibility for any such changes.

A catalogue record for this book is available from the British Library.

ISBN: HB: 978-1-3502-7778-6
PB: 978-1-3502-7781-6
ePDF: 978-1-3502-7779-3
eBook: 978-1-3502-8075-5

Series: Bloomsbury Studies in Modern German Philosophy

Typeset by Integra Software Services Pvt. Ltd.

For product safety related questions contact productsafety@bloomsbury.com.

To find out more about our authors and books visit www.bloomsbury.com
and sign up for our newsletters.

Contents

Translator's Introduction	viii
Glossary of Key Terms	xxxviii
Prologue	xlv
Acknowledgments	xliii
A Note for the Reader	xliv
Introduction	1
1 Nothingness and the Ens Rationis	21
2 Nothingness and the Nihil Privativum	39
3 Nothingness and the Ens Imaginarium	61
4 Nothingness and the *Nihil Negativum*	91
Notes	126
Index of Names and Subjects	152

Translator's Introduction

As I write this introduction, *Kant and the Problem of Nothingness* is still, at least to my knowledge, the only book-length analysis of Kant's massively overlooked discussion of the concepts of "nothing" in the *Critique of Pure Reason*. This very brief portion of the *Critique* serves as the closing piece of the *appendix* to the most important division of the book (the "Transcendental Analytic") entitled "On the amphiboly of the concepts of reflection through the confusion of the empirical use of the understanding with the transcendental." It is perhaps no wonder, then, that it is often overlooked![1] However, not only does Kant's division of "nothing" into its own table (the "table of nothings," or TON hereafter) provoke interesting discussion of the place for nothingness in transcendental philosophy, it is arguably essential for understanding the structure of philosophy itself. A study of Kant's TON makes it apparent that Kant is not operating without a deep understanding of the need for an account of how both "being" *and* "nothing" have a logical place in the system of philosophy. Ever since Parmenides identified thinking and being (thereby ruling out even the possibility of *thinking* nothing), it became necessary to find this logical place for nothingness. This is not lost on Kant, but it has been lost or obscured along the way in Kant scholarship.[2] One place where Kant's discussion of nothing has not been entirely lost is in the meeting place, between twentieth-century Kant studies and the twentieth-century "Continental" tradition. Particularly, Heidegger's intensive study of Kant's *Critique of Pure Reason* at least does not ignore this part of the text. But, in addition to this more well-known study of Kant, a fascinating book examining in great detail Kant's approach to the concept of nothing appeared in the Spanish-speaking world in 1965, written by a Venezuelan philosopher named Ernesto Mayz Vallenilla.

Ernesto Mayz Vallenilla (1925–2015) authored many books along a wide spectrum of philosophical topics. While his best-known philosophical work was on the topics of technology and science, education, and humanism,[3] he notably published focused exegetical texts on Dilthey, Husserl, and Kant.[4] He also wrote widely on the idea of the university, a topic which Mayz Vallenilla knew quite intimately, serving as founding rector (Rector-Fundador) of Simón Bolívar University in Caracas from 1969 to 1979. His academic decorations include having held the UNESCO chair in Philosophy, and, not least, being designated twentieth century's most outstanding Latin American philosopher by the Argentinian Philosophical Society in 2001.

Mayz Vallenilla begins *Kant and the Problem of Nothingness* (*KPN*) with the remark that "To think is to hold a dialogue with problems" (p. xliii). As he spells this out, it becomes clear just how he plans to hold a dialogue with Kant, whose "critical" turn in philosophy was a turn away from a simple beholdenness to the objects. When introducing the central problematic of the *Critique of Pure Reason*, Kant argues that the success of any science (*Wissenschaft*) rests on its ability to know what reason itself puts into it. Hence, even the empirical sciences do not proceed through the mere passive reception of data, but by *compelling* nature to answer its questions, just like a judge who compels the witness to answer his questions under legal oath (Bxiii). For Mayz Vallenilla, holding a dialogue with philosophical problems "means forcing them to reveal the path that leads to their encounter and makes them testify to the truth they hide" (p. xliii, prologue). Indeed, he uses here a term that appears over and over specifically in *Heidegger*—"interrogate" (*befragen*, for Heidegger).[5]

I submit that the best tribute that can be made to a philosopher of Mayz Vallenilla's caliber is to confront and interrogate his own dialogue with the important problems raised in this book. Or, at the very least, to faithfully interpret and hold up Mayz Vallenilla's argument to some questions that may serve the future development of the project that he has initiated for us. In what follows, we will encounter an approach to Kant that is largely absent in the contemporary scholarship, as it presents a distinctive *phenomenological* interpretation of Kant that results from a confluence of variables present in the Latin American philosophical world at the time of the book's publication. We will also see that Mayz Vallenilla's approach is unique in adopting, much like Heidegger before him, an approach of what we might call *sympathetic criticism* (or what Heidegger, with a decidedly different emphasis, would less politely call a "violent" reading[6]). According to *KPN*, Kant's "critical" approach to what Mayz Vallenilla calls "the problem of nothingness" is itself subject to critique, even though Kant had developed basically all of the right tools for the endeavor. In fact, the basis of Mayz Vallenilla's critique is Kant's own transcendental-idealistic insight that all experience has an essentially *temporal* structure. If so, Mayz Vallenilla argues, then insofar as the concepts of nothing are concepts of *knowable and experiencable nothings*, they too must have an essentially temporal structure. But, as the argument goes, this implies that the TON requires a discussion about its *own* kind of temporal structure, even its own *schematism*—one that is not first and foremost a schematism of *ontological* concepts, or concepts of *being*.

With an eye to situating his central argument in relation to Kant's discussion, I will present a brief set of remarks about Mayz Vallenilla's philosophical context, and then focus on presenting an overview of the general problematic of the text as well as Mayz Vallenilla's unique approach to this set of questions. I will conclude by highlighting some important questions that ought to inform our engagement with this text going forward, with Kant in mind, of course.

Mayz Vallenilla and His Context

To begin surveying the environment out of which *KPN* arose, a bit of a (mostly philosophical-) biographical aside will help to orient us. There are two important points which I would like to highlight here. The first is that "official" biographical information regarding Mayz Vallenilla is somewhat scarce. The second point is that the most important thing for the reader to know about Mayz Vallenilla the person is not, I think, any bit of personal biography, but rather what constituted the philosophical context he inhabited when *KPN* was written. The reason for this is simply that what marks the importance of *KPN* is precisely the distinctive philosophical approach it represents. In part, this involves understanding the text just as it is presented here. But, in part, it also helps to see that the text as it is presented represents a philosophical environment unique in its time and place. Hence, I'll say just a few words about this philosophical context before developing an introduction to *KPN*'s argument on its own terms.

Mayz Vallenilla's education took place between Venezuela and Germany. He earned his bachelor's degree in philosophy and literature (*filosofía y letras*) at the Universidad Central de Venezuela in 1950, taking also his Ph.D. there in 1956 with a thesis on Husserl. His education occurred at a time when European philosophy had long since taken root throughout the Spanish-speaking world, thanks to exposure to figures such as Henri Bergson, followed by the massive influence of Spanish philosopher José Ortega y Gasset's twist on the "vitalist" philosophy present in both France and Germany (work that sought to unify figures such as Bergson, Dilthey, Husserl, and Heidegger). For Ortega, at least in this regard, one absolutely central concept was that of *raciovitalismo*, which emphasized what he called *razón vital* (a "vital" or living reason). On this view, in opposition to classical versions of "realism" and "idealism," the unity of thinking and being is determined neither by an abstract faculty of reason nor by an entirely mind-independent reality, but by the organic activity of *human life*.[7] The significance of Ortega for Latin American philosophy is hard to overstate, but in the case of *KPN* the influence is mostly registered only indirectly by Mayz Vallenilla. One concept that may especially signal Ortega's influence here is that of the "intrabody" (*intracuerpo*), which Mayz Vallenilla periodically uses in the text. Ortega's notion of the "intrabody"[8] is a kind of embodied-phenomenological counterpart to the externally visible body. What makes up the intrabody, on Ortega's view, is a complex set of organically unified *inner* bodily awarenesses. Mayz Vallenilla does not credit Ortega with this concept, but uses it in a curiously *Kantian* way by associating the *categories of the understanding* implicitly or explicitly expressed by language, and the *schemata* that mediate categories and intuitions, with the concept of an intrabody. It is plausible, given the explicitly Kantian (and indeed, Hegelian) context in which this emerges for Mayz Vallenilla, that he speaks of an "intrabody" of such representations precisely to indicate their unity in a *self-conscious* nexus of representation. Hence, Mayz Vallenilla refers (particularly in sections I & II of the Introduction) to the *meaningful intrabody* of logical and conceptual relationships that make up the sphere of pure thought (p. 2). This, of course, would necessarily be a self-conscious unity of representations for Kant and for Hegel. While Mayz Vallenilla does not explicitly connect the use of "intrabody" here to an inner *bodily* awareness, it emerges later in the text that the meaningfulness of such a logical or conceptual nexus is conferred not by pure abstract thought itself, but by the temporal form characteristic of finite human experience generally. Indeed, for Mayz Vallenilla, the paradigmatic *experiences* of nothingness are found in phenomena such as deep sleep and anxiety (pp. 48–9).[9] It is in such states that we are directly presented with a nothingness that is pure and original (not requiring the negation of any prior sensory representation, viz., of being), and yet also revelatory of the kind of *temporality* that remains even when what is "present" to us is nothingness as such. What we ought to take away from this brief encounter is that Mayz Vallenilla's philosophical context is not simply that of a student of German Idealism and post-Kantian European philosophy, but of a student whose understanding of the German tradition is apparently infused with an appreciation for the *raciovitalismo* of human life.

Aside from this connection, it is noteworthy that Mayz Vallenilla and Ortega were educated in overlapping spheres of German philosophical culture, albeit at different times. Ortega had studied with both Cohen and Natorp, from the Marburg school of neo-Kantianism. Mayz Vallenilla, from 1950 to 1952, would study in Freiburg (where, incidentally, Heidegger had been allowed to return to teaching in 1950, after being banned for four years during the French occupation's "denazification" program), Göttingen (where Husserl had taught until his move to Freiburg in 1916, and Nicolai Hartmann until the year of Mayz Vallenilla's arrival), as well as Munich. At these universities, Mayz Vallenilla would surely have been steeped in the philosophical milieu of Heidegger's "existential" brand of phenomenology, the remnants of Husserlian phenomenology, as well as neo-Kantianism.

While the cultural context is important for a *partial* explanation of the philosophical confluence of variables leading up to *KPN*, the most important explanation can only be given through a study of Mayz Vallenilla's book itself. The most important point to emphasize about his cultural context, in my view, is that there is an undeniable gap between philosophical writing in Latin America and in the Anglophone world, and the gap is glaringly one-sided. As we have seen, the European influences in Latin America were extensive. However, even now in the twenty-first century there is a whole world of interesting philosophical work that has been and continues to be done in Latin America, but which often does not break through this one-sided barrier into the Anglophone world. Mayz Vallenilla's *KPN* is just one example of that. But, I would suggest, it is a very important example. The reasons are twofold. First, it should be noted not only that this is Mayz Vallenilla's only book dedicated to a study of Kant, but also that it is hardly known yet in the English-speaking philosophical world.[10] Second, precious little has been written *at all* on the topic of Kant's TON, but in recent years the topic has begun to attract some notice. The burgeoning interest in the TON is, however, still lacking in two important respects. First, it lacks the depth and systematicity of a book-length study. Second, it so far lacks the kind of *post*-Kantian perspective that Mayz Vallenilla's book brings. This study, with the distinctive approach I have just outlined, will therefore be invaluable for the emerging literature on this and related topics.

The Problematic of *KPN*

My hope is that readers of this book will recognize that Mayz Vallenilla is making a convincing case that the concept of "nothingness" is quite central to Kant's philosophy. But we should first ask ourselves: doesn't Kant himself dismiss this? In the *Critique of Pure Reason*, in the only section that explicitly takes up the concept of "nothing," Kant indeed states that his brief analysis of the concept "nothing" is "not in itself especially indispensable" but "nevertheless may seem requisite for the completeness of the system" of transcendental philosophy.[11] While he therefore accords the division of the concept of nothing some importance (after all, it has *a place* in the system), he would seem to think that it does not occupy a central role. However, this is not such a simple matter.

A Quick Overview of Kant's Critical Treatment of Nothingness

Kant's TON appears in the all-too-brief appendix of the Amphiboly chapter of the *Critique of Pure Reason* (in both the 1781 or "A" and 1787 or "B" editions). While this is Kant's most careful treatment of the concept of nothingness,[12] the first significant precursor to the TON occurs in the 1763 essay "Attempt to introduce the concept of negative magnitudes into philosophy" ("Negative Magnitudes"). Here, Kant's aim is, as he puts it, to *introduce* the concept of negative magnitudes to philosophy. What exactly is being introduced? After all, non-being is an issue that has received ample attention since philosophy's very inception. The answer lies in Kant's proposal that distinguishing *logical* opposition (contradiction) and *real* opposition (contrariness) corresponds to a distinction between absolute nothingness and a nothing that can be known—indeed, curiously, a nothing that is (perhaps in a different sense) *something*.[13]

A body which is both moving and, simultaneously and in the same sense, not moving is *nothing at all* (*nihil negativum*). By contrast, the result of equal opposing forces on the same body is *something*—namely, rest. But this "something," Kant says, is "nothing in another sense to that in which it occurs in a contradiction." Kant calls this "nothing" zero = 0, and says that it carries the same meaning as "negation (*negatio*), lack, absence [...]."[14] How is this "nothing" a "something"? That which can be expressed as *zero* is not thereby contradictory, and is not thereby an absolute nothing. It is, instead, a "relative nothing." In the case of a body at rest, for example, it is "a certain motion which did not exist."[15] This places non-existence *within* the sphere of the real.

The significance, particularly for our purpose of examining the TON, is that by 1763 Kant had already decided that the concepts "something" and "nothing" are not unidimensional. "Something" comprises not only the well-known "table of the categories" (what Kant later calls the "table of something," A291/B348), but also that which contains the *division* between "something" and "nothing." Kant's hierarchy of concepts looks like this:

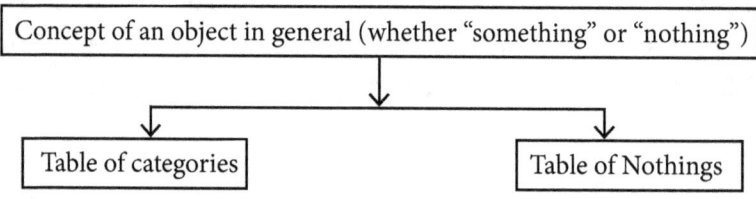

In the *Critique*, Kant introduces the systematic role of nothingness by pointing out that there is a problem with the way the concept had been dealt with by his rationalist predecessors. Baumgarten's *Metaphysics* (which Kant himself lectured from in his own metaphysics courses) argued that ontology begins with the distinction between the (logically) *possible* and the (logically) *impossible*.[16] "Nothing," for Baumgarten, was therefore synonymous with contradiction. Kant takes issue with this starting point on the grounds that all distinctions presuppose a higher concept that is divided. That is, as long as "the ontologically possible" is opposed to "the ontologically impossible," they must share in some higher concept. Kant calls this higher concept "the concept of an object in general," which is *prior* to any consideration of whether it is "something" or "nothing." This concept of an object in general is therefore *neither* something *nor* nothing. It is worth asking, then, *what* it is, if not "something" by another name. And, indeed, it may be "something" in a sense quite distinct from the senses elaborated in the table of categories.[17] In any case, this highest concept of ontology is useful not just as a kind of notational correction to Baumgarten. Baumgarten's view was that *ontological nothing* was synonymous with *logical contradiction*. And, indeed, logical impossibility *absolutely* resists the logically possible, making it appear that they share no higher representation whatsoever.[18] But in the "Transcendental Analytic," Kant had undertaken great efforts to demonstrate that what can be known—the *real* in appearances—has its being only in being determined in accordance with the categories (the pure concepts of the understanding). And to be determined in judgment is, among other things, to *exclude* all contraries to the determining predicate. For Kant, the sort of exclusion that takes place in judgment is necessarily defined by the parameters of the forms of intuition—space and time. To add a predicate that goes beyond the subject concept of a judgment (hence, to judge *synthetically*), the predication must be grounded in concepts of understanding that have application only to appearances—i.e., to what can appear in space and time. The sphere of appearance, as the sphere of what can sensibly affect us, is the sphere of the *real* and the *actual*.

Hence, synthetic judgment (which all substantial knowledge consists of) does its excluding (negation) on the basis of "real" opposition and not logical contradiction. All determinate ontological concepts, then, are concepts of *real* being and *real* negation. For this reason, the tables of something and nothing are divided by sharing in the concept of an object in general, which must be the concept of the *real* in general.[19]

The concepts of real or knowable nothings are then spelled out as follows:

(1) *Ens rationis* (being of reason): The empty concept without an object; the concept to which no intuition can correspond. What Kant has in mind specifically is the noumenon—the object of an infinite intellect, which can never be given to a finite, discursive intellect like ours.

(2) *Nihil privativum* (privative nothing): The empty object of a concept. This is the concept of an absence, such as "shadow" or "cold."

(3) *Ens imaginarium* (being of imagination): The empty intuition without an object; the merely formal condition of an object. Pure space and time are not appearances, but the condition of the possibility of any appearance.

(4) *Nihil negativum* (negative nothing): The empty object without a concept. This is the nothing of a contradictory concept. The object is nothing because the concept is logically impossible.

(1) & (4) are objects understood to be impossible in relation to principles of possibility that govern being (the principle of non-contradiction, and the first "postulate of empirical thinking," A218/B265). (2) & (3) are "empty *data* for concepts," Kant says. Regarding the latter, it seems strange for Kant to identify the empty forms of intuition with "empty data." When Kant uses the term "data," it is often to indicate the *matter* of a cognition, and specifically the matter given in sensible intuition (e.g., A107). It is possible, however, that Kant means to highlight that the concept of the *ens imaginarium* is the concept of an intuition which, because it is pure or merely formal, *gives* no data. Pure or formal space and time would be "empty data" for their concept, as they are intuitions *of* no object, but that which enables objects to be intuited.

Now we can see that each nothing presupposes being. We would not know the nothing of noumena without the something of "all, many, and one" (under the category of *quantity*). We would not know the nothing of absence without degree of reality in presence (the *quality* of being). We would not know the emptiness of space and time without the perception of extension in space and time (*relations* of being). And we would not reject the absolute nothing of the contradictory object without knowing the highest principle of the possibility of anything real (the *modality* of being). Those familiar with post-Kantian discussions of nothingness might, on this basis, relate Kant to Bergson and Sartre, both of whom argue that all nothing presupposes a *being* that is negated.[20] This is true to an extent. But even though Kant would agree that *being* is logically prior to *nothing*, there is a sense in which that priority is reversed *within* the order of experience. Kant declares that we would not be able to represent darkness without light or space without extended beings (A292/B349); but as suggested above, it must be equally true that the nothing of space is that *out of which* extended beings emerge in experience. The synthetic *a priori* principles of knowledge elaborated by Kant include the ways in which objects are *anticipated* in experience. If we could not in some sense intuit the object prior to its actually being given, then there is nothing to know *a priori* about empirical reality. Pure or formal intuition—the empty intuition without an object—is precisely this *a priori* intuiting, which, because it is *a priori*, is said to "precede" all intuiting of objects (A267/B323; AA 4: 282). In this way, while the light of being precedes the darkness of nothing logically and ontologically, the darkness of the forms of intuition precedes the light of appearances in experience.[21]

In this way, there is room at least for the elaboration of what "being" and "nothing" mean in each of these orders: pure logic, ontology, and empirical experience. Prior to a much lengthier treatment, it is by no means obvious where Kant stands among the post-Kantian theories of nothingness. Or, better: it is not obvious where *they* stand with respect to Kant's systematic placement of the concept of nothingness. Mayz Vallenilla's text is at least a first big step toward getting a better view.

The Structure of *KPN*

The simple overview of *KPN* is: Mayz Vallenilla seeks to vindicate and critique Kant's TON. The table is vindicated as a sound division of concepts of *real* or *knowable* nothingness. Mayz Vallenilla particularly finds that Kant has made significant philosophical headway in illustrating *time* or *temporality* as a kind of nothingness (the "*ens imaginarium*"). The critique, however, can be made from just this vantage point. It is precisely the nothingness of time that, Mayz Vallenilla believes, Kant fails to prioritize above all. If Kant were to follow his own critical philosophy through to its logical conclusions, it would become apparent to him that the presupposition of time as a condition of any cognition, including even as a condition of the possibility of the unity of pure apperception, places the nothingness of the structure of time itself at the juncture between *being* and *nothingness*. To be sure, this would significantly alter Kant's logical placement of the concept of nothingness in the critical philosophy, since the TON could no longer be thought to be the result of acts of *negating* a prior form of being. Like Heidegger, Mayz Vallenilla argues that nothingness is not secondary to or derivative of being, but an original negating or nihilating force. I will now briefly spell out the most crucial moments of each step in Mayz Vallenilla's overall project.

Mayz Vallenilla's Introduction spells out the basic problem to be investigated in the book, namely: how can *time* be the framework (the "horizon") of meaning for the concept of Nothingness? And, correlatively, how does this involve a critique of Kant's TON?

First, though, Mayz Vallenilla introduces and preliminarily addresses two specific problems presented by any pursuit of the broader question. The first problem we might call the *methodological* problem, or the problem of language, and it runs roughly as follows. Speech or language—the expression of thinking—necessarily reveals a connection to objects, what is spoken of. Hence, an investigation into the concepts of nothingness will require the presumption of a sphere of objects. But access to the object is obscured through language as long as it is left obscure what constitutes the objective meaningfulness of the basic categories expressed in language. What is obscured here is the *ontological difference* between beings and the Being of beings (or nothings and their Nothingness).[22] What confers objective meaningfulness on the beings is an understanding of their Being (an understanding of what it *means* for them to *be* this way), and the same would necessarily hold of the knowable nothings. It would seem that if we want to uncover what confers this meaningfulness, then we cannot do it through language itself, as language betrays an obscuring of the ontological difference precisely because linguistic *reference* is not of Being or Nothingness, but *beings* or *nothings*. Mayz Vallenilla's proposal at this point is that while language does not directly refer to or conceptualize the conditions under which *beings* or *nothings* are intelligible or meaningful for us, it does *reveal* or *display* it. Hence, the ontological difference is not discovered in the world, but it is revealed in our thought or expression thereof.

The second problem we might call the *ontological* problem, or the problem of originality. If our understanding of nothingness or non-being is based on ontological categories (Kant's "table of the categories," for instance), then nothingness only appears as the negation of being (p. 11). This, however, does not express nothingness authentically or in its originality. What "is not" is, then, only derivative of what "is." As has been remarked about Plato's encounter with the Eleatic Stranger in *Sophist*, the text does not adequately deal with the really destructive worry that talking about non-being renders *falsehood* absolutely impossible.²³ In order to explain falsehood, we would need to be able to explain how the description "representing in thought what is *nothing*" "does not incoherently represent the thought or speech it applies to as (genuine thought or speech, but) possessing no subject matter."²⁴ In other words, as Mayz Vallenilla similarly suggests, we would need to show how language manages to *refer to* what is nothing at all—not revealing, incoherently, that what it refers to is something that cannot be referred to. This would appear to reveal an anxiety about the limits of language, as Wittgenstein also recognized when he asked: "How can one think what is not the case? If I think that King's College is on fire when it is not on fire, the fact of its being on fire does not exist. Then how can I think it?"²⁵

Mayz Vallenilla's proposal will be, again, that language ("The Word") displays or shows ("testifies to the presence of") nothingness. This is not merely a Wittgensteinian solution, though. It is at least equally, if not more fully, a Heideggerian one. In "What Is Metaphysics?" Heidegger's account of nothingness implies that it is never simply the object of a thought, or the referent of speech. It is, rather, what is *revealed* through the mood of Anxiety (*Angst*), a fundamental mode of human attunement to the world. Indeed, even Wittgenstein recognized himself as following in the footsteps of both Heidegger and Kierkegaard, especially when he described the nature of ethics as being revealed only at the very limits of language or what is expressible in propositional form.²⁶ But, Mayz Vallenilla sets out to address each of these problems not just through Heidegger, but through a turn *back* to Kant's original discussion of the division of the concepts of nothingness. To this I now want to turn.

Why not simply present an analysis of Heidegger's concept of Nothingness (the *nihil originarium*)? One reason for this is that Mayz Vallenilla wants to take advantage of Kant's explicit discussion in the *Critique* of the *schematism* of the categories of understanding. Our categories or pure concepts of understanding—under the headings of Quantity, Quality, Relation, and Modality—are, for Kant, the expressions of the "being" of objects in general (they are *ways* that objects *can be*). But these categories in and of themselves are *empty*; they have significance only in relation to what is empirically given to the senses. But in order for the categories to bring form to what is given to them by the senses, Kant argues, there must be a third form of representation—a *schema*—which amounts to a "time determination," or a consciousness of a determinate relation of objects according to the structure of time. Mayz Vallenilla's insight with regard to the TON is that a complete understanding of the forms of nothing would require a similar *schematism* in the form of a "time determination." So, by looking directly at the relation between Kant's explanation of the schemata and the categories of nothing in the "table of nothing," we can hopefully gain an understanding of the relation between Nothingness and temporality.

But, Mayz Vallenilla also clearly notes, he is not setting out merely to rehearse and imitate Kant's schematism, for we must simultaneously *critique* that schematism in order to get beyond a merely "ontological" conception of Nothingness. Here it is best to simply quote Mayz Vallenilla:

> Seen from there, the original Temporality (*Temporalität*) of Nothing—as purely negative schematism—results as an opposite, if not contradictory, sign with respect to that revealed by the ontological schematism developed by Kant in relation to the corresponding categories. Applying these to the configuration of Nothingness—as opposed to the function assigned to them by Kant as *a priori* constituent forms of Something—they demand from that schematism, as a horizon giving its temporal "meaning", a radically different design. Categories and schemata thus exhibit, from their new "foundation", a completely different meaning from that which they manifest as ontological determinations. From this remains, *eo ipso*, the temporal structure that supports and defines its meaningful intrabody. (p. 18)

The path through the book, and thus through Mayz Vallenilla's critique of Kant's schematism, can be seen as a logical movement beginning from Kant's concept of the *ens rationis* and running through each of the categories of "nothing." Very roughly, we can see the progression as follows: The *ens rationis* is the first glimpse at a determinate form of nothingness for Kant, which takes the shape of a purely intelligible being of understanding—that which cannot correspond to anything given in sensation. The question thus arises whether such a concept of nothingness excludes any intuition of time which Kant otherwise thinks is necessary for schematizing representations. Here we first get into view the idea of an original nothingness, as the *ens rationis* appears pure, lacking reference to positively given sensation. But it is here that we also first encounter the thought that there must be a way of purely schematizing such a concept without its losing originality. The challenge is thus raised: distinguish a kind of nothingness which is derivative of or relying upon something sensibly given, from a kind of nothingness which is pure or original.

The *nihil privativum* arises as that notion of *lack* or *absence* with respect to what is positively given in sensation. But here again is the question whether there is any sense to be made of an *absolute lack* or "*absolute negation*" that is schematized in time. Mayz Vallenilla suggests that there is a determinate form of experience in which an original or pure nothingness arises for us—deep sleep and Heidegger's notion of anxiety—and that Kant's *nihil privativum* is not yet adequate for capturing this.

The *ens imaginarium* is the concept of the pure horizons of space and time themselves, which as such are empty forms of intuition without an object. But as these empty forms, *entia imaginaria* cannot be *perceived* or directly *experienced*. This finally introduces us to the real possibility of *absolute negation*, in this case as an "onto-logical" form of negation (the next category, *nihil negativum*, representing *logical* negation). More specifically, this represents absolute negativity that is essentially *temporal*. But as we investigate this category, the question of the necessity of *categories* (or "anti-categories") of nothingness arises: for time itself, as a mere form of intuition, exists in a way that is pre-categorial.

Finally, the *nihil negativum* arises as the idea of the impossibility of an object. Generated from the logical principle of contradiction, it appears to transcend any condition of temporality whatsoever. However, Mayz Vallenilla seeks to show that there is a "peculiar" and "sui generis" form of temporality, the *Temporality of Nothingness*, which precedes and makes possible the temporality of *ontology* or real being, hence also undergirding even the absolute impossibility of an object. If he can indeed show this to be true, then he will have fully succeeded in showing how a critique of Kant's schematism of the categories can give us a new form of schematism for the "anti-categories" of nothingness.

Nothingness and the *Ens Rationis*

The first chapter is focused on spelling out the first concept of nothing on Kant's table, and more specifically the way in which an analysis of this concept positions us to see the significance of *temporality* for the problem outlined in the Introduction.[27] Mayz Vallenilla argues that, for Kant, the very idea of a concept of Nothing (*None, Kein*) suggests a "canceling" (*Aufhebung*). And the "canceling" function of the concept of *none*, of course, first requires a *material* that may be cancelled or negated.

It is here where Mayz Vallenilla introduces us to the first significant way in which Kant's conception of Nothingness seems to presuppose a "temporal horizon" of meaning, and hence the first step to an investigation into an absolutely negative schematism. The *ens rationis*, or the empty concept without an object, is ostensibly, through Kant's own analysis, the concept of a being of pure understanding and therefore need not (indeed *cannot*) correspond to anything given in sensible intuition.[28] Initially this seems to pose a problem, as Kant speaks of the category of *none* as having the function of *canceling* everything given in sensation, which appears to require our concept of nothing to *rest on* something positively given in sensation. Briefly, the worry arising from this observation is this: if this nothing is to be thought of as a *noumenon*, as Kant suggests, then it is to be thought of as a purely intelligible being (a *being of pure understanding*) and therefore as requiring no *schematism* and no notion of a temporal horizon of significance. The *ens rationis* is a concept arising from nothing but pure understanding or "I" itself, and this pure understanding is characterized by Kant as having a timeless character:

> Now, what guarantees such characteristics in the *Transcendental Unity* of consciousness can only be its *timeless* condition. Permanence, immutability, fixity, and identity with oneself, occur only where, apparently, there is no temporal flow and, therefore, possible change, mutability, or variability; it is worth saying, in an ekstasis alien to all becoming, synonymous with an *instant* paradoxically disconnected from all temporal flow. (Ch. 1, p. 33).

But, Mayz Vallenilla continues:

> [I]f *Transcendental Apperception* is, as Kant himself designates it, a "common function of the mind",[29] whose operation consists in *connecting, composing,* and *uniting* the diverse in the unity of a single consciousness,[30] it is worth asking whether such a "function"—and its corresponding acts of "connecting", "uniting", and "composing"—can be conceived without a meaning or temporal sense. All "action", indeed, is a process that takes place in time: it is "*temporal.*" (Ch. 1, p. 33).

Moreover, because the transcendental unity of consciousness that is presupposed by any cognitive act is, Kant says, "stable" (*stehende*) and "permanent" (*bleibende*) in all cognition ("present at all times," Mayz Vallenilla notes), this unity of consciousness is—must be—*in some sense* temporal. These characteristics are, after all, temporal qualifications of something. Mayz Vallenilla insightfully points out that, perhaps unbeknownst to Kant, this apparently "timeless" character of the "I" or faculty of understanding is time*less* only with respect to the temporality of what is empirically real, and hence the temporal condition of the "I" excludes its being *inside* empirically real time. Most helpfully for this point, Mayz Vallenilla underscores Kant's own point that *time itself* as the pure form of inner sense (and a kind of nothing, the *ens imaginarium*) is not *in empirically real time*. Kant is clear at B183, for instance, that "time itself does not elapse, but the existence of that which is changeable elapses in it." On the basis of this claim, Mayz Vallenilla notes on Kant's behalf that "just as Time does not cease to be Time because of its character of permanence [...] neither does the I, as permanent, reject its temporal condition and become a timeless being" (MS p. 36). Time does not cease to be time (something *temporal*, perhaps we could say) because it does not *pass* in time, and hence nothing bars us from saying that the "I" can similarly retain a temporal characterization. This argument appears to be fundamentally inspired by Heidegger's suggestion that Kant's theory of time lacked a clear-eyed grasp of the ontological distinction.

On Heidegger's reading of Kant, while Kant properly recognized the structure of time as a pure condition under which objects appear to us *in* time, he failed to fully grasp that this pure time as enabling representation or structure reveals its own, more original or "primordial," temporality. To put it simply, Heidegger sees in Kant's theory of time the existence of both the empirically real temporality of appearances *and* the temporality which enables and structures that real temporality. In other words, there clearly exists an *ontological difference* between the passing series of "*nows*" and the temporal *being* of that passage of time and the things in it.

Indeed, in Heidegger's *Kantbuch*, he makes note of the same passage where Kant describes the transcendental unity of apperception as "unchanging and permanent,"[31] and later also clearly registers the point that the temporal character of time itself is that of permanence:

"But time as the pure *now*-sequence is ever now. That is, in every *now* it is now. Time thus manifests its own constancy. As such, time is 'non-transitory and abiding' while all else changes."[32] More precisely: time is not one permanent thing among others, but by virtue of the essential character just mentioned—that it is now in every *now*—it provides the pure aspect of permanence in general [...] time exists as a *now*-sequence precisely because, flowing across each *now*, it remains a *now* even while becoming another *now*.[33]

On this reading, the appearances are cognized in an ever-flowing sequence of "*nows*," but only on the basis of the *one, stable, permanent* time (as pure intuition) that remains *in* each moment. Heidegger later suggests that "Although, on the ordinary plane of experience where 'we take account of time,' we must consider it to be a pure succession of *nows*, this succession by no means constitutes primordial time. On the contrary, the transcendental imagination as that which lets time as the *now*-sequence spring forth is—as the origin of the latter—primordial time."[34] This primordial time, however tied to the faculty of imagination, is no further from the transcendental unity of apperception, for just the reasons we saw above. Hence, on Mayz Vallenilla's Heideggerian reading of Kant, if we are going to render the *ens rationis* comprehensible as a knowable nothing, then we cannot let the (merely) apparent timelessness of pure intellect or understanding get in the way. Rather, we must inquire into the possibility of a temporality that can know not just *being*, but *nothing*.

Now, if there is a "horizon" of temporality which enables us to know this nothing, then there must also be a corresponding *schematism* for the concepts of nothing. As Kant demonstrates in the "Transcendental Analytic," the pure categories of the understanding—as entirely universal concepts, and hence entirely *heterogeneous* with respect to radically *singular* intuitions—require a form of representation that would link them to intuitions of objects. This form of representation, the "schema," is what comes into focus next.

Nothingness and the Nihil Privativum

The second chapter seeks to demonstrate how Kant's second concept of nothingness, the *nihil privativum*, explicitly brings us to the question of the *schematism* of this nothingness. The *nihil privativum*, Kant says, is the "empty object of a concept." Specifically, the object in question here is "empty *data*" (*leere Data*) for concepts. Empty data is opposed to *positive* data just as *darkness* is opposed to *light*. Kant explains that "if light were not given to the senses, then one would also not be able to represent darkness" (A292/B349). We represent *darkness* by representing the *absence* of light. Indeed, the *nihil privativum* is "a concept of the absence of an object, such as a shadow or cold" (A291/B347). It is also here that Kant reminds the reader of what he had explicated in the preceding "Schematism" and "Anticipations of Perception" chapters—namely, that "reality is **something**, negation is **nothing**" (A291/B347). The concept of an absence of something positive is, then, a negation of some prior reality (something given under the conditions of possible experience). It is not surprising, then, that we encounter at this point the problem of how a total negation of that which is given in intuition—a degree of *zero* in intensity of sensation—could nevertheless have a *phenomenal* structure in a way similar to an object, or a something. That is, how could an absolute absence of all reality be *something* for us, at least to the extent that it figures in relations of real opposition and not merely the absolutely impossible "relation" of logically contradictory opposition?

It is here where Mayz Vallenilla suggests that we face a Kantian *aporia*. It appears that if the *nihil privativum* is a knowable nothing, then it must have the structure of a knowable object, and hence a "phenomenal" structure. But, the phenomenal structure of this nothing would involve our knowing something with a sensible degree of *zero*. This would initially appear to conflict with Kant's claim that, since every sensation has a degree of reality, we cannot intuit or perceive a total absence of reality (B214). In short, we are then forced to think either that absolute negation is impossible (because there is no phenomenon that could correspond to it) or that absolute negation is not a condition of the possibility of knowable objects ("phenomena," loosely speaking). But from the perspective of the *nihil privativum*, it does not appear that we are ready to accept either horn of this dilemma. Because of this, the concept of an absolute form of negation must await another category—and indeed, as Mayz Vallenilla notes, Kant reserves this for both the third and fourth categories, where *time* as a form of sensibility and *contradiction* are considered.

However, one thing we can do while we remain in the vicinity of the *nihil privativum* is to sketch what it must mean for there to be a *positive nothing* in experience, even if this means going beyond Kant's own discussion of this concept. While Kant seems to exclude the possibility that we could positively *and directly* apprehend a nothingness in experience, Mayz Vallenilla argues that we do in fact apprehend such a nothingness in, for instance, deep sleep. This brings us to one of the most curious and fascinating parts of Mayz Vallenilla's text. While he gives a decisive nod or two to Heidegger's own example of *anxiety* as that which most decisively reveals original nothingness to Dasein, Mayz Vallenilla believes that other such "phenomena" can testify to the presence of this nothingness, including that of sleep. Without taking us too far afield: one might wonder how this could be any example of a positive and direct experience of nothingness, since deep (presumably dreamless) sleep involves the lack of consciousness of any object whatsoever. We would therefore appear to be acquainted with it only in a moment when we apprehend (indeed, indirectly) an interruption in our otherwise-continuous conscious experience. But Mayz Vallenilla introduces deep sleep as something much more interesting. He seems to be motivated at this point by the idea that ordinary "phenomena" of absolute negativity (absolutely "empty" or negative "data," if you will) are worth preserving in a full description of human life. And, while much could be said about the use of deep sleep as an example at this juncture, there is plausibility at the very least because such a feature of ordinary human life does *not* seem capable of being simply relegated to the proverbial trash bin of barely noticeable gaps in human experience, as though one goes "missing" from life until one awakens.

From his example, it appears that Mayz Vallenilla is introducing to us a *new* division of the concept of nothingness—one which is not strictly speaking a *nihil privativum*, given that it is not a mere privation of a previously given reality. In general, it becomes clear that Mayz Vallenilla hopes to discover that experience which represents an authentic encounter with the nothing itself, and it becomes clear that he thinks neither the *ens rationis* nor the *nihil privativum* comes quite close enough.

Now, the most important point to take away at this stage of the discussion is that the positive *appearance* of nothingness in deep sleep or anxiety does not reveal the absence of time itself (as Mayz Vallenilla argues would happen in Kant's conception of the *nihil privativum*, where the cancellation of all sensation would at the same time be the cancellation of that which enables an intelligible passage of time). Rather, to think this form of original nothingness (which positively intrudes or "irrupts" into the realm of existence), we must think it as having a temporal form. But time itself "is" not, while providing the condition of the possibility of this original positive nothingness. As Mayz Vallenilla puts it:

> But with *nihilation* or *deep sleep*, as we have said, Time does not *disappear*. Time is still there and we have a certain understanding of it. But how is Time still there? What "is" Time viewed from Nothing? This question is meaningless. From Nothing, Time "is" not. And this not in the sense of a Non-Being, but because Time reveals itself and then "appears" as Nothingness itself. And just as it is only possible to say *"there is Nothing"*, it is only possible to say also: *"there is Time."* Both expressions, however, reveal the factum of an *understanding* (p. 58).

Nothingness and the *Ens Imaginarium*

Having seen that time itself (which, per Kant, is a mere form of intuition, not an object intuit*ed*) is a nothing which is yet not *absolutely* nothing, we now must investigate it. The third chapter seeks to explain and/or clarify *why* the mere forms of intuition are not things intuited and the meaning of this non-thinghood or nothingness, what their mode of being is, and their relation to the faculty of imagination.

Cutting to the heart of the matter, the *ens imaginarium* is a mere form of intuition which "exists" while lacking *real presence* (this is the meaning of "mere form"). This alone is a fascinating thought which needs to be explored in much more detail by Kant scholars. Kant himself declares more than once in the *Critique of Pure Reason* that the representation "I think" already brings with it the "I exist," though *not* originally as the *category* of existence (see: B422–3n.). Kant's remark suggests that there is a non- or pre-categorial sense of "existence". Moreover, Kant is clear that this non- or rather pre-categorial sense of existence has a strictly *temporal* meaning when he says that the representation "I think" is a determination *of my existence in time*. Kant recognizes a form of existence which is not first a *category* of being, but something that the categories may *determine* in various ways. But this would seem to imply that there is a "primordial" or original sense of existence which does not, at least not yet, bear the determination of any category of thought.[35] Time as a pure form of intuition may also have existence even as a nothing. It is nothing, Kant says, because it is a mere form of what *can be*. It "is in itself not an object, but the merely formal condition of one" (A291/B347). In Mayz Vallenilla's estimation, what Kant gets right is that time, as an *ens imaginarium*, is no object of intuition, and therefore is in some sense a nothing. But, according to the same point of view, it may be asked whether the *ens imaginarium* is a nothing that itself admits of a kind of *temporal* characterization. Returning to Mayz Vallenilla's claim that it is absolutely essential for Kant that time serve as the horizon of meaning of any possible cognition, we may then ask whether time as a pure form of intuition is cognized *under some temporal condition*. Do we need *temporality* to render *time itself* intelligible as a form of our sensibility? A paradox lurks. But, if one follows Mayz Vallenilla's lead, it will be seen that time as an *ens imaginarium* is not the original or "primordial" time that serves as the horizon of all cognition. The "time" that is lost when all reality is absent is, Mayz Vallenilla says, merely the "instrumental" time of a series of "*nows*" or present moments that gain their determinate orientation with respect to the sensation that is now missing. So, one point of the utmost importance in this chapter is that a study of the *ens imaginarium* further reveals the need for a more original notion of temporality—one that can serve even as the horizon of meaning for the *loss* of temporal experience in empirical reality.

We have also seen, in connection with this thought and by sketching "the strict meaning of" the nothingness of Time or Space themselves as forms of intuition, that Mayz Vallenilla is raising the important question of the precise role of *conceptual determinacy* in understanding nothingness. As he states at the end of chapter 3:

> In this respect, it is not only possible to ask whether one can speak in general of "categories" of Nothingness—or of "anti-categories", as we have called them elsewhere—but, more radically, whether Nothing is constituted by such "categories", or whether, on the contrary, all possible idealistic perspectives—however nuanced or subtle—should be abandoned when trying to think about this problem (p. 89).

In one way, it is clear that Mayz Vallenilla hopes for his critique of Kant's TON to pave the way past such a clear logical *table*, since the very existence of a table of concepts presupposes a notion of what these are concepts *of*—i.e., whether of *being* or *nothing*. Even Kant points this out by saying that all previous attempts at transcendental philosophy have failed to see clearly that the division of concepts of being and non-being presupposes an even higher concept, since any *division* presupposes something that may *be divided* (A290/B346). So, Mayz Vallenilla might ask Kant, whence the concept of *nothing* which enables categorial (or "anti-categorial") distinctions among the *types* of nothing? This is just to ask, again, for the primordial or original notion of nothingness. And the suggestion would seem to be that such an original notion of nothingness will forever be obscured unless and until we ask, like we do for the notion of *existence*, for the "phenomenon" itself which is given determinate character through the various "anti"-categories.

Nothingness and the Nihil Negativum

The final chapter is by far the most philosophically challenging, but also the most philosophically rich. Mayz Vallenilla is concerned with the question how the temporal horizon of meaning can inform our understanding of nothingness as *nihil negativum*, or the "empty object without concept"—i.e., the concept of a contradictory object. Here, naturally, the question arises how a *temporal* horizon of meaning should be possible at all, since the thought of a logical contradiction (or rather the thought of the *impossibility* of contradiction) appears to be a thought *beyond* the conditions of time; a logical contradiction cannot, by definition, agree with the conditions of mere thinking, let alone of time.

The key to what Mayz Vallenilla does in this concluding chapter can be found in his discussion of Kant's example of the *nihil negativum*: the two-sided rectilinear figure. In the TON, Kant emphasizes that the example exhibits a logical contradiction. But, Mayz Vallenilla suggests that the logical contradiction of the concept of a two-sided rectangle may be grounded in the *ontological* impossibility of the figure. He points out that elsewhere Kant is happy to say that Euclidean geometrical impossibilities are not logical, but synthetic. The concepts "two straight lines" and "the intersection of lines" do not negate the concept of "figure," Kant says. Rather, the impossibility of a figure enclosed by two straight lines is grounded on the attempted spatial construction itself—i.e., grounded in intuition. This case, it seems, would be susceptible to Mayz Vallenilla's suggestion that temporality is the horizon even of impossibilities or nothings, at least of a certain kind.

But, from there, Mayz Vallenilla sketches an account of a *sui generis* temporality (indeed, he calls it "Temporality," to indicate just how alien it is from the sphere of ordinary ontological being and non-being) which provides the possibility of thinking the strictly impossible. This is because the *logical contradiction* is rooted in the *ontological* (in the construction of space, for instance) only by being completely excluded from it. Once the boundaries of the ontological are violated and broken, a sphere of pure negativity opens up, precisely on the basis of a rejection of the temporal lawfulness of the ontological:

> Is the *im-possible*, which manifests itself in it, therefore also something *a-temporal*? Or could it be that in Reason—by abolishing the borders of Experience and therefore the limitations of the natural *understanding of Being*—a sui generis "Temporality" is established? Is it possible, perhaps, to bear witness to such a "Temporality," experienced in the uprooting of Being and therefore of the phenomenal world that encircles Experience? (p. 122)

Now, the absolute impossibility represented by the *nihil negativum* is not only a rejection of the limits of ontology, it also results in a self-cancellation of its own concept. As Kant says of any contradiction, the thought destroys itself. Why should we think that it is even possible to become "uprooted from Being" in *this* way, though? It is one thing to *think* beyond the bounds of experience, but it is entirely another thing to attempt to think beyond thought.[36] Mayz Vallenilla's suggestion at this point does seem to break with Kant. For Kant, a contradiction cannot be thought. Two logically incongruent concepts cannot be held together in one unity of consciousness, which is precisely why they cancel the thought itself (*The Jäsche Logic*, AA 9: 51). But Mayz Vallenilla suggests a different route when he says that it will be necessary to admit that "Reason possesses a distinct logos," a "logos" which comprehends the absolute Nothing of the *nihil negativum*. Reason possesses such a "logos," he thinks, because he takes it to be clear that we can *think* this Nothing. We can think the failure of the concept of the two-sided rectilinear figure, and hence there is just as much a "logos" of this Nothing as there is of Being. And what Mayz Vallenilla now takes himself to have established is precisely this *sui generis* form of Nothingness and its "Temporality" which he had been seeking from the beginning. Reason becomes pure negativity when it disregards and violates the bounds of possibility, but because it comprehends what it does as pure negativity, it constitutes a *sui generis* form of nothingness, grounded on the absolute rejection of ontological temporality, and consisting of the characteristic experiences of this peculiar "Temporality" in the phenomena of deep sleep and anxiety.

A Question on Kant's Behalf

I will close by posing a question that I believe will be worth pursuing for readers—particularly after a first reading of Mayz Vallenilla's text. Well into the "Transcendental Analytic" of the first *Critique*, Kant pauses to consider whether he can make sense of how one and the same "I" can belong to *empirical* and *transcendental* apperception. How, that is, can the "I" that intuits also be the "I" that thinks? The difficulty arises because the "I" that intuits is shown to presuppose the "I" that thinks as its condition. "I" am both, and yet each is distinct. While Kant admits the puzzle, he claims that it is not *especially* mysterious (no more than how I can be an object for myself in general, B155–6). Nevertheless, the puzzle has proven stubborn for interpreters of Kant.

We may now ask Mayz Vallenilla, with equal interest: how can the "I" that belongs to the structure of ontological temporality be the same as the "I" that belongs to the structure of the "Temporality" of the absolute Nothing? The question is pressing because *if* the logos of Being and the "logos" of Nothing share their name in some non-accidental way, it is presumably because they are united by something higher. Indeed, this is exactly the idea with which Kant inaugurates his TON: any division presupposes a higher concept to be divided. Mayz Vallenilla's answer, I suspect, will merge with Heidegger's interpretation of Kant. For Heidegger, it is clear that the temporality of imagination is the "hidden root" of Kant's two stems of cognition. Still, for those grappling with Heidegger's reading of Kant, it must be asked how that root can be the unity of two heterogeneous elements. And for Mayz Vallenilla, it can be asked whether such a root is possible, either for Kant or for Mayz Vallenilla's Kant. In any case, it is most definitely a worthwhile project to take up.

What marks the importance of studying Mayz Vallenilla's treatment of Kant is that it represents a unique point of entry into understanding Kant, and specifically for understanding how Kant's thought opened up the possibility of certain traditions following the monumental Copernican turn that he initiated in the late eighteenth century. The importance of this book therefore does not lie in the value of a narrow set of questions about the concept of nothing. That is, Mayz Vallenilla is well-aware, as any student of German philosophy should be, that the analysis of such a basic concept as that of "nothingness" is nothing less than a systematic undertaking. And the concept of nothingness is not chosen arbitrarily.

As Mayz Vallenilla cuts a distinctive Heideggerian path in the spirit of his own Latin American context, it would not be improper now to note the similarity in my translation of the original title (*El Problema de la Nada en Kant*) and the title of Heidegger's *Kantbuch* (*Kant and the Problem of Metaphysics*). I do not think it is a stretch to suggest that Mayz Vallenilla sees this book as offering his own "violent reading" of Kant, in a spirit that is nothing short of enthusiastic and positive about Kant as the one who lays down the absolutely indispensable foundations for thinking through the relation of *being* and *nothingness* by way of the temporal structure of human experience.

Addison Ellis
Cairo, Egypt
June 2023

Notes

1. Kant himself even says that this discussion is "not in itself especially indispensable" (A290/B346). More on this later.
2. Most secondary sources on Kant do not even mention the TON. The few that do pay very little attention to it, or else cast it aside as unimportant. As an example of the latter, Norman Kemp Smith criticizes Kant, in *A Commentary on Kant's Critique of Pure Reason*, by suggesting that the TON elaborates concepts that "do not properly come within the denotation of the term 'nothing.'" He claims that this "is very evident in the examples which Kant cites. Cold is as real as the

opposite with which it is contrasted, while pure space and pure time are not negative even in a conventional sense" (2003, p. 424).

3   *Universidad, ciencia y técnica* (Caracas: Universidad Central de Venezuela, 1956); *Esbozo de una crítica de la Razón Técnica* (Caracas: Equinoccio (Universidad Simón Bolívar), 1974); *Hombre y naturaleza* (Caracas: Universidad Simón Bolívar, 1975).

4   *La idea de la estructura psíquica en Dilthey* (Caracas: Universidad Central de Venezuela, 1949); a detailed treatment of Husserl is found in *Fenomenología del Conocimiento* (Caracas: Universidad Central de Venezuela, 1956); and, of course, the present treatment of Kant was originally published as *El Problema de La Nada en Kant* (Madrid: Editorial Revista de Occidente, 1965).

5   Heidegger's use of "interrogate" closely parallels Kant's notion of compelling, and putting questions to, nature. See, for example, *BT* 5–6.

6   Heidegger, *KPM* 207. The "violence" Heidegger refers to is not incompatible with deep philosophical kinship and sympathy, as can be seen from any study of Heidegger's interpretive texts, including his extensive engagement with Kant.

7   See, for example, *El Tema de Nuestro Tiempo* (Austral, 2003).

8   Introduced and explored, for example, in Ortega y Gasset, José (1963). "Vitalidad, Alma y Espíritu," in *Obras Completas, Tomo II* (Madrid: Revista de Occidente, my translation): "One might say that in 'I walk' we refer to walking seen from within what he is, and in 'he walks,' walking seen from the outside, in its external outcome… Both our psychic life and our external world are founded upon that internal image of our body that we always carry with us and which comes to be like the framework within which everything appears to us."

9   Ortega's concept of an *intrabody* certainly shares something in common with what is often called simply "proprioception." However, as the term functions for Mayz Vallenilla, it seems chiefly to signify an *organic whole*—that is, a whole in which the parts mutually inform one another. This could then make proprioception—which concerns mainly the feeling of bodily position, orientation, and movement—a *species* of the higher genus "intrabody." What is indicative of an intrabody is its referential (perhaps even self-referential) organic totality. This makes it infused with a kind of life or vitality, even prior to the more spatially oriented notion of proprioception. For an influential discussion of the latter, see Evan Thompson's *Mind in Life* (2007, pp. 244–52).

10 Translations into German and French already exist: *Le problème du néant chez Kant* (L'Harmattan, 2000), *Die Frage nach dem Nichts bei Kant* (Neske, 1998).

11 A290/B346.

12 Aside from brief asides in student transcriptions of Kant's lectures on metaphysics.

13 "Negative Magnitudes" AA 2: 171.
14 "Negative Magnitudes" AA 2: 171–2.
15 Ibid.
16 *Metaphysics* (p. 100., Bloomsbury, tr. and ed. by Fugate and Hymers).
17 See, for example, AA 28: 544: "*Something* means any object of thinking; this is the *logical* something. The concept of an object in general is the highest concept of all cognitions. One also calls an object a something, but not a metaphysical, rather a logical something."
18 I believe that Kant would disagree with this too, since logically possible thought and the *rejection* of logically *im*-possible thought both contain or have in common the logical "I." However, he would agree in the sense that the logical "I" is not a *concept* and hence not a common genus (B404).
19 I suspect that *this* is the key to understanding how even "nothing" is a "something," for Kant. The TON specifies concepts in accordance with conditions of *the real*.
20 Henri Bergson, *Creative Evolution* (New York: The Modern Library, 1944). Sartre (1956).
21 For more on this, see Béatrice Longuenesse, *Kant and the Capacity to Judge* (Princeton: Princeton University Press, 1998, pp. 308–09).
22 This marks Mayz Vallenilla's first explicit use of Heidegger's phenomenological framework.
23 McDowell, "Falsehood and Not-Being in Plato's *Sophist*", p. 17.
24 Ibid.
25 Wittgenstein, *The Blue and Brown Books*, p. 31.
26 See Wittgenstein's "Lecture on Ethics," but also, importantly, Murray, "A Note on Wittgenstein and Heidegger."
27 Note that in the TON passage, Kant does not refer to the concepts of nothing as "categories," even though the division *follows* the division of the previous "table of the categories." I believe this is because Kant takes *categories* to be, originally, concepts *of being* (ways that objects can be), and hence the concepts of *non-being* would not themselves be categories. This aligns with MV's ultimate suggestion that an account of the concepts of nothing in Kant would require the existence of "anti-categories" (pp. 12, 25–8).
28 Interestingly, Kant defines the *ens rationis* as the concept of an object "to which no intuition that can be given corresponds" and hence "a concept without an object" (A290/B347). He then gives as an example *not only* the noumena, but "certain new fundamental forces, which one thinks, without contradiction, to

be sure, but also without any example from experience even being thought, and which must therefore not be counted among the possibilities" (A290–91/B347). It can seem as though the latter example opens up the *ens rationis* to include not just noumena, but also objects that are simply thought without contradiction, whose actuality we *happen* not to have grounds for asserting. But it is important to keep in mind that Kant seems to be focused on the stronger point (and hence more interested in the *noumena*), when he says that the *ens rationis* is the concept of an object which *must not be counted among the possibilities*.

29   A109. Mayz Vallenilla translates Kant's *Gemüts* as "espíritu" or "spirit" rather than "mind," but for consistency with the standard English translations, we will continue to use "mind."
30   A108
31   *KPM*, p. 88
32   The reference is, once again, to A143/B183.
33   *KPM*, p. 112
34   *KPM*, p. 181. It is also worth noting that Heidegger's reading of Kant as treating time as a series of *nows* has been disputed, for instance in Melnick (2009, pp. 107–8). If this criticism of Heidegger is correct, then Kant could be taken as already closer to giving an account of original or "primordial" temporality in the *Critique of Pure Reason*.
35   Kant's opaqueness regarding this issue may be what goes to the heart of Heidegger's critique, for instance when he criticizes Kant for not earnestly asking after the "subjectivity of the subject" (the *Being* of the "I"), *BT* 24. And connected to this point is Heidegger's claim that, for Kant, my "existence" essentially refers to my consciousness of being "objectively present," in much the same way as Descartes conceived of the ego, rather than my *being-in-the-world*, *BT* 203–4.
36   Cf. Wittgenstein, *Tractatus Logico-Philosophicus*, Preface.

Citations of Kant

Note: all citations of Kant's *Critique of Pure Reason* follow the standard "A" and "B" pagination. All other citations follow the standard *Akademie* edition pagination.

Critique of Pure Reason. 1998. Trans. Paul Guyer and Allen Wood. Cambridge: Cambridge University Press.

Notes and Fragments. 2005. Trans. Curtis Bowman, Paul Guyer and Frederick Rauscher. Cambridge: Cambridge University Press.

Theoretical Philosophy, 1755–1770. 1992. Trans. David Walford and Ralf Meerbote. Cambridge: Cambridge University Press.

Theoretical Philosophy after 1781. Trans. Gary Hatfield, Michael Friedman, Henry Allison and Peter Heath. Cambridge: Cambridge University Press.

Citations of Kant's *Critique of Pure Reason* from the Spanish:

Crítica de la Razón Pura. 2009. Trans. Mario Caimi: Fondo de Cultura Económico.

Citations of Heidegger

Note: all citations of Heidegger's *Being and Time* follow the standard "Heidegger" pagination.

Being and Time. 1962. Trans. John Macquarrie and Edward Robinson. New York City: Harper & Row.

Being and Time. 2010. Trans. Joan Stambaugh. Albany: SUNY Press.

Introduction to Metaphysics. 2014. Trans. Gregory Fried and Richard Polt. New Haven: Yale University Press.

Kant and the Problem of Metaphysics: Fifth Edition, Enlarged. 1997. Trans. Richard Taft. Bloomington: Indiana University Press.

Off the Beaten Track. 2002. Trans. Julian Young, Kenneth Haynes. Cambridge: Cambridge University Press.

On the Way to Language. 1982. Trans. Peter D. Hertz. New York: Harper & Row.

On Time and Being. 1972. Trans. Joan Stambaugh. New York: Harper & Row.

Pathmarks. 1998. Ed. William McNeill. Cambridge: Cambridge University Press.

Bibliography

Aristotle. 1991. *The Complete Works of Aristotle, Vols. I-II*. Ed. Jonathan Barnes. Princeton: Princeton University Press.

Blattner, William. 2021. "Temporality," in *The Cambridge Heidegger Lexicon*. Ed. Mark A. Wrathall. Cambridge: Cambridge University Press.

Ernesto Mayz Vallenilla. 1965. *El Problema de la Nada en Kant*. Madrid: Editorial Revista de Occidente.

Haugeland, John. 2013. *Dasein Disclosed*. Ed. Joseph Rouse. Cambridge: Harvard University Press.

Hegel, G.W.F. 2010. *Science of Logic*. Trans. George di Giovanni. Cambridge: Cambridge University Press.

Mayz Vallenilla, Ernesto. 1960. *Ontología del Conocimiento*: Universidad Central de Venezuela.

Melnick, Arthur. 2009. *Kant's Theory of the Self*. New York: Routledge.

Nicholson, Graeme. 1996. "The Ontological Difference," *American Philosophical Quarterly*, Vol. 33: 4.

Ortega y Gasset, José. 1958. *Kant, Hegel, Dilthey*. Madrid: Revista de Occidente.

Ortega y Gasset, José. 1963. "Vitalidad, Alma y Espíritu," in *Obras Completas, Tomo II*. Madrid: Revista de Occidente.

Ortega y Gasset, José. 2003. *El Tema de Nuestro Tiempo*: Austral.

Sartre, Jean-Paul. 1956. *Being and Nothingness*. Trans. Hazel E. Barnes. New York: Philosophical Library.

Schopenhauer, Arthur. 2018. *The World as Will and Representation, Vol. 2*. Trans. Judith Norman and Alistair Welchman and Christopher Janaway. Cambridge: Cambridge University Press.

Wittgenstein, Ludwig. 1998. *Tractatus Logico-Philosophicus*. London: Dover.

Wittgenstein, Ludwig. 1986. *Philosophical Investigations*. Trans. G.E.M. Anscombe. London, Oxford: Basil Blackwell.

Glossary of Key Terms

What follows is a list of key terms from Mayz Vallenilla's text, along with definitions or explanations of their usage. While the list is necessarily non-exhaustive, I hope that it will offer the reader some guidance and, at least, a point of departure for further exploration of these concepts.

Abseity (*Abseidad*)—Mayz Vallenilla coins this term, playing off the received term "*aseity*." *Aseity* is the quality of being *self-produced*, *self-dependent*, and *self-sufficient*. It is traditional to ascribe aseity to God (as does Aquinas). Others have attributed it to the will; Schopenhauer, for instance, writes: "but such a will must also be accorded aseity, since, being free, i.e. being the thing in itself and therefore not subject to the principle of sufficient reason, it can as little depend on anything else in its being and essence as it does in its deeds and actions. Only with this assumption is as much *freedom* posited as is needed to maintain the balance with the inescapably strict *necessity* that governs the course of the world (*The World as Will and Representation* Vol. 2, p. 333)."

The substitution of the prefix "*ab*" for "*a*" would suggest, not a *from*-selfness, but an *away*-from-selfness. In the passage where this term occurs (one where the phenomenon of *deep sleep* is used to illustrate the experience of the Nothing), Mayz Vallenilla is therefore suggesting that what is revealed is no longer just the *self-constituted* experience of *being*, but now the *encounter* with something that exceeds any self-constituting act of the subject.

Anxiety (*Angustia*)—While Mayz Vallenilla seems to prefer "deep sleep" (*el sueño profundo*) as an example of the manifest phenomenon of the Nothing, he also indicates his agreement with Heidegger that *anxiety* is such a manifestation. It is worth at least mentioning here the notion that Mayz Vallenilla is registering his agreement with. Anxiety is, for Heidegger, a "fundamental mood" (*Grundstimmung*) of Dasein (his term for our human mode of being). The mood of anxiety has to be understood by the following two points. First, unlike fear, anxiety is not "anxiety *in the face of*" some object in the world, but instead is "anxious in the face of the 'nothing' of the world" (*Being and Time*, 343). But, Heidegger continues, this just means that we are anxious in the face of nothing *but* our being-in-the-world as such. So, being-in-the-world "is both what anxiety is anxious in-the-face-of and what it is anxious about". Second, anxiety is revelatory, in the sense that it places us before, or reveals, the Nothing. In *Being and Time* it is the disclosure of the groundlessness of our being ("the nullity of that with which one can concern oneself," ibid.). In "What Is Metaphysics?" it is made clear that this occurs as the result of finding oneself (as Dasein) before the Nothing ("the nothing rises to meet us," p. 90).

Appearance or Phenomenon (*Fenómeno*)—The text follows other Spanish translations of Kant in using "fenómeno" for both *Erscheinung* ("appearance") and *Phänomenon* ("phenomenon").[1] For both textual and philosophical reasons this has the potential to cause some confusion. While in many cases the difference is not so important, it is good to keep in mind that Kant *defines* "appearance" and "phenomenon" differently. "Appearance" is the "undetermined object of an empirical intuition" (A20/B34), which suggests that *appearances* are objects of the senses that are not yet, as such, determined by a judgment. "Phenomena" are appearances "to the extent that as objects they are thought in accordance with the unity of the categories" (A248–9). Mayz Vallenilla might use "fenómeno" in both cases because the two notions are so closely linked. Both Kant and Heidegger could be understood as holding that "appearance" presupposes the "phenomenon." For Kant, this is because the definition of an appearance presupposes the *determinability* of the appearance (and hence its existence as phenomenon). For Heidegger, "appearance" can be used to mean "phenomenon," although it still seems to carry with it the sense of something hidden (*Being and Time*, 28–31).

Entity/Being (*Ente*)—a being or thing, as opposed to the *being of* beings (see: *ontological difference*). "Entitative" being, then, signifies the being of something as a thing, and typically as present-at-hand (see: *present-at-hand*).

Intrabody (*Intracuerpo*)—For Mayz Vallenilla, this refers to a "meaningful" interconnected nexus (of certain items, e.g., representations, concepts, words) in which the items holistically determine the meaning of one another. It would be appropriate here to think of a meaningful intrabody as an *organic* whole of items, to evoke the sense of "organism," in which the whole is an interconnection of parts which mutually determine one another. As noted in the Translator's Introduction, this term may be derived from José Ortega y Gasset.

Illumination (*Irradiación*)—Mayz Vallenilla often employs the unusual-sounding term "*mutua irradiación*," the direct translation of which would be "mutual irradiation." Despite the initial oddness of such a term, it could easily be seen that "irradiation" can apply to human social or cultural phenomena (e.g., ideologies could *radiate* through culture). The idea of a "mutual irradiation," however, calls more readily to mind the English "illumination." And indeed, "irradiate" has roots in the Latin *irradiare*, which does mean "to illuminate." "Mutual" illumination or radiation suggests that what illuminates or radiates is always an interrelated nexus, not an individual thing.

Nihilation (*anonadimiento*)—In her glossary of Sartre's *Being and Nothingness*, Hazel Barnes notes that Sartre himself coined the term "nihilate" (néantir), and the English term first appeared in Helmut Kuhn's *Encounter with Nothingness* (1956, pp. 631–632). English translations of Heidegger sometimes use "nihilate" as a translation of the German *nichtet* (see, e.g., "Letter on Humanism" and "What Is Metaphysics?"). And, for Mayz Vallenilla, "nihilation" is a translation of *die Nichtung*. The Spanish—*anonadamiento*—would indeed carry with it the connotation of *destruction* or *annihilation*, bringing it closer to the rendering of Heidegger's term. However, this nihilating activity is *not*, as it would be for Sartre, merely the saying "no" to or the negation of some entity (and hence the origin of the Nothing). It is, as in Heidegger's analysis of anxiety, grounded in the Nothing itself. Or, to put it slightly differently, the Nothing performs its *own* nihilating activity (to pay homage to Heidegger's now infamous statement that "The nothing itself nihilates") ("What Is Metaphysics?," *Pathmarks*, p. 90). This nihilation is therefore prior to any negating activity of the thinking subject ("It is neither an annihilation of beings nor does it spring from a negation").

Non-Being (*No-Ser*)—Typically, Mayz Vallenilla uses this term to refer, *not* to the Nothing or Nothingness as such or in its most authentic presentation, but rather to a particular species of it—namely, the *negated* being or entity. Non-Being is thus an "ontological Nothing" in the sense that it gets its meaning from the negation of what structures being (the ontological). But, especially at the end of chapter 4, Mayz Vallenilla emphasizes that any articulation of Nothingness as Non-Being will still leave behind the idea of Nothingness as *pure negativity*.

Ontological Difference (*Diferencia ontológica*)—The ontological difference is a notion deriving directly from Heidegger, but which ultimately has ancient Greek roots. Aristotle's "Metaphysics" is a study of *being qua being*, and recognizes many different *senses* of being. While the exegesis is difficult, it is not difficult to motivate the suggestion that in Aristotle there is already a recognition of the difference between particular beings or senses of being, and being *as such*. This is what Heidegger goes on to take up as a fundamental principle of what is left behind in the history of philosophy (in its oblivion or forgetfulness of being): that there is a difference between *beings* and the *being* that they have.[2] Mayz Vallenilla is using precisely this notion to motivate the project of *KPN* from the beginning. On his view, the only solution to the initial *problem* posed by any attempt to understand Nothingness is an understanding of the way this difference

(1) explains the problem, and (2) shows a way out of the mundane "entitative" conception of being.

Openness (*la patencia*)—Mayz Vallenilla is a phenomenologist, and hence he follows in the tradition of treating the cognition or knowledge of objects as an experience of the things themselves. More specifically, however, he follows *Heidegger* in treating this cognition, knowledge, or experience, as a *letting* things show or reveal themselves. For both Heidegger and Mayz Vallenilla, this "letting-show-up" is best understood through the metaphors of light and darkness, clarity, and obscurity. Hence, in *KPN* the most significant manifestation of a phenomenon tends to be characterized as a *shining* (or even a *gleaming*), or an opening up of what is otherwise concealed. The most authentic form of Nothingness that Mayz Vallenilla is after shows itself in this manner, as an opening or openness.[3]

Present-at-hand/before one's eyes (*Ante los ojos*)—This is a direct reference to Heidegger's distinction between what is merely "present-at-hand" (*Vorhanden*) and the "ready-to-hand" (*Zuhanden*). Presence-at-hand indicates an object as merely standing "there" before the subject, as opposed to the object whose being is inseparable from its being engaged or made use of. Mayz Vallenilla's way of rendering the notion in Spanish is to employ the phrase "*ante los ojos*" (before one's eyes).

Presentation (*aspecto*)—Mayz Vallenilla directly ties his use of "*aspecto*" to the Latin "*aspectus*" (meaning the "appearance" or "presence" of something), and to Kant's use of the Latin "*exhibitio*" in a passage from the *Anthropology*. In this text, Kant describes the faculty of imagination (*Einbildungskraft*) as one that presents an object in intuition either *reproductively*, by recalling or bringing back what has been presented before, or *productively*, by *originally* presenting an object in intuition prior to any experience of it. What is produced or reproduced is what Kant calls a *Darstellung*—an intuitive presentation (not a *representation*, or *Vorstellung*, which could be un-schematized). While the precise distinction between "presentation" and "representation" cannot be drawn here, what is important for Mayz Vallenilla is that a presentation is much like the sensible "look" or "appearing" of a phenomenon.

Temporality (*Temporalidad, Zeitlichkeit; Temporariedad, Temporalität*)— "Temporality" is an enormously important term for Mayz Vallenilla, but it is not used by Kant. The significance it has for the project of *KPN* aligns with the significance it has for the "Existential Phenomenological" tradition more generally (especially Heidegger, but for Sartre as well). Temporal*ity* is something's mode of being temporal. And, since there are different senses of what it means for something to be temporal, there are different corresponding senses of temporality.

Again in accordance with the Heideggerian tradition, two of these different senses of the term are employed in *KPN*. That which is used most frequently throughout the text is *temporalidad*, though he occasionally—near the beginning of the text—uses *temporariedad*. While Mayz Vallenilla does not explicitly tell us this, it is likely that the distinction corresponds to that in Heidegger's terminology between "temporality" as *Zeitlichkeit* and "temporality" as *Temporalität*. *Zeitlichkeit*, for Heidegger, is temporality of Dasein, an understanding of which is necessary if we are, in turn, to understand the temporality of being *in general* (for the very same reason that to understand the meaning of being in general, Heidegger thinks it is necessary to inquire into the meaning of *our* being, as the ones who are characterized by the very fact that we ask about being).

In section IV of Mayz Vallenilla's Introduction, he clarifies that his use there of "*Temporariedad del Ser*" (Temporality of Being) is equivalent to the German *Temporalität des Seins*, an implication of which is that the rarely-used *temporariedad* corresponds to Heidegger's notion of the temporality of being *in general* (*Temporalität*), whereas the much more frequently used *temporalidad* corresponds to Heidegger's notion of the temporality of Dasein in particular (*Zeitlichkeit*).

Notes

1   See, for example, *Crítica de la Razón Pura* (tr. Mario Caimi, B185–6. Fondo de Cultura Económica, 2009.)
2   For an interesting and useful overview, see Nicholson ("The Ontological Difference," *American Philosophical Quarterly*, Vol. 33, 4, 1996).
3   This should be directly correlated with Heidegger's notion of a *clearing* (*Lichtung*; see, e.g., *Being and Time*, 350).

Acknowledgments

The idea for this translation emerged when I was a postdoctoral researcher at the Institute for Philosophical Research at the Universidad Nacional Autónoma de México (UNAM). I would like to express my gratitude to the colleagues at UNAM who supported my work during 2019–21 (and beyond), but especially Pedro Stepanenko and Efraín Lazos. Regular meetings with my friend and distinguished philosopher, Carlos Pereda, were a source of constant encouragement, as were all the fond moments spent with Byron Davies and Marcela Cuevas. My utmost gratitude is also due to the estate of Ernesto Mayz Vallenilla for welcoming the project. Leonor Mayz Wallis and Gladys Arellano Mayz graciously agreed to the publication of this translation, on behalf of the Archivo Mayz Vallenilla. In connection with the development of this project, I would also like to thank Courtney Fugate and Suzie Nash for their support.

Many friends and colleagues were sources of inspiration and support along the way. Discussions with Sasha Newton about Kant's table of nothingness inspired my interest in the topic as a graduate student, and further discussions with Megha Sachdev kept it going. The moral support of colleagues at the University of Illinois at Urbana-Champaign made it so much easier to complete the project. For this, I thank especially Jochen Bojanowski, Kirk Sanders, and David Sussman. During the process of translating, I periodically consulted friends and colleagues who graciously let me think through puzzles of translation with them. For this, I especially thank Ana Lopez and Marcela García-Romero. I would also like to express my thanks to my colleagues at the American University in Cairo, who truly believe in the importance of translation work.

A Note for the Reader

In what follows, all text occurring in square brackets is the addition of the translator. In order to keep with the standard of modern Kant scholarship, all English quotations from Kant are from the Cambridge Edition translations, except where otherwise noted.

Prologue

To think is to hold a dialog with problems. But the authentic problems, walled in their mysteriousness, not only refuse to give an answer to anyone who wants to interrogate them, but they obscure their true face under subtle tricks that mislead the quest. Dialoguing with them means forcing them to reveal the path that leads to their encounter and making them testify to the truth they hide. In order to do this, thinking must besiege them and penetrate their dwellings. Only through this intimacy can dialog be born: authentic thinking.

But there is nothing easy in this task. More powerful than the power of thinking is that of those mysteries which constitute the finitude of man. It is impossible to fight against them. Anyone who faces their quest with sincerity must be willing to fail in such an attempt. Their failure must bear witness to the very finitude of their thought.

Sometimes, however, something unexpected happens. After the sustained and fruitless struggle, an unexpected face shines forth: in that which veils its presence the nameless is insinuated and sensed as that which hiddenly appears. They who have not sought it admire and startle at its call.

These are moments of extraordinary joy, prodigious lucidity, and communion with the unknown.

Whether this book uncovers a similar finding, it is up to the reader to decide.

Caracas, July 1, 1964

Introduction

Every attempt that pretends to confront the problem of Nothingness, before undertaking its specific task, must become explicitly conscious of the difficulties that surround and limit it. Not only because of the abstruse and complex topic, but because of the impediments that arise from its own ontological bases, the development of such a problem inevitably stumbles over serious obstacles that make it difficult, and sometimes bewildering, to access the phenomenal data in which it manifests itself. Authentic philosophical work consists not only in trying to overcome these obstacles—arduous and risky work—but, also, in indicating at the same time the source from which they arise and their reason for being.

The present *Introduction* aspires to accomplish such a task. Before we confront the problem of Nothingness, we consider it necessary to explain certain difficulties that arise, in the form of resistance and ontological barriers, making impossible or disrupting our understanding of the problem. In this way, in addition to alerting the reader to them, we will have the opportunity to clarify a series of aspects that are essential for achieving an adequate grasp of the primary issue that we will investigate: the Temporality [*Temporalidad*] of Nothingness.

I

One of the greatest difficulties stems from language. Traditional in this regard has been the dispute surrounding whether or not philosophy requires a special terminology in order to carry out its specific task. Considering that the forms of thought are consigned to and exhibited in human language, and that every expression implicitly contains a category, hidden or mixed in the intrabody [*intracuerpo*][1] of meanings, Hegel believed that it was unnecessary for philosophy to have to resort to any trick in order to express its ideas [*intelecciones*]. Indeed, if its task consists in exhibiting the realm of thought in its own immanent activity, that is, the development or unfolding of the categories through which absolute spirit finds its manifestation or epiphany, and these also find faithful and adequate expression in ordinary language, nothing prevents the employment of such an instrument from fulfilling the proposed purpose. On the contrary, the conscious use of language will provide an opportunity to make the greatest discoveries [*hallazgos*], and a careful study of its objectified forms will be able to reveal the fine and interwoven fabric of meanings wherein the categories have been placed and form the intrabody of logical relationships that constitute "the realm of pure thought." Even, he [Hegel] himself says, the most difficult and delicate ontological realities (e.g., that which defines the dialectical method) find faithful and adequate expression in ordinary speech, which in this sense would come to be like the living reflection of the speculative work of spirit.[2] So—as he expresses it verbatim— "philosophy does not in general require any special terminology."[3]

But, as can be observed, all of this depends on a prior and determinate task assigned to philosophy, as well as an assumption on which the meaningful evidence of language is allowed to rest in its transparent expressive function of categories. Now: is this indeed the task that Hegel assigns to philosophy, and is the character [*la textura*] and configuration that he assigns to language as an expressive instrument of the secret work of spirit also evident? Is, perhaps, the categorial reality that is expressed through it synonymous with what philosophy must aim to apprehend and exhibit as a desideratum? Our age is not so sure.

On the contrary, with respect to the categories, one of the aspirations that our era has pursued with the greatest enthusiasm has been to revise ontological-categorial assumptions. Under this is included not only a formal consideration of the theory of the categories—trying to improve or correct the existing ones in order to adapt them to the complex plot of reality discovered by scientific or technological advances—but the attempt to subject to a truly radical critique the same foundations on which they rest and from which they spring. The ontological supposition of any category is Being and, therefore,

Nothingness. It is a question, then, not simply of examining the categories in which Being (or, what is the same, Nothingness) unfolds, but of centering the analysis on their very foundation as that which confers their meaning.

In this respect, when in our era there is talk of "overcoming metaphysics," this would be misunderstood if in such a motto one believed to see an outdated return to positivism or an attempt to suppress the notion of Being. On the contrary, behind this statement, if it is understood, there is hidden an attempt to overcome "metaphysics"—since the "metaphysical" notion of Being is unsatisfactory—with a view to acquiring a new notion in which the *ontological difference* shines forth. Only by starting from this, having in clear view an instance in which an adequate meaning is conferred on the categories, could the latter be taken as authentic indicators of ontological reality.

But if that which enables and sustains the categories themselves is what has fallen into crisis, and language, on the other hand, is a reflection of those categories, then language could hardly be an adequate instrument for the tasks of philosophical work, if one intends (even without categorically denying Hegel's goal) to examine the most radical ontological assumptions and achieve an adequate expression for the new ideas that arise from there. On the contrary, as long as language reflects categories that are the expression of an unsatisfactory concept of Being, and through which they want to formulate new ideas, their meaningful intrabody, as well as their expressive instruments, will fail in the attempt to capture that which by its very nature exceeds its own limits and even contradicts the semantic roots on which it feeds. Cradled within the framework of a vision of Being (or of Nothingness) in which the *ontological difference* does not prevail, the meaningful resources of language, and even its syntax, refuse to adapt to a radically different expressive function from that assigned by its own categorial intrabody.

Such is one of the primordial difficulties that we will have to examine and test throughout our investigation. Without making us completely supportive of the thesis exhibiting the notable validity of the so-called *ontological difference*—nor to subscribe to all the assumptions and metaphysical implications that accompany it—we must investigate whether the use of ordinary language, or even of technical language coined under the influence of a certain *understanding of Being*, is capable of serving as an ideal instrument for expressing a notion of Nothingness under which the very "ontological" assumptions that sustain such a thesis are called into question. For this, as can be easily understood, it is necessary that, if only briefly, we point out a series of aspects connected to the previous ones.

II

The Word, certainly, testifies to the presence of Being: it is its expression. But it is a fact—historically and philologically verifiable—that in Western thought, almost from its origins, a *forgetfulness of Being* has prevailed. This *forgetfulness* must not be understood or interpreted as *ignorance*, or in the manner of a loss of *memory* [*desmemoria*], *amnesia* or *omission*, but, rather, as a *distraction* or (to put it more precisely) as *carelessness* or *negligence*. In his dealings with Being—insofar as ek-sistence means being exposed and open to comprehension—man has neglected Being and has been distracted by entities. In this way, the Being with which he deals is not an instance in which his absolute transcendence shines forth with respect to entities, or even to the entitative en abstracto—as a radical or vast difference—but, on the contrary, summarizes and expresses a notion discovered in view of entities. Being is, as the highest or most universal genus of entities, the "Being of entities," but not Being as such. "Metaphysics"—Heidegger has said in this regard—"does indeed represent beings in their being, and so it also thinks the being of beings. But it does not think being as such, does not think the difference between being and beings."[4]

> The oblivion of being makes itself known indirectly through the fact that the human being always observes and handles only beings. Even so, because humans cannot avoid having some notion of being, it is explained merely as what is "most general" and therefore as something that encompasses beings, or as a creation of the infinite being, or as the product of a finite subject. At the same time "being" has long stood for "beings" and, inversely, the latter for the former, the two of them caught in a curious and still unraveled confusion.[5]

But if this has happened with Being, the same seems to have taken place with Nothingness. Or rather: beginning from the thought of a concept of Being wherein there is no radical difference between it and entities, Nothingness, as a notion opposite to or contradictory with respect to Being, has been thought and elaborated from within a similar horizon. As a negative notion of Being (non-Being), Nothingness is conceived either as the negation of an entity, of the entitative in general, or, in short, of the Being itself of entities. But just as Being is confused with the entity or the entitative in general, in the thought of Nothingness, the difference between the Nothing of the entity and Nothingness as such does not prevail, which implies that this notion does not correspond to a Nothingness of Being as Being, but to a Nothingness of entities or of the Being of entities. Moreover, since Nothingness consists of a negation of the Being of entities or of the entities themselves, it goes unnoticed that this negation itself, as a positing, has its origin in the ontological sphere (i.e., that it is an ontological position), which clouds and diverts thinking when it tries to apprehend Nothingness as Nothingness. In this way, having its origin and foundation in an ontological negation, Nothingness "is" and is inevitably confused with its own contrary.

The Word, certainly, can constitute the expression of Being (or of Nothingness), but when this occurs, it is *eo ipso* impossible to express Being as Being or Nothingness as Nothingness. Taking root in and sprouting from such a *forgetfulness of Being*, the *ontological difference* does not come to express itself in it. Metaphysical language, says Heidegger, speaks about Being, but refers to the entity.[6] One may want to speak of Nothingness, but necessarily she remains a prisoner of negation and expresses only an "ontological" Nothing. Such is a primary fact that makes understandable the reason allowing us to think that a language arising from such a situation is incapable, in principle, of serving as an ideal instrument in relation to our ends. But then it becomes urgent to ask: what path or recourse have we left for overcoming such a difficulty?

It would be very easy to say—in order to escape luckily and avoid the obstacle—that one can, through a certain effort, dominate or overcome this *forgetfulness of Being*. That is: that such a phenomenon is only a temporary historical situation, as such, contingent and even surmountable. In truth, we do not deny this. But if we do not deny it, it is necessary to specify that this is not because we believe that the *forgetfulness of Being* is a mere historical situation. On the contrary, in that which has reality, such a phenomenon is established or rooted in an *existential a priori* and, as such, springs from the very ontological structure of the human being. If perhaps it is possible to think of an overcoming—since the opposite would be to condemn man to a situation that does not correspond to him—such a conquest can be thought only from the conditions of possibility offered by the very context of human Existence. But in this, precisely, is where the problem of the matter lies and the circumstance that does not necessarily guarantee the possibility of overcoming it.

Indeed, we do not deny man the ability to overcome the *forgetfulness of Being*. His own ontic-ontological constitution, in exceptional moments of fullness or authenticity, makes him capable of envisaging the *ontological difference* and of attaining an idea of where the radical transcendence of Being (or of Nothingness) shines forth with respect to entities. But it is a factum, also rooted in such a constitution, that his own existence inevitably tends to project his own ontological understanding from the horizon of the *world* where he lies seized as a *being in the world* that is. From such a horizon, insofar as he exists immersed and situated amongst the entities, his *understanding of Being (Seinsverständnis)* does not exhibit the features or marks that are shown in it when it is projected from the distinctive validity of the *ontological difference*. The *forgetfulness of Being* (or of Nothingness) is, in such a way, an event rooted in the very ontological-existential constitution of the human being that Heidegger has called its *state of thrownness and fallenness*.[7]

The Word springs from the bosom of Existence. As such, establishing its roots in its own ontic-ontological constitution, it has the power to testify to an *understanding of Being* (or of Nothingness) in which the *ontological difference* prevails. But just as Existence is constantly liable of falling into a world commanded by entities, the Word is subject to a similar phenomenon. Projected from such a horizon, and inserted into the fabric of intraworldly relations and entitative involvements [*transferencias*], it becomes a mere signifying-instrument that is used or employed to designate entities and their multitude of relations. If one tries to mention Being (or Nothingness) with it, its meaning picks out and expresses that of a Being (or Nothing) in which, obliviously and inexplicably, a forgetfulness of the *ontological difference* prevails.

Conceived from such a perspective, it is important to observe that the Word is not denied—in an absolute or radical manner—its power or capacity to express the idea of Being or Nothingness as such. But, at the same time, the condition to which it is exposed is that of losing sight of or failing to achieve such a task. Either because it originates from a horizon where an *understanding of Being* that acknowledges the *ontological difference* does not prevail, or because of the use and constant reinterpretation to which it is subjected in ordinary language (where the domain of entities prevails), its illuminating force turns weak, opaque, or non-existent. Although in some cases it is capable of revealing the presence of Being, or of rising up as a testimony of the possibility of saying Nothing[8], its illuminating power or force is lost, confused or weakened, until it becomes expressionless. Instead of naming Being or Nothingness as such, transposed from a purely entitative meaning, its original apophantic function is distorted. Therefore, according to Heidegger, "the difficulty lies not so much in finding the Word of Being in thinking as in retaining purely in genuine thinking the Word found."[9]

But as it should be noted, Heidegger assigns to the Word (in strict correspondence with the ontological assumptions that sketch his conception of language) an innate and original capacity to serve as a revealing instrument of Being or of Nothingness as such. Since language is the home of Being—*its templum*—nothing seems more natural than the possibility of expressing, through the Word, the presence of Being itself.[10] But precisely in this lies the most dubious thought of such a suggestive doctrine. In effect, the question to be examined consists not only in asking if the Word can be deprived of its original condition of becoming a merely expressive instrument of entities, but, on the contrary, whether its true and original condition is not precisely the latter and if it can, *in principle*, be overcome. According to Heidegger, as is well known, the eventual overcoming occurs thanks to the modal dialectic of Existence (which develops between the extremes of *ownedness* and *unownedness*)[11] and on the basis of this, as a phenomenon rooted in that same Existence, language acquires the corresponding modalities and possibilities of expression.[12]

But, apart from the existential assumptions implied by such a doctrine, and even without going into them in themselves, it is a question of wondering whether a Word could be conceived whose function is purely *ontological*, and, as such, exempt from any entitative or *ontic* reference. Heidegger himself has said that Being never presents itself without an entity,[13] and it is a question then of whether it is possible to imagine a Word that could surpass or overcome such a condition. In effect: does not the comprehensibility and meaning of every word require its insertion into a *world*, in order to be understood and interpreted by those who hear it? And does this *world* not imply necessary and inevitable references to a horizon of entities? Heidegger himself seems to have seen this problem when he says: "Is it a matter of chance that initially and for the most part significations are 'worldly,' prefigured beforehand by the significance of the world, that they are indeed often predominantly 'spatial'? Or is this 'fact' existentially and ontologically necessary and why?"[14] It is not that we wish to reduce the Word to being mere *meaning*—viz., that its essence is reduced to "meaning"—but, without a doubt, this "meaning" (as such) is inherent in the function of the Word as an instrument of communication between men. Now: can the "meaning" be displayed without referring to entities? In our judgment, even within the assumptions of the Heideggerian conception, such a question must be denied. Both for the first purely ontological reason (the impossibility that Being presents itself without the required co-presence of the entity) and by the very dialectic of Existence (the state of thrownness in which man finds himself), such an assumption is forced and even lacking a basis. It is true, however, that the Word can name entities and refer to Being, but the question is, even in doing so, whether it can ever fully escape its ontic design. Thinking or imagining otherwise—whatever the metaphysical explanation that is provided to justify the "theory"—means as much as exempting man from his original condition and assigning to him a *Creative Word* that, in truth, does not correspond to him. On the contrary: isn't the Word's essential impossibility for having a pure ontological reference rooted in the very *finitude* of ek-sistence?

This is not to say that, falling to the opposite extreme, language is denied any possibility of expressing a situation or reality in which it attempts to apprehend the *ontological difference*. As a result of his first investigations on language, Wittgenstein coined a famous aphorism that has gained suspicious popularity: "What can be said at all can be said clearly; and whereof one cannot speak thereof one must be silent."[15] But this would mean—taken literally—that all questions over which "darkness" prevails would have to be abandoned or silenced, refusing to deal with them or declaring them "mystical."[16] As such, the *ontological difference*, insofar as it is not expressed clearly, should be taken as one of those questions proper to "mysticism" and, consequently, separated from all genuine philosophical consideration. In our judgment, however, instead of solving such a problem so trivially, it would be better to ask ourselves about the basis of the same phenomenon shown. Indeed: for what reason or principle in the situation mentioned can something not be spoken of clearly? Does it not reveal the existence of this same fact that sometimes questions arise about which language fails when it wants to express itself? And can such questions therefore be declared merely non-existent or unworthy of philosophical consideration? Doing so means refusing to investigate phenomena, or, at the very least, putting yourself in a position that *a priori* assigns language a certain function, while, also *a priori*, closing off others by the simple fact of its limitations. More precisely, this *fact*—the "failure" language is accused of due to its precariousness and limitation—is, in our judgment, the phenomenon most worthy of study and in-depth analysis if it wants to clarify its own essence.

Now: does not the same failed aspiration reveal an essential feature in which the very finitude of language is shown and, at the same time, man's painstaking effort to break or exceed his limits? In our judgment, just as it is wrong to attribute to language a purported ability to overcome this finitude—assigning to it a supposed creative or pure ontological faculty—it is also improper to want to condemn it to the condition of being a mere designative instrument of entities and bare entitative relationships. On the contrary, neither a purely ontological function, nor this other merely conventional and ontic one, seems to correctly interpret the authentic and essential manifestation that it reveals in its dialectic. Language—we have said—"fails," but in its "failure" the effort to break the frame of the world that marks the limits of its own finitude is witnessed. The Word "fails," but in its "failure" the attempt to capture and express the *ontological difference* is revealed.

In his dealings with Being (or with Nothingness), man already encounters a set of Words that, always and necessarily, bear witness to some "ontological" ideas shown from the horizon of entities that make up his world; but in constant struggle with this language, painfully uprooting that reference to entities, and trying to show its pure ontological reference, it manages to capture a repertoire of mediating expressions which limits and outlines the domain of a trans-entitative, and in a certain way, trans-worldly, region: the one where the *ontological difference* prevails, is discerned and manifested. In this way, language is not creative—in the sense that through it a Being separate from entities is created—although, by apprehending and expressing the *difference*, it is capable of moving and unfolding in that illuminated border area that mediates between Being (or Nothingness) and entities. The Word, in this sense, names the *difference*, already cleared by understanding,[17] and establishes or founds that trans-entitative region as a field of pure intelligibility, at the same time as it reveals or testifies to the vain effort of man to break the frame of his radical finitude.

This attempt to overcome and transcend his own finitude is, besides, nothing strange or novel. This occurs generally in all fields, and, especially, where man insists on trying to appropriate and intelligibly express that which, being not created by himself, but an ingredient of the world in which he finds himself thrown, offers opacity and resistance to his desire to reveal Truth. In this fight—as science and technology testify to in an exemplary way—human language has been creating codes that allow us to name, organize and decipher entities, establish their laws and relationships and, in short, project order and intelligibility among them.

But if this has occurred in this field, all the more necessary and comprehensible is that it has also manifested itself where First Principles are concerned: Being and Nothingness themselves. In this sense, all that language reveals is man's constant effort to achieve mastery of the *ontological difference*. Thus, not having a creative recourse, because his Word is established and rooted in the essence of his own finitude, through it he has tried to name and illuminate the area where his highest and most worthy idea dwells, although what he always stumbles on—as an ultimate resistance—remains in obscurity and darkness. But not for being clear and evident does man seek Truth, but, on the contrary, for knowing or sensing that, after the apparent obscurity that surrounds him, he can, through his epistemic effort, reveal the light and implant the desired clarity. In this sense, "failing" over and over again, his effort testifies to the desire to find and express what appears obscurely: the Truth of Being or Nothingness as such.

Our attempt begins from such a situation and is conscious of what it implies. The problem of our own language presents us with an opportunity to face one of our most arduous tasks: that of trying to capture and express Nothingness where the available resources are not suitable for doing so. If one is aware of the difficulties this entails, and of the complex plot of questions that underlie it, everyone who wants to share it with us must be willing to experience the "failure" of their own language. Only in this experience, coming to understand where such a "failure" comes from, and seeing through its own foundations, can one also see what the investigation intends to show: Nothingness as such, while it reveals itself *through* a language that refuses to express it. Only in this experience does one *eo ipso* attain the language to comprehend what its "failure" means and says as a testimony to human finitude. But coming to understand this root or the foundation of its precariousness and limitation, it also glimpses the meaning of its effort and what it tries to transcend.

III

But just as language obstructs an adequate expression of Nothingness, it is possible to verify historically that this is compounded by another obstacle closely linked to the previous one: it is represented by the horizon of concepts and notions from which—as tacit assumptions—it is thought of and from whose referential basis its idea finds development.

Only by way of demonstration—and without the intention of verifying the extensive analysis that the detailed exposition of such a subject would require—can we point out that Nothingness has always been thought in relation to concepts such as those of *beginning, origin, source, foundation*, etc., in whose ontological treatment notions such as *cause, potency, act*, etc. are brought into play.[18] To these notions and concepts, as determinations of Being, is added or inferred, eminently, a *negation* whose effect consists in transforming Being—or its respective determination—into a Non-Being.

Now, the difficulty is that all these concepts and notions have an ontological meaning (when not ontic), and thinking Nothing on the basis of the indicated *negation* (which in turn implies an ontological positing), it appears only when Being is negated, ultimately finding its notion burdened by a surreptitious meaning derived from those other concepts or from the negative (ontological) position that is inferred from them. Therefore, generally speaking: resting upon a repertoire of ontological notions, and originating from a *negation* of the same nature, Nothingness is doubly affected by this irreducible ontological background that hinders and even distorts its positive concept. In such a way, instead of being apprehended in its originality—that is, shown plainly in its absolute negativity—the presentation under which it is offered conceals its true face and undermines its meaning.

What to do, then, in the face of this state of affairs?

The situation that is thus outlined contains a problem of the highest magnitude. Now, with a certain glibness it could be thought that its solution consists in replacing the notions and concepts mentioned by others in whose meaning the "ontological background" causing the disturbance is not found. But is it possible to achieve this? The crux of the matter lies in the fact that Thinking—and with it the entire repertoire of notions and concepts that constitute the heritage of philosophy—has been shown to have as a horizon of reference the Being or the Entity as such. Because of this, such Thinking (and the set of fundamental concepts) shows the indelible mark of its *ontological* origin and, through its application, it hardly achieves access to a region where all reference to such a nature should be eliminated.

However, this should not be an obstacle that leads one to abandon the attempt. An attempt to understand this situation, and to get clear about the root from which it springs, must strive to modify the foundations and find the appropriate path to carry out its task. The plan for such an attempt cannot be other than to invert the perspective and make Nothingness appear in its originality without the danger of being distorted by ontological interferences; this is: *to discover a path leading to a possible idea of Nothingness as such.* From there, Nothingness understood in its originality, Thinking could implement the resources for achieving its apprehension and expression through a repertoire of concepts and notions ("categories," or, perhaps better, "anti-categories") that serve as indices or models of its positive and original negativity.

But in the *uncovering* and *explanation* of this path is where the greatest problem lies. However, a step of remarkable importance has been taken in contemporary philosophy—especially notable in the thought of Martin Heidegger—by putting into relief Time as the *meaning* of Being. Following this, it has been shown that the idea of Being as such, and therefore that of all its determinations and concepts, reveals a marked and conclusive reference to Time. From Time, as a horizon of meaning, Being is understood and it is from such a perspective that all the notions that express its determinations are contained.[19] *Then won't Time also be the horizon of Nothingness?*

But what "Time"? If the attempt to apprehend Nothingness is obstructed by the *ontological* perspective dominating Thought, and if this perspective manifests a temporal meaning as its root, the question now lies in asking about the possible connection between Time and Nothingness in order to see if it is possible to discover a *sui generis* Temporality that offers a new horizon of meaning from which to coin the necessary determinations that the idea of Nothingness as such requires. But is this possible? Or is Time also condemned to being seen and apprehended from Being?

A *circle* seems to appear here.[20] Is this *circle* insurmountable, or is it precisely from its circular structure that the possibility is glimpsed and clarified? In any case, these questions must be posed if we intend to seriously investigate the possibility of breaking the ontological frame that obstructs any attempt to apprehend Nothingness in its originality.

IV

An inconvenience similar to that exhibited by ontological notions and concepts in relation to Nothingness arises in reference to Time when, clad in the usual meaning attached to it, it is intended to be used as a possible horizon for interpreting Nothingness. The obstacle comes—as we have hinted—from the undeniable existence of a *circle* of mutual illumination between Being and Time, which inevitably leads to Temporality being included in a surreptitious [*subrepticio*] ontological background that prevents or disrupts its proper use in order to achieve the precise idea of Nothingness as such.[21] The *circle* mentioned is revealed and developed from the attempt to think about the connection that mediates between Being and Time by highlighting the mutual dependence shown by both due to their respective conditioning.

Indeed, since Time is the horizon of Being, it is nevertheless historically verifiable that it is a certain conception of Being—in which even the *ontological difference* does not shine—from which that Time that serves as a meaning-giving horizon is "understood"; and it is, conversely, from such a Time thus "understood"—which functions as a horizon of meaning— that Being is interpreted and "ontologically" determined. But, finally, Being thus reinterpreted reaffirms the rights of the dominant "understanding" of Time that serves as a general and immediate horizon of interpretation.[22]

Given this ground, we can now say that such Temporality exhibits an "ontological" root; and, as Time here displays the structure of an entity among entities, its conception not only reveals a deficient perspective—since it is not even elaborated from the prior clarification of the *ontological difference*—but, at the same time, it would only be adequate for granting an interpretive scheme of Non-Being as long as it is conceived as an (ontological) negation of the Being of those entities. Thus, when "ontological" Temporality is used as a "meaning" of Nothingness, what can be apprehended through its determinations is the temporal schema of a "Nothingness" interpreted as the negation of an entity, of the entitative in general, or of the Being of entities. In brief: an ontological-temporal Nothing whose "meaning" is far from expressing the authentic temporal structure that Nothingness, as such, should exhibit as original negativity.

But does this mean that by this we postulate the possible existence of a Temporality of Nothingness that is independent of the Temporality of Being? Not at all. When speaking of a Temporality of Nothingness, this is not to say that Time as such duplicates its existence, as if there were one Time separate from another, or as if the Temporality of Nothingness subsisted, as a reality per se, alongside another reality that would be the Temporality of Being. Time—it seems obvious to say and will be shown through our investigation—is always one and the same, that which varies in it being only the result of its immanent temporalizing and the autonomous configuration of its ekstasis.

However, what requires emphasizing is that "ontological" Time—Temporality viewed and interpreted from the horizon of entities or from the perspective of a notion of Being in which the *ontological difference* does not prevail—is incapable, in principle, of serving as an index or exhibition of "meaning" for conceiving Nothingness. In this regard, it is necessary to emphasize and reiterate that, at least, as in the previous step, it is essential to acquire an idea of Time where that *difference* does prevail and that only on the basis of such *Temporality of Being*[23] (Temporalität des Seins [*Temporariedad*]) is it possible to attempt an idea of the *Temporality* [*Temporariedad*, Temporalität] *of Nothingness as the Nothingness of Being as such* and not, simply, as the "Nothingness" of an entity or of the entitative in general. This *Nothingness*, certainly, implies a "negation," but this cannot be conceived now as a mere negation of ontological modality, but as one that arises and finds its "foundation" in the original and absolute negativity of Nothingness itself. As will be shown in due course, if the Temporality [*Temporariedad, Temporalität*] of Nothingness is to emerge from a prior *understanding of Nothingness* (which reiterates the persistence of a circle similar to that already shown), it must establish itself in that absolute and original *negativity* that shows Nothingness itself when it manifests itself as the essential heterogeneity of Being. From that understanding of Nothingness as such, and from the original power of its absolute negativity, a Time must be conceived that can serve as an authentic "meaning." Instead, then, of displaying the characteristics of an entitative Time, or of an "ontological" Time, it is possible to detect in its particular temporalizing, and in the configuration of its ekstasis, the trace of that which serves as the ground soil of its comprehension.

Now, this implies that there are "phenomena" in which, or from which, the understanding of Nothingness is established. But isn't any phenomenon … phenomenon of Being? Or are there "phenomena" where Nothingness as such is shown and revealed? Such a question can only be exhibited through a precise description. Our work, committed to such a plan, is obliged to show the evidence and adduce the testimonies that can confirm such a hypothesis. In any case, although the term *phenomenon* is saddled with an ancient and manifold "*ontological*" meaning, nothing nevertheless prevents us from resorting to its most obscure meaning so that it may serve as an expression of what is manifested and shown insofar as it is obscured. And this is, like Being in relation to entities, Nothingness itself in relation to Being.

However, one last objection may be raised. In effect, we have established that Temporality [*Temporariedad*, Temporalität] *is* the "meaning" of Nothingness. Now: can something to which "Being" is imputed function as an indication or exhibition of precisely what seems to refuse such a condition? Or, expressed in this complementary perspective: can Time, as a "meaning," serve as a horizon for what precisely seems to deny all "meaning"? Such objections, despite their appearance, are no more than formal obstacles. The question lies—and this is where our efforts should have a bearing—in thinking deeply about the problems without being sidetracked by the difficulties of language or the pitfalls of using certain terms. If one proceeds in such a way, taking into account the reflections that have been made in relation to the *ontological* structure that the usual concepts reveal, one can understand the emptiness that such objections entail. For just as Nothingness is not without "meaning," nor is it a merely empty name of all "reality," it is not identical to Being or entities. Nothingness "*exists*," and all that the manifestation of its "existence" requires is that it be apprehended and witnessed. For this, certainly, a "λόγος" is required to verify the apophantic and phenomenological function that its manifestation requires. Overcoming the indissoluble connection that "λόγος" has with respect to Being due to its origin and tradition, and achieving through the sustained effort of the dianoetic function that which remains obscured (which implies the emergence of a "λόγος" that testifies to the positive negativity of Reason),[24] is exactly what should be attempted.

In order not to become demoralized in such a task, and to avoid the suspicion that it is only a vain effort that tries to find and apprehend something that does not exist—a ghost, a breath, a chimera—it is always necessary to reinforce the search with the testimony that the things themselves offer. Who would dare doubt what they themselves tell us, when, in addition to revealing to us the undeniable *understanding of Being* available to man, they also confirm the factum of their *understanding of Nothingness*? If he who undertakes such an attempt does not have adequate words to express this factum, if the concepts he uses are unsuccessful, if his Thinking fails, and if the "ontological" Time that serves as the "meaning" of his ideas in Thought presents enormous difficulties, there is nevertheless a secret impulse which guides and forces him to ask about that which he understands without being able to express it with lucidity and perfection. From such a root our attempt has been born. Only those who understand it in this way will be willing to experience in their own Thinking what this means and will be able to find in our investigation a stimulus—and perhaps a path forward—for the attempt to confront Nothingness.

V

It is not very difficult to explain the reasons that we have for choosing Kantian thought—and the fourfold notion of Nothingness that is systematically exhibited in the *Critique of Pure Reason*—as a point of reference on which to center our analysis. While it is true that those notions do at first glance denote originality in content—but, on the contrary, summarize the rich fabric of a tradition that is admirably placed and collected there[25]—their value to us lies in Kant's approach to and development of them by including them within the general meaning of his doctrine, and by conferring on them a meaning that is closely related to the already announced proposal of clarifying the connection between Time and Nothingness.

Indeed, each one of these notions of Nothingness—*ens rationis, nihil privativum, ens imaginarium,* and *nihil negativum*—being closely linked to the different groups of *categories*, and each one implying the existence of its respective *schematism* as the source of its temporal meaning, it is easy to see now the close connection that can be discovered between the problem of Time and question of Nothingness. To clarify such links, and develop their problems, has been one of the primary proposals of our attempt.

However, our work is not a matter of simply repeating or explaining Kant's ideas with regard to the *schematism* (an issue that is hardly elaborated in his own thought) but, fundamentally, of seeing what limits these schemata of ontological categories, as determinations of a temporal meaning, making them adequate or operative for referring to Nothingness and establishing their authentic temporal interpretation. As it will be shown—and this was already pointed out in mentioning the existing *circle* between Being and Time—the surreptitious ontological background of Temporality [*Temporalidad*, and presumably, *Zeitlichkeit*: see translator's note 23, and Glossary], which also undeniably operates in the Kantian conception, prevents the schematism of such categories from fully fulfilling the attempt to highlight that connection and strives to think radically from a notion of Nothingness in which the attempt is made to overcome "ontological" limitations. For this reason, through the exposition and discussion of Kant's own *presuppositions*, we have always had as a goal the search for new temporal exhibitions [*exponentes*] that offer a "meaning" in accordance, and at the same time compatible, with a notion of it conceived from such a perspective. However, this task has not been easy. For although Kantian thought provides us a certain frame of reference— thus revealing the extraordinary greatness of his original intuition—it is no less certain that its own limits represent an obstacle that cannot be overcome without help from arduous and prolonged work. Explaining and criticizing his thought, in this sense, is an extraordinary task for the depth, rigor, and lucidity that are required, both to interpret it correctly and to make corrections in those places where the new perspective requires it.

Our attempt has been confronted with such a task. Supporting ourselves with the framework of Kantian reflection, and seeking to illuminate those points susceptible to critique in his own doctrine, we have tried to sketch the grounds that can sustain the attempt to think Nothingness from Time. At the same time, aware of the *circle* that underlies such an attempt, we have tried to understand and interpret Time itself—its ekstasis and temporal configurations—from the horizon of Nothingness itself and from that border or limit-area where, in light of the *ontological difference*, it manages to manifest its positive, original, and absolute negativity. Seen from there, the original Temporality [*Temporariedad, Temporalität*] of Nothingness—as purely negative schematism—manifests as an opposite, if not contradictory, sign with respect to that revealed by the ontological schematism developed by Kant in relation to the corresponding categories. Applying these to the configuration of Nothingness—as opposed to the function assigned to them by Kant as *a priori* constitutive forms of Something—they demand from that schematism, as a horizon giving its temporal "meaning," a radically different form [*diseño*]. Categories and schemata thus exhibit, from their new "foundation," a completely different meaning from that which they manifest as ontological determinations. From this, *eo ipso*, the temporal structure that supports and defines their meaningful intrabody is modified. Sketching this new structure, and indicating the strange configuration that such a negative Temporality [*Temporariedad, Temporalität*] assumes, has also been one of the primary objectives pursued in our investigation.

Such a venture—as is easy to understand—is surrounded by dangers. To the merely exegetical difficulties are added, eminently, those that come from the impetus to reform. It is difficult, for those who have set out to challenge these dangers, to say whether they have managed to dominate them. It is up to the reader to judge this and ultimately decide the value of such an attempt. On the other hand, although we are aware of the possible defects that could be attributed to it, we are left with the intimate certainty of having always tried to overcome them. If this has not been possible, it is the product of our own limitations, as we do not have the superior strengths required to carry out such a task successfully. But man does not decide what he must face when he dedicates his life to thinking. From the things themselves the enigmas appear before him and do not give rest. It is then impossible to turn your back on them, ignore or forget them. Whoever respects himself must face them because only in tough battling with them can he reach the Truth or, at least, have the intimate awareness that in his passage through the world he has not been a fearful fugitive.

1

Nothingness and the Ens Rationis

§1 Nothingness as Noumenon

The first determination that Kant ascribes to the notion of Nothingness is that of being-qua-*noumenon* (ens rationis).[1] As such, as with what occurs in the case of the noumenon, Nothingness exhibits the character [*textura*] of an "*empty concept without object,*"[2] that is, of a concept to which no sensible intuition corresponds and that, therefore, lacks objective reality.[3] If it is characteristic of all *phenomena* to have a sensible intuition as a foundation—by which they obtain their necessary reference to an object[4]—Nothingness is exhibited precisely as this "empty concept" because it is impossible to point out the necessary reference to such intuition. Therefore, being devoid of all objective reality or a possible phenomenal exhibition, it cannot be counted among the possibilities, although it should also not be declared impossible. Just like the *noumenon*, by being a merely intelligible construct devoid of contradiction, it assumes the guise of a mere entity of reason (Gedankending) or of a mere fiction (Erdichtung).[5]

But in identifying the notion of Nothingness with a noumenon, one must remember the dual modality that this has within the Kantian doctrine; that is to say, its positive and negative sense. While in the positive sense the noumenon becomes "*the object of a non-sensible intuition*"[6]—already ruling out its possible affiliation with the notion of Nothingness—in the negative sense the result is a *boundary-concept* (Grenzbegriff),[7] through which we represent a "thing" (Ding) that is not the object of our sensible intuition, while we abstract from that "thing" our way of intuiting it and we are left with the purely intelligible structure that holds its representation as merely thought, or as an entity produced by the activity of our own understanding (Verstand). As such, as an entity born of our own understanding (Verstandeswesen), and taken in such a merely negative sense, this noumenon is like Nothing in its purely intelligible character [*textura*]. The Nothing is, in this mode, a noumenon in the negative sense.

But from such a characterization—by means of which the noumenon and the Nothing are formally identified thanks to the common lack of an intuitive basis—a series of corollaries can be extracted, which, although Kant considers them only in relation to the noumenon, it is also possible to apply to the notion of Nothing, thereby achieving greater precision and breadth in the characterization of its noumenal character [*textura*]. Indeed, just as the noumenon is not properly an *object* (Gegenstand)—since to be so would require the cooperation of an intuition—the Nothing, similarly, *eo ipso* repels such a connotation. Despite the fact that it is an entity produced by the intelligible function of the understanding, and that even without any intuition whatever, the manner of thinking remains (i.e., the way of determining an object for the manifold of intuition)—for this reason, the understanding's sphere of activity seems to extend beyond sensibility, precisely outlining the possibility of certain autonomous entities such as the Nothing and noumena—despite such activity being *empty* or devoid of matter, and, therefore, unable to constitute by itself a true *object*. If this means the phenomenal correlate of a cognition [*conocimiento*], integrated by the synthesis of intuitive matter with the categories, then the Nothing, like the noumenon, is only the product of a mere segmentation of the intellect, that is, of a purely intelligible structure, just as it is a fiction (Erdichtung) as *ens rationis*. However, despite these features, the Nothing or noumenon should not be declared inane chimeras devoid of any meaning and invented on an arbitrary whim.

Indeed, is it possible, just like that, to cast aside the understanding's own activity? Are the entities it produces through its self-sufficient activity absolutely meaningless? Although it is true that we can only *know* phenomena, it is no less true that there is also the possibility of *thinking* those "things" constituted or embodied by the purely intelligible activity of understanding. Nothing—as noumenon—is one of those things or notions that appears before us not as phenomenon, nor as object of the senses, but as a true *thing in itself* thought through the pure understanding.

Now, such a notion—as with the noumenon—has the value and meaning of a *boundary-concept* (Grenzbegriff), and is in no way arbitrary, but imposed by the constitution of "the things themselves." Indeed, just as the reality of the noumenon must be established in order to limit the pretensions of sensibility[8] and to affirm the rights of the understanding,[9] the notion of the Nothing would come to function as a boundary for establishing "the distinction of whether an object is Something (Etwas) or Nothing (Nichts)."[10] Its function, in this sense, is anything but arbitrary. The notion of Nothing, as opposed to that of Something, would be imposed as an absolute necessity for distinguishing the ontological function of the categories—that is to say, the one in which they participate as constitutive modes of phenomenal objects—from the other in which, acting as pure Forms of a Thought that has been stripped of all intuitive content,[11] they express only a merely formal function and secrete those purely intelligible products such as Nothingness or the noumena themselves. The Nothing or the noumena would come to be, in such a way, expressions of the activity of the categories as pure Forms of the understanding, devoid of any content and therefore without objective reality, that is, merely intelligible structures, such as that exhibited by an "empty concept without object," as the Kantian expression says.

Now: can we simply accept such an identity between Nothingness and the noumenon? Or do the most serious and intricate problems spring from this? Indeed, this is the case; and it is only a matter of reflecting a little on what it implies so that those problems appear on their own. Let us see, then, what they consist of and what the consequences are for our goal.

If the noumenon taken in a negative sense constitutes that sort of merely intelligible correlate or structure which remains in the representation of a thing if it is abstracted from our way of sensibly intuiting it,[12] and this noumenon is also the same as the Nothing ... Would it then be unnecessary to carry out such an abstraction from the intuitive basis, so that what functions as a purely intelligible character [*textura*] of the representation shows up synthetically combined or fused in the reality of a phenomenon? Is it then sufficient to think[13] that the purely intelligible Forms (categories), which give the entitative character [*textura*] of the noumenon and the Nothing, are filled with intuitive data, so that both become "phenomena"? What would this mean? It would mean—to put it roughly—that the noumenon or the Nothing would have only the abstract structure of a phenomenon, and that between it and them would stand only a difference of *content*. Is this true? And if it were ... what would it reveal? What this would reveal is a pregnant problem of the most serious consequences, namely: that the entire structure of the understanding—and with it that of its possible representations—has an exclusively ontological nature. Or said more simply: that the Nothing and noumena are only ontological modifications, since the categories as Forms of Thought—which constitute their original root—are conceived in a narrowly ontological sense, that is to say, as categories of Being or modes of possible representation. The noumenon and the Nothing, in this sense, would be correlates of an ontological representation simply stripped of its sensibly intuitive content or basis.

In their concise formulations, the above questions place us before a field fraught with intricate problems. Suddenly it is revealed to us that the Kantian doctrine—to identify Nothingness with the noumenon and conceive it as an abstract counterpart to phenomena—has a cross-bred background of ambiguous darkness. Nothingness as noumenon, and this as a purely formal concept, is sketched in view of Being and is a mere ingredient of Something. And just as there is no radical difference between the noumenon and the phenomenon—except that there is no sensible content in the former—there would be only a similar difference between Nothingness and Being: the former would become pure (empty) Form of the latter.

But the Nothing, if in truth it opposes the Something, should not be a mere Form for possible appearances of Being, but on the contrary a notion that, in its radical heterogeneity with respect to that Something, negates Being and all possible phenomena and expressions of it as that Something. If it can be conceived as a mere "Form," it could not in any way be the "Form" of Being or Something, but in any case, the "Form" of Nothingness itself, that is to say: "Form" negating ["*noth-ing*," *nadificante*] and canceling with respect to possible contents of an ontological nature. Is there any indication of this in Kant's own doctrine?

Indeed, as far as Nothingness is concerned—and in this it is possible to discover a mark that seems to distinguish it from the noumenon and place it on a level of "ontological" distinction[14]—Kant himself is responsible for indicating a feature quite symptomatic of it. If we carefully review the first notion of Nothingness that appears on his table, we will notice that, despite its formal origin from the concepts of understanding, Kant points out that, instead of having its foundation in traditional quantitative categorial concepts (all, many, one), it comes from the "categorial" function of the concept of *None* (Kein), which when applied or functioning as such "*cancels out everything.*"[15]

Now, in addition to the surprising fact that this indicates—since nowhere in his famous table of categorial concepts does *None* appear in such terms—the above implies an innovation of profound consequences for the "ontological" aspect of the problem. Indeed: does the above mean that the concept *None* lacks an *ontological* character [*textura*]? If we attend to what Kant himself says about this concept, we see that he assigns to it a *canceling* (aufheben) function, whose final end is to eliminate any intuitive mark or content in the corresponding object. In this sense, such a concept produces the notion of Nothing not because it is a mere empty Form, but precisely because it has eliminated that intuition upon which its canceling function as a Form rests. In this way, Nothing would then not be the mere expression of a noumenon in the ordinary sense—although its formal character [*textura*] reveals a corresponding appearance—but the product of a "categorial" (or perhaps "anti-categorial") activity whose correlate would be a perfectly negative "phenomenon." Nothingness would become a "phenomenon," but a "negative phenomenon" and opposed in its structure to all phenomena of Being. If the latter, in its phenomenal aspect, appears as Something endowed with a *positive magnitude* (modulated under the framework of a Totality, of a Plurality, or of a Unity), through the effect of the "anti-category" of *None*, the respective "phenomenal" correlate appears as a privative Nothing or devoid of any positive quantity.

But the terms in which the problem is now presented are of crucial importance for our purposes. Indeed, interested as we are in clarifying the Temporality [hereafter, all uses of "temporality" translate "*temporalidad*"] of Nothingness, it is already possible to glimpse the radical diversity of perspectives offered by the preceding interpretation regarding the problem of such Temporality. The next section is devoted to showing this and to pointing out the profound consequences derived from it for Kant's own doctrine.

§2 The Twofold Possibility of Nothingness in Its Noumenal Structure

The objective reality of knowledge is only produced, according to Kant, by the synthesis of *a priori* forms with the phenomenal matter provided by experience. In order for there to be knowledge, and for it to possess true objective reality, the categories must be applied to the data of intuition, or even more precisely, of empirical intuition.[16] In this sense—for example—the categories of quantity are applied to the indeterminate *Something* that provides sensible intuition, classifying the way or manner in which it becomes the *object* of a possible experience: that is, as *Something* conceived in terms of Unity, Plurality, or Totality. Acting as ordering and meaning-giving forms on the manifold of intuition, the categories prescribe the logico-ontological profile of the known *object*. In the case of a cognition of reality, that *object* is always and necessarily *Something*—a "positive Something"—to which being or existing is imputed, as *Something* to which corresponds, at least, the fact of being material composed of a manifold of intuitive data.

But what if instead of the categories that prescribe the way of being of *Something* as Unity, Plurality, or Totality, it is a concept of understanding, in its "categorial" function, which has as its characteristic function that of canceling everything? Such is the concept of *None* (Kein), as opposed to the concepts of *All*, *Many*, and *One*. In this case, as Kant says, the consequence is that the "*object*" arises from a concept for which there is absolutely no intuition indicated, that is, a *Nothing*, which is strictly speaking a concept without an object, with the same structure as that of the *noumenon* in the negative sense.[17]

Now: on what obscure ground or basis does some specifiable intuition not correspond to that concept of Nothing? Why is the "object" of it *negative*, i.e., non-existent or unreal, making it in fact a *concept without an object* in a strict sense, as the Kantian formula says? Raised thusly, this question observes the twofold possibility of interpretation which, from here, arises with respect to the presence of a noumenal structure in the notion of Nothingness. Indeed: there may be a lack of intuitive data either because there is no intuition that corresponds to the concept—then the conceptual structure is the product of a merely intelligible activity—or because, with an indeterminate sensible manifold existing as preliminary intuitive data, the "categorial" activity itself, being of a nihilating or canceling nature (such is the function exerted by the anti-category represented in the concept of *None*, in Kant's own words) cancels in the "object" any quantitative mark or sign, shaping it as a *Non-Being*, as a *Nothing*, as *pure negativity*.

Such diversity in possible interpretation—as will be shown in more detail below—is of fundamental importance in reference to the problem of the *schematism* and, therefore, in relation to the possible Temporality of

Nothingness. Indeed: if the Nothing has the structure of a *noumenon* because it is the product of the merely intelligible activity of the understanding itself—with absolute abstraction from all sensible intuitive data—it seems that there is then no possibility that there is a *schematism* for that *noumenon*;[18] but if, on the contrary, the Nothing results from a nihilating or canceling activity of the "category" of *None* on those intuitive data, such a nihilating activity necessarily requires a *schema* that produces negativity and, therefore, as in all *schemata*, a "temporal" horizon defining its meaning.

§3 The Notion of Nothingness as Zero or Negative Magnitude

The twofold hypothesis posed cannot be settled formally, nor can it be referred back to Kant's own explanation. Even the latter is not without contradictions. Indeed, in establishing that the notion of Nothingness, as *ens rationis*, is like that of the *noumenon*, Kant is inclined to impute to its origin the same reason for being as to that of the latter. As a *noumenon in the negative sense*, the Nothing would arise from an absolute lack of intuitive data on which to carry out the object-producing categorial synthesis. But in this case ... why then introduce the concept of *None* as a genetic component of it? If the noumenal structure of Nothing came from the absence of intuitive data—that is, from the merely intelligible function of the concepts of the understanding—then this sole function, performed by the positive concepts of the understanding corresponding to the categories of quantity, would suffice for it to emerge as an *ens rationis*. Why, then, does Kant not use these positive concepts of understanding and introduce, instead, the concept of *None*, attributing to it the characteristic function of "cancelling out everything"?[19] But on the other hand ... what can this "cancellation" that implements the concept of None refer to—in close parallelism, but in the opposite direction, to the concepts of *All, Many, and One*—if not to intuition? For the operation of "cancelling" to make sense, there needs to be a term to which it applies and upon which it exercises its particular action.

But, in addition to this circumstance, it must be added that if the notion of Nothing were equated with that of the *noumenon*, the consequence would be that, in the same way, Nothing should be included among those "things" (Ding) which, due to their own ontological character [*textura*], do not have true objective reality (they are not "phenomena," in a strict sense), but, counting themselves among those that cannot be positively declared possible or impossible, they are reduced to being merely problematic and limiting concepts.[20]

Now, for Nothingness to exhibit and present an objective reality, it is not necessary that we resort to the famous Kantian hypothesis of an *intellectus archetypus*,[21] possessor of a kind of creative *intellectual intuition*. Perhaps what condemns Nothingness to being merely an intellectual notion devoid of contradiction but without objective reality is the fact of being excluded, as such, when the positive categories of quantity—since these are, in a strict sense, *ontological* categories—are synthesized with the manifold of data coming from sensible intuition. Certainly not presenting it in this way—and at the same time closing off the hypothesis of an intellectual intuition for man's own *intellectus echtypus*—Kant only discounted as an explanatory possibility of its "reality" the comparison of it with the structure of a noumenon in the negative sense.

But in Kant's own explanation—as we have indicated—an issue is pointed out which is worthy of being observed because of the profound consequences it entails. The characteristic function of the "category" of *None*, as he himself says, is to "cancel everything," and this canceling function necessarily requires a material to which it applies and on which to exercise itself. The second hypothesis that we have outlined thus takes on great potential. Demonstrating and explaining it—filling it with concrete content—is, however, not easy. Indeed, to suppose that the anti-category None acts as a negating function on the data of sensible intuition, bringing about its "cancellation" (Aufhebung) and therefore its negativity, requires laborious work, parallel almost to that carried out by Kant with respect to the positive categories. But only in this way—when it can be verified that the intuitive material is marked by negativity by the negating function of the "category" itself—will it be possible to understand why Kant succumbed to the mistake of taking that *negativity*, in the mode of being of these objective data, as synonymous with the lack or absolute lack of *intuition*, and believed he could equate Nothingness with a noumenon.[22] But the important thing about such an explanation lies not only in this, but also in making transparent how the Nothing—having a negative "objective reality"—also has a temporal structure rooted in the same sense of schematism that enables the synthesis of intuition with the corresponding "category."

Referring to the categories of quantity, Kant points out that the concept of magnitude in general can be clarified by saying that it is the determination of a thing through which one is permitted to think the unity of the *number of times* contained within it. And then he adds—and this is of the utmost importance—that this "*number of times*" is based on a successive repetition, consequently on Time and on the synthesis (of the homogeneous) in Time.[23] Now, such a suggestion not only makes clear the function of Time in the categorial synthesis, but at the same time makes transparent the reason that *Number*, as a schema, would be the concrete representation of the temporal flow of consciousness in its operation of gathering synthetically into a Unity the manifold of intuition quantified by the corresponding category. "The pure schema of magnitude (quantitatis), however, as a concept of the understanding"—Kant expressly says—"is **Number**,[24] which is a representation that summarizes the successive addition of one (homogeneous) unit to another. Thus, number is nothing other than the unity of the synthesis of the manifold of a homogeneous intuition in general, because I generate time itself in the apprehension of the intuition."[25] Number, as a schema, thus encloses and defines the temporal—ontological—sense of cognitive synthesis, outlining the horizon of its possible temporal interpretation. Only on the basis of this temporal horizon—which lends it support and gives it meaning—could the task of an ontological hermeneutics of magnitudes in general be attempted.[26]

It is not our proposal to develop such a theme, but only to indicate its intimate connection with the problem of Nothingness as a negative determination of a quantity. Then, in close parallelism with positive magnitudes (whose pure schema has turned out to be Number), the problem of negative magnitudes is presented, whose schema cannot be other than Number except understood as "negative," just as the result of the announcement [*notificación*] of itself as a negative quantity or magnitude. As early as 1763 Kant had studied such a problem in a work entitled *Attempt to Introduce the Concept of Negative Magnitudes into Philosophy* ["Negative Magnitudes"],[27] and in it he explicitly pointed out the definition of such magnitudes by indicating that the concept of the "negative" that was ascribed to them could not and should not have the meaning of a negation produced by a logical contradiction with respect to the positive magnitudes, but rather that such negative magnitudes expressed a truly real opposition—that is, rooted in the phenomena themselves—without being themselves contradictory with respect to the positive magnitudes.[28]

Now, the characteristic and primordial function of negative magnitudes, insofar as they truly express a real opposition and not simply a logical contradiction, is to *cancel* (aufheben) totally or in part the positive magnitudes exhibited by the phenomena.[29] The same operation is carried out by the concept of *None*, in real opposition, when applied to phenomena—and hence its exceptional importance for our purposes. Indeed, beyond a merely logical and contradictory opposition with respect to the concepts of understanding that express a positive quantification, the concept of *None* is the condition of "categorial" possibility that corresponds to the presence of negative magnitudes in the phenomena themselves. And just as positive Number is the pure schema of the positive magnitudes—when expressing the successive addition of homogeneous units in Time—negative Number expresses this same temporal condition ... but in a Time whose "ontological" horizon is marked by the negativity of the Nothing from which it is understood and of which it is the schematic expression. Applied to the manifold of intuition, the concept *None*—via its temporal schema—has the characteristic function of canceling the positive, producing *eo ipso* its opposite: a negative reality that confronts it and causes a Nothing to emerge whose numerical representation is defined by Zero.[30]

But for what reason did Kant not reach such conclusions, instead making the concept of *None* the originating condition of a noumenal reality? In addition to the reasons already expressed at the beginning of this section, the following should be added: the consequence of interpreting the Nothing as an objective reality of a negative nature led directly to considering it as a *privation*.[31] But *privation* is privation with respect to phenomenal qualities. By contrast, Kant was interested in pointing out the possibility of a Nothing as *ens rationis*: a Nothing originated and sustained in a pure intelligibility. For this reason, he attributed to such a notion—within the first concept that he uses in his systematic exposition—a noumenal structure. His attempt thus opens up the possibility not only of pursuing Nothingness in intuition, but, at the same time, as purely intelligible reality. While the former already hints at the presence of a characteristic Temporality—that of its negative schema—it is worth asking about the possibility of that Temporality in the latter.

§4 The Temporality of the Nothing as Noumenon

At first glance, and even with the support of the text, it could be said that noumena lack structure and temporal meaning. The explanation seems very simple: since noumena are the products of a purely intelligible activity, carried out exclusively by the concepts of the understanding, they lack the temporal unity that comes from the schematism and which makes possible the application and objective validity of those concepts in their categorial function. "Where this temporal unity cannot be encountered, thus in the case of the noumenon"—Kant says with total precision—"there the entire use, indeed even all significance of the categories completely ceases; for then we could not have insight even into the possibility of the things that would correspond to the categories [...]"[32] Reason, in its merely intelligible aspect, would seem to transcend, or at least to remain separated, in the face of any temporal limitation. This is what Kant affirms when trying to explain the antinomy of its possible freedom in the face of the universal necessity of Nature. "Pure Reason, as a merely intelligible faculty, is not subject to the form of Time, and hence not subject to the conditions of the temporal sequence."[33]

But in the face of such resounding statements a problem arises, or at least an apparent contradiction. Is it not Kant himself who at the same time affirms that all our representations—whatever their origin, modality, or nature—are subject to Time? And isn't the *noumenon*, strictly speaking, a representation?[34] By way of an "observation," intended to clarify the foundations of the Deduction of the categories, Kant himself affirms the following:

> Wherever our representations may arise, whether through the influence of external things or as the effect of inner causes, whether they have originated *a priori* or empirically as appearances—as modifications of the mind they nevertheless belong to inner sense, and as such all of our cognitions are in the end subjected to the formal condition of inner sense, namely time, as that in which they must all be ordered, connected, and brought into relations. This is a general remark on which one must ground everything that follows.[35]

Thus, the problem or the simple contradiction that arises from Kant's own thought is posed, in its concise formulation and wording.

But where do we look for the common thread or the clue that enables us to clear up such a difficulty? Without a doubt, the text cited last indicates this. Indeed: Time—which is the structure in question—is explicitly identified with *Inner Sense* and it is in this, as the axis of the "mind," where all possible representations that the Subject may have find their order, relationship, and unity. The question is thus outlined in the following way: does *Inner Sense* remain absolutely necessary in the case of noumenal representation, that is to say, is it a structurally indispensable condition even in the case of the merely intelligible function of Pure Reason?

One cannot attempt to answer this question without going directly to what things themselves offer to us as data. What Kant calls *Inner Sense*, ascribing to it a temporal structure, cannot be understood except by consulting the very face of the appearances in which it is incorporated. All representation, in fact, being the moment of a cognitive process, is inserted into the flow of a consciousness. This flow or process itself, as such, exhibits a temporal aspect or structure. *Inner Sense* is therefore what is otherwise called the temporal flow of consciousness. The representations are embedded in it, as they occur one after another, as conscious appearances. Now, everything that is a phenomenal moment of consciousness is therefore subjected to that expressly temporiform condition of its flow. *Inner Sense* is the expression of *Time*—and all representations are subject to Time because consciousness itself is, in itself, temporiform.

But this could be objected to by saying that the problem posed does not refer to the empirical—that is to say, to *Inner Sense*—but, justly and properly, to the intelligible. In this sense, Kant's truest intention—in distinguishing the *transcendental* direction of his inquiries from the style of the *psychological* and *empiricist* investigation of a Locke or a Hume—was not simply to address the apparent description of psychic realities that shows a factual consciousness at a given moment of its course, but rather to clarify how those same realities, thanks to the *a priori* conditions of possibility of a transcendental Subjectivity, could become objective knowledge—even marked by universality and necessity—exercised by a Subject. The specific transcendental inquiry consists therefore in the discovery and fixation of those *a priori conditions of possibility* whose structures are, to be sure, purely intelligible. In this sense, with almost mathematical precision and extreme finesse, Kant took care to point out the difference between *Empirical Apperception*—which is identified with *Inner Sense*, and therefore with *Time*—and *Transcendental Apperception*.[36] While in the first—which is psychologically identified with consciousness of the self given subjectively in the form of a *temporal continuum* marked by a certain *empirical unity*—Kant points to the marks proper to all intraworldly and factual temporal appearances (mutability, contingency, and variability),[37] in the second—as an absolutely necessary condition a priori demanded by Pure Reason itself so that the manifold of what is given in intuition can be brought together with strict *objectivity* in the *transcendental unity* of a single *I*—Kant himself points to *immutability, permanence*, and *fixity*[38] as characteristic marks, describing the structure of the resulting unity of consciousness as "*numerically identical*."[39] Now, what guarantees such characteristics in the *Transcendental Unity* of consciousness can only be its *timeless* condition. Permanence, immutability, fixity, and identity with oneself occur only where, apparently, there is no temporal flow and, therefore, possible change, mutability, or variability; that is to say, in an ekstasis alien to all becoming, synonymous with an *instant* paradoxically disconnected from all temporal flow. Only in this way does the "I think" of *Transcendental Apperception* seem to ensure—in the strange temporal configuration of a uchronic instant—the characteristics of universality and necessity that it needed to register as the ultimate foundation of the *objective validity* of knowledge or (as "Practical *I*") of the *autonomy* of freedom in the face of the temporal structure of the causality of Nature. As a merely intelligible function of Pure Reason, *Transcendental Apperception* (and, in this sense, also the *noumenon*) would seem to exhibit a manifest *timelessness*.

But if such an explanation gives us the clue for understanding the difficulty posed, it does not, however, adequately solve it. The Kantian formulation, although from a systematic point of view it provides a formal answer to the problem—apparently confirming the existence of a twofold structure in the Subject, each with different ontological features—cannot however fully satisfy the aim of confronting the data arising from the things themselves and of following the evidence that springs from them.

Indeed, if *Transcendental Apperception* is, as Kant himself designates it, a "common function of the mind,"[40] whose operation consists in connecting, composing, and uniting the manifold in the unity of a single consciousness,[41] it is worth asking whether such a "function"—and its corresponding acts of "*connecting*," "*uniting*," and "*composing*"—can be conceived without a temporal meaning or sense. All "*action*," indeed, is a process that takes place in time: it is "*temporal*." Now, supposing that, despite this, what Kant confronted was the fact that since it does not have the ontological structure of a *reality* (psychological or factual), the function of Transcendental Apperception does not take place in time (or, more precisely: that it is not circumscribed by the *hic et nunc* that defines a real existence), this factum—which ties the structure of Transcendental Apperception to a merely *logical* function and, therefore, to an *ideal* nature—should be the object of special attention. So then, could the ontological-temporal structure of Transcendental Apperception be identified with an ideal entity? Kant himself, when referring to *Reason* (which, in a sense, due to its merely intelligible aspect, would have the same marks that characterize the function of *Transcendental Apperception*), seems to leave space for holding this view. "It, Reason, is present to all the actions of human beings in all conditions of time, and is one and the same, but it is not itself in time, and never enters into any new state in which it previously was not."[42] Is he not saying that Reason—and the function of Transcendental Apperception—does indeed possess an ideal ontological structure that is manifested in its "supratemporal" condition?

    So it seems; with the sole exception that the transcendental apperceptive function is also the *condition of the possibility* of the ideal entities themselves, and, therefore of the ontological structure that exhibits its own constitution. But what meaning or consequence can this superior hierarchical position, which is now insinuated in and ascribed to *Transcendental Apperception*, produce in relation to the problem of its "temporality"? Without going into greater detail, let us simply say the following: if, on the one hand, the criterion of a simple and apparent *timelessness* of Transcendental Apperception is rejected (as it seemed to be, derived from the initial Kantian formulation of the problem), since contrary to being timeless it now turns out that it is "*present*" at all times and also while performing certain self-generating functions of *supratemporality*—understanding that its "not being in time" only refers to the fact that it is not present in the way or manner in which any *real entity* occupies a time—on the other hand, "*being present*" at all *times* (as if it were an *ideal entity*) is a determination that must be specified in its details. Well, could it not be that this determination of supratemporal plenitude or permanence, which characterizes ideal entities, is created or instituted in themselves by their own original "condition of possibility"? And then won't the *"being present" at all times* of Transcendental Apperception (and the essential and necessary *temporal* meaning that must be given to its characteristic actions of "connecting," "uniting," and "composing" the manifold, by means of which it *is present* at all times, *is* temporal, and even institutes the *supratemporality* of ideal entities and their own constitutive structure) be of another modality or origin than the simple *"being present" at all times* that guarantees the invariance, identity, and permanence of the ideal entities made possible by itself?

But, before proceeding further, let us note another factum which is decisively as important as the previous one for understanding the problem of Temporality itself, and which is characteristic of *Transcendental Apperception*. Effectively: the *I* of this Pure Apperception is characterized by Kant himself with the properties *"standing"* (stehende) and *"permanent"* (bleibende).[43] Now, what sense, if not *temporal*, can such determinations of the *I* have? "Standing" means, in fact, that which does not change ... in time; "permanent" that which, as a numerically identical unity, is present ... at all times. Faced with the determinations of the *empirical I*, Kant himself is obligated, even in order to stress the supposed *timeless* characteristics of the "I think" of Transcendental Apperception, to use criteria that do not escape temporal determination.[44] What is he saying? Neither more nor less—in our belief—than what was already revealed in the previous reflection. Indeed, it is not that the *transcendental I* is *timeless*, but simply that it does not exhibit the same temporal characteristics of the *real* and *empirical I*. The determination *permanent* that characterizes it does not define an *absolute absence* of Time, but rather expresses its *absolute presence*—which as *"presence"* is *temporal*—in the midst of the changing flow of empirical consciousness.

But what we say is even confirmed—at the same time that it raises the problem in its greatest depth—if we appeal to a strange coincidence that is possible to track in the *Critique of Pure Reason* itself. Indeed, when referring to Time as such and trying to define it, Kant characterizes it by means of the same marks that he uses to refer to the *pure I* of Transcendental Apperception.

"Time"—he says—"does not pass."[45] What is he expressing—we ask—with this strange parallel?

Leaving aside all formalism, it can be said that the foregoing fully confirms the temporality of the *I* and, therefore, of *Transcendental Apperception*. For just as Time does not cease to be Time because of its character of *permanence* (although with it is demonstrated the need to postulate the *permanence* of Time in order to understand the *change* and *mutability* of the real-temporal), nor does the *I*, as *permanent*, reject its temporal condition and become a *timeless* being. That the *I* is *permanent* and *standing* only means that it assumes a temporal modality different from that of any *real entity*, which changes and varies in time. Its way of being in time is to *remain identical in its absolute presence*.

This permanence in its identity exhibited by the I could be taken as a criterion for affirming the *ideal* structure of its ontological constitution. So, indeed, it could be. But the caveat must be made—already made by us in the previous reflection—that such an ideal structure by which the *I* is thought to be informed has its *condition of possibility* in itself as a necessary instance of the transcendental apperceptive function that requires every "something" (in this case the "I" represented as "ideal") to be the *object* of consciousness. In this sense, just as the mark of *permanence* in Time does not only define a merely ideal structure of Time itself—but also indicates its originating condition as *Temporality*, and allows us to think about the possibility of an essential variability in the modes of being of Time as such[46]—thus the *permanence* of the *transcendental I* seems to indicate the originality of the *I* and its correlative *Temporality*, different not only from that of any *real entity* (temporality of the real world), but from the very temporality that defines the meaning and the mode of being of the mere *ideal entities* marked by *permanence* through the work of Transcendental Apperception itself.

But, of the approaches we have taken, what are the repercussions for the problem of the *noumenon* and the *Nothing* conceived as noumenon? Their influence—if you now reflect carefully—is absolutely decisive and determinate. Indeed: shall we persist in affirming that the *noumenon*—as a merely intelligible representation and, therefore, not subject to the *schematism*—is *timeless*? Does the Nothing remain excluded from all temporal determination insofar as it is a product that makes up a merely noumenal structure? Let's continue and slowly extract the consequences of our own approach.

In the first place, let us say that it would be wrong to identify, without further ado, the *noumenon* with *Transcendental Apperception* or *Pure Reason*, applying to one the traits and characteristics that the others have. Our attempt—although for understandable reasons it has apparently approached, at one point, this situation—should not be understood in such a way. What we have wanted to highlight—by insisting on pointing out the Temporality of Reason and of Transcendental Apperception—is to show that, despite being merely *intelligible* structures, it is improper to ascribe to them a supposedly *timeless* condition. In this sense, also to the *noumenon*, as a merely intelligible structure, it is necessary to impute a Temporality.

Kant's possible error, by limiting the temporal condition to exclusively phenomenal entities—that is to say, to those in whose constitution *schemata* participate—comes perhaps from identifying Time with a constitutive condition of *real entities*, excluding its presence in the constitution of the *ideal, merely intelligible entities*, or, if you like, the *a priori* and *transcendental*. But surely there is no decisive reason to hold this point of view. The Temporality of Reason is not exhausted in *Inner Sense*, nor does Time as such have to be considered an exclusive property of real intraworldly entities.[47] Along with the intra-temporality of real entities—everyday and vulgar, as Heidegger would call it—there is a *Transcendental Temporality*. In it, as we have seen, there are even different temporal modalities, viz.: a temporality of pure ideal (intelligible) entities and an original and constitutive Temporality (that of Pure Reason).

It is not possible to discuss at this point—since the elements required not only to understand, but even to establish the assertions would be missing— whether the Nothing simply participates in the temporality proper to intelligible entities, or if it has yet a higher rank or hierarchical position, participating *eo ipso* in original Temporality. Within the Kantian conception, Nothingness as *noumenon* is simply a merely intelligible entity.

Now, if it were to be shown that Nothingness—as such—is a constitutive ingredient of Pure Reason, then a certain original Temporality should be ascribed to it. But, to characterize that original Temporality of Nothingness, it would not be enough to appeal to its simple noumenal, nor merely intelligible, structure. Being, God, and Soul are also purely intelligible structures: products or constituents of Pure Reason. Nothingness, in any case, is also a *negative* structure. Original Temporality should spring and be characterized from that *horizon of negativity* proper to it. In this sense—as was hinted from the *Introduction* itself—the very structure of Temporality must be rooted in the horizon of understanding that Nothingness itself offers.

The reflection ceases, for now, in the present stage. We are not interested at this moment in advancing any claim that escapes the control of a strict and rigorous phenomenal confirmation. And the above, apparently, already exceeds this limit. It will be necessary to reinitiate the meditation in its due time—and renew it with direct phenomenal evidence—to finally elucidate what is now only posed in a problematic way, or rather as a mere hint that prompts Thought to continue its search.

2

Nothingness and the Nihil Privativum

§5 Nothingness as Nihil Privativum

The second notion of Nothingness expounded by Kant is the one corresponding to the *nihil privativum*, which he explains is the "empty object of a concept"[1] or (like the *ens imaginarium*) the "empty data for a concept."[2] As *nihil privativum*—as its own title indicates—this notion of Nothingness has its origin in a *privation* and, as such, its structure reveals the effect of a *negation*. Now, since *privation*, as *negation*, is synonymous with the *lack, absence,* or *deficiency* of positive qualities in the *object*—as happens, for example, when it comes to coldness or darkness—the notion of Nothingness that it represents remains embedded in the *categories of quality* and it is from these (and, therefore, their respective *schematism*) that it gains its meaning.

But the terms "absence," "lack," or "deficiency," insofar as they indicate a *privation*, assume a *Something* (thought or conceived as *Something* marked by *positive qualities*) in relation to which the *privation* is presented or made present precisely as an *absence, deficiency,* or *lack* of those qualities. Now, such an ontological presupposition relates the Kantian conception to the Aristotelian notion of *privation* (στέρησις). But if the Kantian doctrine basically repeats the Aristotelian one—by assuming the primacy of a *Subject* or of a *Something* as the original ontological substratum—nevertheless there is a radical difference between both conceptions, which is undoubtedly important to point out in relation to our purposes.

In effect, the Aristotelian notion of στέρησις assumes not only a Subject or Substance with respect to which the *privation* occurs, but at the same time admits that the qualities it has (and of which it is deprived) belong to it properly or essentially. In this sense, that Subject naturally possesses the qualities of which it is deprived and whose lack brings about the στέρησις.³ The same is not true, however, in the Kantian conception. For Kant it is not possible to speak of a Subject or Something substantial that possesses in a natural, essential, or paradigmatic way, a certain quality, whose absence or lack decrees *privation*. *Privation* is certainly the absence or lack of a quality, but it is reduced—neutrally—to a mere quantitative gradation of sensation, which may now fill, now leave empty, *Inner Sense* or *Time*. Understood with this meaning, *privation* (and therefore the Nothing as *nihil privativum*) comes to be the expression of a determinate aspect assumed by *Something* as modified by the *categories of quality*. As such, this categorial function necessarily requires the intervention of a *schematism* and it is in such a way, also in this case, that the Nothing assumes a structure and a temporal meaning.

It is the purpose of what follows to demonstrate this in its details.

§6 The Constitution of the Nihil Privativum

In accordance with the tradition in which he worked, Kant thinks the notion of *Nothing* in constant opposition to that of *Something*. "Something" (Etwas) and "Nothing" (Nichts) are seen as poles of a manifold and variable relation. To *Something*, as existent, corresponds a *reality*; the *Nothing*, in opposition, is synonymous with the non-existence of this *Something*, that is to say, with a *negation*. "Reality is **Something,** negation is **Nothing,** namely a concept of the absence of an object."⁴

But Kant's true thought cannot be interpreted as though in it a true ontological assumption is made between Being and Non-Being, between Something and Nothing, in which they are irreconcilable extremes that express between themselves the coexistence of two contradictory and diverse principles. That which exists in truth, according to Kant, is the *object in general*, a kind of empty X, which is modalized by the constitutive set of categories, giving it the ontological aspect that it exhibits in each case. *Reality* and *negation* are, precisely, qualitative categorial forms and this is why the *object in general* may appear now as *Something*, now as *Nothing*, that is to say: as existent or non-existent.

In this sense, as *a priori* conditions of the possibility of Experience, the categories sketch the formal aspect that the phenomenal appearance of the object assumes in the former. For this reason, the category of *reality* is such that it functions as an a priori condition of the possibility of Experience, and corresponds to the appearance of a real, existing object, present in a determinate time and space. To *negation*, by contrast, corresponds the absence or lack of that object.

Now, how does Experience respond to this formal schema of a presence or an absence, which in the manner of mere possibilities sketches in it the categories of *reality* and *negation*? To *reality*—Kant asserts—corresponds in Experience the presence of a *sensation* provided by *matter*, by means of which the object is represented as something existing in space or time; to *negation*, by contrast, corresponds in Experience the deprivation, lack, or absence of such a *sensation* contributed by *matter*, for which reason that object is merely formal—as in the case of the *ens imaginarium*—or it assumes the profile of a non-existent, unreal, phenomenal object, that is to say, deprived of qualities just as it happens in the case of the *nihil privativum*.

But *absence* and *presence* are not absolute terms. On the contrary, they are *degrees* of a certain opposition. All sensation, indeed, has a *degree* and it is the reason that there exists "a relation and connection between, or rather a transition from reality to negation,"[5] and vice versa, which makes all *phenomenal reality* representable as a *quantum* susceptible to increase or decrease. In fact, "every sensation has a degree or magnitude, through which it can more or less fill the same time, i.e., the *Inner Sense* in regard to the same representation of an object," with a variable intensity and, in accordance with such, produces precisely *reality* or *negation*, *existence* or *non-existence*, in the ontological structure of the object in question.[6] That is why Kant says with precision: "the schema of a reality, as the quantity of something insofar as it fills time, is just this continuous and uniform generation of that quantity in time, as one descends in time from the sensation that has a certain degree to its disappearance or gradually ascends from negation to its magnitude."[7] Between total *negation*, represented as zero, and the *reality* of the object extends a whole range of intensities or degrees of sensation, reflecting the degrees of *privation* and defining the structure of a *Nothing*, gradually and progressively, that is expressed in the notion of the *nihil privativum*.

But this conception of Nothingness as *nihil privativum*, despite its apparent simplicity, contains serious problems. It is necessary for our project to specify and clarify them, in order to take possession not only of the "ontological" structure that this notion of Nothingness exhibits, but at the same time to introduce ourselves to the problem of Temporality that it presupposes.

§7 The Phenomenal Structure of the Nihil Privativum

Both *reality* and *negation* are *a priori* conditions of the possibility of Experience. For this reason, objective qualities and phenomenal features correspond to them. Indeed, Kant defines *reality* as *realitas phaenomenon*.[8] In this sense, to *negation* also—and therefore to the *Nothing* as *nihil privativum*—there should correspond a phenomenal structure. For this reason, when it is alluded to in the second notion of the Kantian table, it is expressly defined—as *nihil privativum*—as the "*empty object of a concept*."[9] This "*object*," it seems, must exhibit—in opposition to the noumenal structure that was ascribed to it in the first sense as *ens rationis*—a phenomenal aspect.

But this assertion—that the *nihil privativum* refers to a phenomenon or that it necessarily has a phenomenal structure—raises serious problems in relation to the explicit constitution that has been given to it. Indeed, it is clear that if the *nihil privativum* stems from a continuum of sensations, the assertion of its phenomenal structure can be sustained up to the point at which the sensation does not disappear completely and there remains, therefore, the necessary *material* inherent to all phenomenal reality. But what happens when the absence of the sensation is not only greater than zero, but when the sensation disappears completely and, instead of *reality*, *negation* appears? Can it be argued that this *negation*, as the absolute absence of any positive quality, also corresponds to a phenomenal structure? Is it not lacking in it, simply for the reason that it implies the absence of a *material*, an essential and necessary ingredient for the very existence of all *phenomena*? At this point the Kantian conception is shaken by apparent contradictions. Having posed the problem in the proposed terms, there is no other path than to confront it decisively in order to clear it up and find the way that truly takes us to the bottom of the matter.

Such a path cannot be other than to analyze the very structure of *negation* in Kant. A fundamental question is to see, from the very beginning, that *negation* is a category of Being and, as such, this ontological primacy implies an assumption that has decisive consequences in its constitutive function. In effect, as an ontological category, *negation* means exhaustively a *negation of Something*. Its primary function is precisely to *negate* the qualities of that Something. Now, the qualities of the Something are always and necessarily *positive* qualities. The Something, in itself, is represented as the structural unity that brings together all the positive qualities that are predicated of or attributed to it. But these positive qualities are embodied in the Something by the data of sensation. "*Negating*" means, in this sense, depriving the Something of the positive data represented by the qualitative matter that provides the sensation.

But every sensation—as Kant points out in the Proof of the "Anticipations of Perception"—has a *degree*, and, in this sense, everything real insofar as a sensation corresponds to it, exhibits an *intensive continuum* for this very reason. Because of this, between *reality* and *negation* in phenomena there is a continuous nexus of possible intermediate sensations, "*whose difference from one another is always smaller than the difference between the given one and zero, or complete negation.*"[10] But this factum—the necessary presence of a sensation in everything real, however minimal its degree—implies consequences of unusual gravity. Indeed, Kant notes, with words that leave no room for doubt, that because of this "no perception, hence also no experience, is possible that, whether immediately or mediately (through whatever detour in inference one might want), would prove *an entire absence of everything real in appearance.*"[11] But what is he saying here? Effectively, this indicates to us that *total negation* cannot occur in Experience, and that, therefore, there cannot be an objective correlate of it (a phenomenon that is the example of absolute negativity from the qualitative point of view) in which the presence of such a category could be apprehended or detected. In Experience—in the field of appearances—what is presented as a "negative" form is *privation* and, therefore, as an objective correlate, the *nihil privativum*. But the *nihil privativum* implies, insofar as it signifies the presence of a degree of positive reality (however minimal it may be), the presence of a *Something*: of a real Something, merely deprived of certain positive qualities. In this sense, *privation* does not imply or decree the total abolition or disappearance of that Something, but simply its presence deprived of certain qualities, that is, a nihil *privativum*. The "Nothingness" of this nihil *privativum* is, as a strict consequence, "Something": part or counterpart of Being qualitatively modalized through one of its categories. *Absolute negation*, due to this circumstance, cannot be apprehended phenomenally. For—as Kant says—"first, the entire absence of the real in sensible intuition cannot itself be perceived, and, second, it cannot be deduced from any single appearance and the difference in the degree of its reality, nor may it ever be assumed for the explanation of that."[12]

Such a conclusion places us—as we are seeing—before a true aporia. Indeed, if there is no possibility of apprehending *absolute negation* in appearances, there are only two equally extreme consequences. Effectively, either the assumption that this *absolute negation* exists is denied—since there is no appearance whatsoever that testifies to its possibility—or it is declared that *absolute negation* is not an authentic condition of the possibility of appearances.

Conscious of this, Kant is obligated to attempt the apprehension and deduction of *absolute negation* through other means, on pain of accepting those consequences. To do so, as we will see, he postulates two new notions of Nothingness, where it appears as *ens imaginarium* and as *nihil negativum*.

Such are his paths. However, before rehearsing his journey, we must ask ourselves—more thoroughly—whether the very categories of *quality* (in which term we have encountered the obstacle that it represents in the *nihil privativum*) are truly incapable, in their constitutive function, of giving us an *absolute negation* in the sphere of appearances. Not in vain, the assumption from which all the argumentation begins—that is, affirming that they are *ontological categories*—is, strictly speaking, an "assumption." Or does it turn out that *negation*—because it is a negation of positive qualities—is not, by itself, a *quality*? Does zero cancel every quality, or does the realm of *negative qualities* begin with and from it? Isn't *negation*, in addition to an *ontological* category (whose function constitutes exclusively the *nihil privativum*), a category of Nothing?

But already the very formulation of such problems exceeds the limits and assumptions in which Kant posed them. All of them assume, in effect, that Being and Nothingness confront each other as two opposing principles. For Kant, on the contrary, what existed as a merely formal nucleus was an *object in general*—an empty X—with respect to which *reality* and *negation* were or expressed only its constitutive modalities. But that empty X, that *object in general*, however, was strictly speaking a *Something* and, as such, surreptitiously credited with a primacy of Being.

With this underlying and unexplained assumption now discovered, nothing prevents us from rehearsing its discussion and judgment, even if it means abandoning our own Kantian perspective. But true philosophizing is not about blindly following a thinker. The real philosophical work consists in discovering and discussing the assumptions that animate and support your claims. The extraordinarily useful thing about Kantian approaches lies in the virtue they have of not obscuring their own limits and consequently granting the possibility of confronting the truth that testifies to them.

§8 Nothingness and Negation

Metaphysical thinking—oriented toward Being from its earliest manifestations—is for this very reason, strictly speaking, an *onto-logical* thinking. Being and Thinking, λόγος and ὄν, have been and continue to be, within the Western tradition, two inseparable terms. The most complete exposition of their synthesis is Logic: the science of Thinking ... but of a "thinking" oriented and directed by the categories of Being. In its maximum and most refined contemporary expression—in the Hegelian formulation—the "Science of Logic" is, for this very reason, *Ontology*.[13] Logic—and with it the Thinking by which it constructs its laws and indicates its limits—serves therefore only to think Being. It would be from every point of view suspicious for Thinking—if it wishes to be considered a "logical" thinking, and, therefore, rational, coherent, and normative—to attempt the adventure of thinking Nothingness.

But that is what it is about, and it is precisely for this reason that one of the fundamental difficulties encountered by an attempt such as the one we propose lies here. Indeed, if the intention revealed by the previous approaches is fully understood, it soon becomes clear that it is not simply a matter of thinking of the Nothing as a Non-Being (for which, starting from hypostasizing Being, its opposite negation is formulated) but, rightly and radically, of thinking the Nothing in and of itself as a principle that does not spring from the simple negation of Being—that is, only as the result of an *ontological negation*—but, on the contrary, as the original source of a *negativity* that is distinct and different from the *ontological* one: of an *absolute negativity*, if the expression fits. For this, as it is now understood, more than an *Ontological Thinking*—of an Ontology or a Logic oriented and built from the perspective of Being and rooted in its implicit *understanding*—we require a Thinking that sprouts from and develops in view of pure Nothingness (and its original *understanding*), without reference or a mediate or immediate relationship with Being (which it would simply "negate"), but which begins and is sustained in *absolute negativity*. Is such an undertaking so much as possible? Does it make any sense? What purpose would it pose?

Seen from the perspective of Being—where the "Something" (Aliquid) is an entitative representation—the "Nothing" comes to either the negation of a singular real "Something" (negation of an entity), or the negation of everything real (of the entitative in general, of the Being itself of entities), at which point it is then synonymous with Non-Being, the non-real, that is, of a negation of Being. But this apparent distinction shouldn't confuse our purposes. Well understood in its foundations, both the "Nothing" that refers to a singular real entity as well as that which is relative to everything real are only the expression of a *nihil privativum*, already conceived in an ontic dimension, already with an "ontological" order. Indeed, referring to *quality* (be it that of the entity as a whole or that of a singular entity), as every quality is supposed to be positive, "Nothing" expresses or defines the absence of such qualities in Being or in the entities, that is, a *nihil privativum*, where the "*privative*" is understood as the *privation* of positive qualities.

Now, it is not a matter of following this path, which always leads to the same thing. What should be attempted is to think the Nothing in and by itself, as *absolute negativity*, and not as a result of the negation of the positive qualities of Being or of entities. Or, put more bluntly: one should try to think *absolute negativity* as a *quality* of Nothing itself.

But is it possible to speak of a *quality* of the Nothing itself? Is this not, in itself, a contradiction? How can that which is the *negation* or *absence* of all "quality," and is for that reason "Nothing,"[14] have *qualities*? Let us not forget, however, that such a way of thinking hypostasizes *quality* as something merely *ontological* and *positive*. Indeed, for Kant, *quality* is proper only to the ontological categories and therefore it only makes sense to predicate it of Being: of what "*is*" and, therefore, *really* exists or as a *real* "*Something.*" Hence, the typical category of quality is *reality* because the real corresponds to Being.[15] When speaking of *negation*—as a quality—it is conceived as a "negation" of *reality*, that is, as absence, lack, or deprivation of positive qualities, that is, of those that constitute *reality*: Being or Something. Moreover—as has been seen[16]—in Experience, even *total negation*, the absolute absence of positive qualities, cannot be apprehended, because Experience is also, strictly, Ontological Experience. Only Being (or Non-Being, insofar as it is that Being deprived to some extent of positive or real qualities) can shine forth in phenomena.[17] There are, therefore, only phenomena of Being. Nothingness, in its purity, is in principle unable to appear as a phenomenon. As a "phenomenon" of Nothingness, the only thing that can appear is a *nihil privativum*, that is, a "Something" deprived of positive qualities, although as such "qualities" they always and necessarily carry a degree greater than zero. As all positive degree of quality disappears, the possibility of apprehending Nothingness disappears because in the first place "the entire absence of the real in sensible intuition (viz., the *total negation*) cannot itself be perceived, and, second, it cannot be deduced from any single appearance and the difference in the degree of its reality, nor may it ever be assumed for the explanation of that."[18] Therefore—Kant adds—"no perception, hence also no experience, is possible that, whether immediately or mediately (through whatever detour in inference one might want), would prove an entire absence of everything real in appearance."[19] The *nihil privativum*—it is concluded—insofar as it appears as a *phenomenon, eo ipso* reveals a *reality*, that is, a positive or ontological quality (diminished, if you like, to its minimum but *real* threshold). That is why, following this path, one arrives at an aporia: either it is impossible to predicate any quality of Nothing—because it is the absolute lack of all (positive) quality—or the qualities that it exhibits, as *nihil privativum*, are *ontological* qualities resulting from a "negation" of Being: a privation of Being. Nothing, as such, does not appear as a *phenomenon*. Every phenomenon is a phenomenon of Being. As a "phenomenon," "Nothing" (the *nihil privativum*) is only the *absence* of Being, never the *presence* of an *absolute negativity*. It lacks that which is real, the quality, required in order to be an authentic phenomenon.

But neither path is the one we have proposed to follow. Indeed, we do not think it necessary to affirm that all qualities are *positive*—and therefore that the lack of these implies an *absolute lack of qualities* in Nothing—nor that the alleged "qualities" of Nothing are only *negative ontological* qualities arising as a result of a *negation* of Being. On the contrary—we ask—what happens if this assumption that proves a twofold *ontological* preeminence is destroyed? What happens if *negation* is conceived not only as the *absence* of *positive* qualities, but on the contrary as the *presence* of *negative* qualities? On the other hand: is it, perhaps, that all qualities must be—in order to be such—*positive*? Are there not thoroughly *negative* qualities? Isn't the *negative quality* a quality?

The crux of the matter here lies in showing the existence of these *negative qualities* and in defining their true meaning. What would those "qualities" be? How is it possible that, without being positive, they can affect us as such "qualities"?

For now, the explanation that they are the product of diminished sensations must be discarded. A diminished sensation, even down to its minimum threshold, would contribute only a quality greater than 0 and less than 1, that is to say, a mere *privation* of *positive qualities*. On the contrary, what is sought is a quality that is *negative* in and of itself. In this sense, what then must be asserted as a synonym for such *negativity* is the *absolute emptiness of all sensation*, since sensation, being necessarily accompanied by a degree, cannot but be a source of positive qualities.

But can such an *emptiness of sensations* affect us? Within the Kantian conception, this *emptiness* of sensations is impossible to apprehend (just as it is also impossible to apprehend the Nothing, which it would boil down to) as a phenomenon. To be a phenomenon, Nothingness requires a *material*—precisely which provides the sensation—and it is precisely such *material* that is missing here. The absolute lack of sensations, the *emptiness* of them, makes it impossible for "Something" to affect us, or for "Nothing" to be apprehended as a phenomenon.

But, we ask, are there not situations lived and confirmed by all, including phenomenally, in which we directly experience an *emptiness* of sensations? Let's imagine, for now, the state into which deep sleep plunges us. All sensations are erased for us, we lose consciousness of what surrounds us, even our own body and our individuality. A deep and limitless "emptiness" envelops us and takes us in. The experience is so real that we can even relive and describe it. It is true that language fails and even hinders the work—because the words we use resonate inappropriately—but it is not impossible that, trying hard, we can find expressions that allow us to communicate to others, at least through allusions, the quasi-ineffable lived "experience." What happens—and hence the fundamental difficulty that is shown in language and even in any intellectual effort that is made to re-live and describe the "experiences" of the deepest substrata of dreaming—is that, in addition to the *ontological* ground that supports every medium or instrument of human communication (language, the discursive process of reconstruction, etc.), instead of being confronted in that experience with the reality of the world with the sole help of our consciousness—and having as a correlate from our apperception the presence of Being constituted and ordered by it—what is shown and appears there is precisely a "world" (if the expression fits) where the "presence" of Nothingness is evident (hence, as "phenomenon"). In the *emptiness of sensations* that swallows us up in our sleep, what is revealed is not merely an *absence* of positive qualities, but the *presence* of "qualities" of the Nothing itself. In the "emptiness" of deep sleep—erasing the sensations that tie us to the real world of the vigilant senses—we feel the strange "presence" of the Nothingness that surrounds our existence as absolute *negativity*. In that trance we have the "experience"—and there is no other term to refer to what is an authentic "phenomenon" framed within the sphere of Existence—of the total possibility of a non-existence of the real world, of our Self, and everything that can be correlated with our consciousness.[20] This *non-existence*, moreover, does not speak against Being, but reveals the forgotten Nothing. Right through it, Being shines as what "is," but at the same time the evanescent frontiers of *abseity* are glimpsed.[21]

The situation described is, however, a somewhat extreme case. But if the Kantian thesis is based on the fact that all phenomena require the presence of a sensation—which as their *matter* contributes the corresponding degree of their *reality*—then it was precisely necessary to point out the existence of certain "phenomena" (and those that develop in the deep substrata of dreaming served us for this) where the presence of sensations—in their function of qualitative material—ceases completely. The "transcendental matter" of dream phenomena was revealed, in this sense, as *absolute negativity*: as a negative quality in itself because it is not the fruit or the result of a mere privation of positive qualities, but instead testifies to a "negative quality"—and therefore the existence of a "material"—marked by *positive negativity* in itself.

But there is no need to employ such an extreme device—and which, incidentally, is inexplicably relegated to oblivion in Western philosophy, at least as regards the meaning and possibilities offered by its non-"ontological" interpretation—to find other ways that testify to and discover the "presence" of the Nothing. Indeed, if the hypothesis that everything *real* is constituted by *sensations* is discarded—which in fact has been convincingly demonstrated by *Gestaltpsychologie*—then there are *phenomena* like *wakefulness* itself that testify to the "presence" of the Nothing. Heidegger, for example, has existentially described the experience of *anxiety*. In it, as he clearly expresses it, "*the Nothing is made manifest.*"[22] Such revealing of the Nothing comes about—as he says in his masterful description—neither by the work of nihilating the entity, nor by springing forth from its negation, but because Existence is *given*—and unexpectedly bursts into—the "presence" of Nothing. Such is what occurs in the phenomenon of *nihilation* (die Nichtung)—made possible by anxiety—and which, expressed technically, makes the Nothing evident as the absolutely "other" and opposed to what "is." But such a phenomenon—it is important to underline—originates not by saying "no" to the entity, nor by logically denying its attributes or positive qualities, but because the Nothing itself makes an irruption into Existence and nihilates it.

"The saturation of Dasein by nihilative comportment testifies to the constant though doubtlessly obscured manifestation of the nothing that only anxiety originally unveils."[23]

"The not"—he adds for this reason—"does not originate through negation; rather, negation is grounded in the 'not' that springs from the nihilation of the nothing."[24]

"But the 'not' can become manifest only when its origin, the nihilation of the nothing in general, and therewith the nothing itself, is disengaged from concealment."[25]

But what is this *Nothing* that thus reveals itself to us through the *anxiety* and *nihilation* that it brings? It would be necessary to re-emphasize their description in order to make the point that this *Nothing* cannot now be understood as a mere Non-Being, as a Non-Being or a Non-Something (i.e., as a simple "negation" of ontological qualities), but as Nothing in its *positive negativity*: as pure and absolute Nothing and nothing else. Such Nothing would be a *nihil negativum*—not in the sense that Kant understands this term and whose later elucidation will occupy us—but as an authentic phenomenon that surrounds and configures the finitude of Existence.

But at the moment we are not sufficiently prepared to try to demarcate such a phenomenon. Our intention has been guided exclusively by the purpose of pointing out the phenomenon of the Nothing as the origin of a possible *absolute negativity*. What has been said so far confirms the existence of such a possibility. Nothingness, as such, has revealed itself as a source of negative qualities. The *negativity* of the qualities themselves testifies, in effect, to the "phenomenon" of the Nothing itself. What the structure and physiognomy of such a "phenomenon" is, is something that remains to be specified. But if *Temporality* is that which gives "meaning" to the phenomena of Being, this is indicating to us that we must now limit the *Temporality* of Nothingness itself in order to appropriate its "phenomenal" structure and to specify the temporal meaning of the *negativity* exhibited by it.

§9 The Temporality of Negation

As a result of the analysis and interpretation that we have made of *negation*—considered as a category of quality—two distinct and radical meanings have been pointed out in it: the one it has as an *ontological negation* and the one it exhibits as *absolute negativity*. The first intervenes in the constitution of Nothingness as *nihil privativum* (that is to say, as a "Something" deprived of positive qualities), while the second sense—not expressly seen or emphasized by Kant—determines the notion of Nothingness as an absolute principle and opposed to Being. Its correlate—although it is inappropriate to connote it with a term that Kant technically reserves for another notion—would be the *nihil negativum*.

But, as has been announced, we must now delve into the structure of Temporality that functions as the *meaning* of these two notions. For this, as it is easy to foresee, we must connect our reflection to the problem of *schematism*. Now, divided as the categorial field has been into two perfectly discernible regions, we propose to develop the whole problem by keeping the specific limits of each notion separate. To do this, we will first study the function of *schemata* in their concrete application to the sphere of *ontological negation*, while later we will study the *schematism* of *negativity as such*, which contains some problems that, due to their originality and importance, are exactly those that I would like to emphasize with greater emphasis in our investigation.

It is more or less easy to follow the Kantian line of thought regarding the schematism of the ontological categories of quality. Instead of referring to the *series* of Time (Zeitreihe)—as happens in the case of the categories of quantity—the schematism of those categories assumes the aspect of a determination of the *content* of Time (Zeitinhalt), insofar as this Time functions as the horizon of the presentation of every possible object.[26] For this reason, the schematism of the categories of quality—of *reality* and *negation*—does not attempt to explain how the *successive synthesis* of the apprehension of an object is produced and connected, but precisely the one that occurs in a single *instant*, thanks to which that object is endowed with a qualitative content through the determination of *Inner Sense* (Time). Kant's words are clear and precise in this regard:

> Reality is in the pure concept of the understanding that to which a sensation in general corresponds, that, therefore, the concept of which in itself indicates a being (in time). Negation is that the concept of which represents a non-being (in time). The opposition of the two thus takes place in the distinction of one and the same time as either a filled or an empty time.[27]

Now, *sensation* is—as a "transcendental matter"—that which fills an *instant* of Time with a *content*. The explanation of its possible variability (and therefore the possibility of an *object* endowed with the corresponding qualitative marks) comes from the fact that every *sensation*, as such, has a *degree*, that is, a *magnitude* (Grösse)—not *extensive* as in the case of quantities whose production is carried out by the *successive addition* of the Parts into the Whole (and whose representation is *number*)—but an *intensive* magnitude, which is immediately captured in the *instantaneous presence* of the sensation itself. The degree of magnitude, Kant says, "is not, however, encountered in apprehension, as this takes place by means of the mere sensation in an instant and not through successive synthesis."[28] In this way, just as *number* is the schematic representation of the categories of quantity, *degree* would become the schema of the categories of quality. Thanks to it—as in the case of the other schemata—the application of these categories to the phenomena is possible. Through its function, it is possible to represent *negation* and *reality* in objects and make them appear under the aspect of a *Something* or a *Nothing* (*nihil privativum*).

But the fact that the *sensation* has a *degree* projects enormous consequences for the determination of the *content* of Time and, therefore, in the very structure of Temporality that gives *meaning* to the categories. Indeed, if *Inner Sense*, in the series of *instants* that make it up, functions as a Time whose *content* is always determined by the presence of a *sensation*, and this—whatever its *degree*—is always *real*,[29] then it is necessary to conclude that it is impossible to conceive or represent an *empty* Time, since its *content* will be that of a more or less positive sensation, but necessarily given a certain degree of *reality* always greater than zero. Or as Kant expressly says: "a proof of empty Space or of empty Time can never be drawn from Experience."[30] The structure of Temporality is thus determined as that of an *onto-logical* Time whose series of *instants* is always and necessarily marked by some *reality*.[31]

Now, if this Temporality, thus conceived, is the one that confers *meaning* upon the categories, it is also necessary to conclude that among the categories of quality it is impossible to conceive *absolute negativity*, since this is essentially repugnant to the conception of that Time. Or put another way: it does not find its corresponding *schema* among those that function as such in reference to the categories of quality. Such a category either has no objective validity—that is to say, is inapplicable to phenomena—or, if it does, it demands the introduction of a *schematism* (and therefore of a structure of Temporality) that goes beyond the limits strictly set by the Kantian conception.

But before developing such a claim, let's reflect on the *presuppositions* that have led us to the situation. In effect, the question is to see that to arrive at the determination of the *content* of Time where it is "full" of a sensation that carries a *degree*, we have begun from the *presupposition*—which we must still examine and not accept without further reason as "understandable in itself"— that Time, in its schematic structure, necessarily refers to Being. The temporal schema of *reality* is that of a concept that shows a *Being* in Time, while that of *negation* shows or indicates a *Non-Being*, but this *Non-Being* is hardly (as we already know) a privation of Being, that is to say, a Being diminished in its degree of reality. In such a way, the schema being an intermediate representation between the categories and the sensible, it always displays a physiognomy similar to what it connects and from where it originates. This primacy of Being therefore subordinates the entire structure of schematism, and therefore that of Temporality, to this ontological primacy. Inasmuch as all possible phenomena are, *stricto sensu*, phenomena of Being, there is no other possibility than that *schemata* are *ontological schemata* and, likewise, that the Temporality that they constitute and define gets its meaning and structure from Being. The prior *understanding of Being*—and of a Being conceived as a *gradated reality*, that is, provided with an *intensive magnitude*—thus operates as a fundamental *presupposition* in the production of the very character of Temporality.

But our reflections have opened up a totally different perspective to that configured by these deductions. We have shown the possibility—without abandoning the realm of the "phenomena" themselves, but, rather, by means of their methodical expansion—that Nothingness itself, conceived as *absolute negativity*, irrupts into Existence. In this sense, the prior assumption does not retain its compelling and limiting necessity. There are, in fact, "phenomena" where Nothingness itself becomes apparent and in which *sensations* are abolished in the face of given *realities* with *positive degrees*. Now, what structure of Temporality emerges and stands out from such a horizon of understanding? What structure is imposed on the schematism if it is to promote—in the strict Kantian sense—the application of *absolute negativity* to the corresponding "phenomena" seen from this new perspective? And what is the meaning of these "phenomena" if Temporality is thus transformed?

What is implied here, as can easily be inferred, is the existence of a *circle*—which thought must try to traverse—between Time and Nothing. For just as there was an opportunity to show the existence of a similar *circle* between Being and Time, now the reason we had for wanting to transport it to this sphere is clearly evident. Technically expressed and described, this *circle* implies the following: since there exists an indissoluble connection between Time and Nothing—just as there is between Being and Time, as evidenced by the understanding of the latter from the horizon of the former—it is necessary for the investigation to begin by delineating the structure that Temporality exhibits when its horizon of understanding is drawn by Nothingness and not by Being. But once this new perspective of Temporality has been obtained, just as Being is retroactively interpreted from *Ontological* Temporality, it is necessary to attempt the reinterpretation of the Nothing from the newly achieved Temporality.

Viewed from the natural *understanding of Being*, Time is an entity among entities, that is, an *intraworldly* entity. As such, inserted into worldly relationships, Time appears as an entity "ready to hand" (Zuhandene) and "present at hand" (Vorhandene),[32] whose specific function is to serve to distribute and arrange tasks, distinguish the succession of events, establishing an order—chronological or chronometric—in the world populated by entities, which is possible because all intraworldly entities are susceptible to receiving such an ordering since they are also, in some way, "temporal." In such a way, Time is shown or presented as a "something," *in* or *within* which other entities *pass*. Its importance or pre-eminence derives from the fact that, as the tool or instrument that it is, it allows other entities, and the entire universe as a totality of entities, to receive an intelligible order that extraordinarily facilitates their handling and use.

To meet these ends—and to serve as a horizon or coordinate that facilitates the domination by intraworldly entities—either in the form of its simple and immediate everyday use, or in the aspect that it assumes when entering as a quantitative factor in the physico-mathematical formulas and equations that are used to calculate the events of Nature, Time as such is assigned certain properties that allow its instrumental handling and specific functions. Thus, for example, it is endowed with a certain *direction* (for which, as it is easy to deduce, it must first be "specialized"), and that *direction* is generally interpreted as *irreversible*.[33] In addition, to facilitate its calculation, it is quantified, dividing it into *points* (representing instants), resulting in its *continuity*,[34] as well as its necessary *infinity*, since each *instant* ("*now*") becomes subdivided up to the infinite, always retaining, however, its *instantaneous-now* character. Interpreted in this way, Time is conceived as an uninterrupted infinite sequence of *nows*, each of which occupies a *present-instant* (present-now), continuously passing in a certain determinate direction that goes from "*not yet now*" (future) toward the "*no longer now*" (past). Or as it was said in the Aristotelian definition itself: "For Time is just this—number of motion in respect of 'before' and 'after.'"[35]

But what happens if Time, instead of being viewed from such a *natural understanding of Being*, reflects the features of Nothingness manifested and also understood in Existence?

Let's recall, for now, the ways of revealing Nothingness. In this regard, we have highlighted *nihilation* (on the level of waking, when this is made possible by anxiety) and the trance of *deep sleep*. Both phenomena imply a kind of loss or fading of the real and everyday world, whose borders disappear when the ties of meaning dissolve, or when the total absence of sensation occurs.[36] Now, having lost this horizon of *meaningfulness*, it is a matter of seeing that Time (whose "instrumental" function acquires meaning only within the total horizon of the world in which it is inserted) also loses that character. But does Time disappear with it? Absolutely not. With the loss of *meaningfulness*, what vanishes is the *instrumental character* of Time, that is, that aspect that makes it possible to use it as a tool or appropriate instrument to measure, calculate, and anticipate worldly happenings and events. But Time, as such, does not disappear. On the contrary, nihilation or deep sleep also occur and develop in Time, that is, they are not events that imply their absolute cessation or disappearance. Or, put more strictly: causing the disappearance of the instrumental aspect of Time, those phenomena promote the appearance or unveiling of another face of Time. But what "Time" is it that appears like this and is now discovered? It is not a question of inventing the specter of an imaginary Time here, but of bringing the description to the things themselves and capturing there the characteristics that it is now possible to discover.

In effect, real and worldly [*mundano*] Time is a Time composed of *present nows* and instants. Such *nows* and instants are *present* because *something* in them, a *reality* (a sensation, an event, etc.) is *presented* within the world. But this is precisely what is extinguished in the phenomenon of nihilation or deep sleep when the frame of the real world vanishes.[37] There is, in effect, an "emptiness" of *real contents*, and a "presence" of *negative* "*contents*" *eo ipso* arises: absence, Nothing, in its pure negativity. The Time of nihilation or deep sleep *presents nothing* or "presents" … Nothing. This Time—non-presentative, non-meaningful, "empty—," therefore has no "signs," "things," "meaningful events," in which it can recognize and set its course. Moreover, if the *now* is synonymous with a point or an instant individualized by its meaningful content, this Time has neither individualized *nows* nor *instants*, nor can the course and direction of them be set with the same criteria as those used in worldly Time to mark the passage from the future to the present and the past. Such location boundaries—established on meaningful assumptions—are also blurred.

This is what happens in deep sleep and even—with certain variations—in some dream strata where the disarticulation of the world is partial. In deep sleep, Time seems to "cease" in its course: there is not that passage of events spread out from future to present and past that animates and sustains wakefulness in the order of their temporal succession. Time, here, seems to "not exist," since there is nothing that is present in consciousness and it seems extinguished in its presentative activity. Only a deep cavity seems to surround Existence and welcome it in its bosom, dissolving all borders. For this reason, when we wake up, we are overwhelmed by a kind of daze and disorientation: we do not know "how much time" has passed (it could well be a minute, an hour, maybe more), nor can we "calculate" the precise time except by resorting to the clock or orienting ourselves again by surrounding signs. Time has lost for us its aspect of having a *quantum*.[38]

Something similar occurs in other less profound dream phenomena. When dreaming, for example, certain images turn to the subconscious in which not all the meaningful temporal resonances that have been united with them in wakefulness have been completely extinguished. But then it happens that the "course" of Time—and its strict order of staging—is strangely mixed up and confused. "Past" events—prior in chronological order with respect to others—appear in an "illogical" context, in "situations" that do not correspond to those experienced in waking, or linked to other events that we have never really "lived." It is the "time" of the "melted clocks," as the surrealists usually represent it in their symbolic language to indicate that in it the established temporal order does not prevail, that its "direction" is not irreversible, nor that its "now" can be fixed by the common delimiting boundaries that are used in the everyday world. On the contrary, having disarticulated the *meaningfulness* conferred by its insertion in this world, its course also exhibits a parallel dis-articulation, losing *eo ipso* the "logic" that governs it in wakefulness. Or as Vicente Huidobro puts it poetically:

Reason for day is not reason for night and each time has a distinct implication.[39]

These phenomena—but especially that of deep sleep, where the fading of the real world is more visible—make us understand that, as Time loses its worldly character, it *eo ipso* loses its topological properties, that is, those which through an interpretation are assigned to its course so that it can be used by all using a conventionally established system of references. But no less than its *topological* properties, Time also loses the properties or *metaphysical* marks that, in a certain way derived from its scientific and technical consideration, lack any reality when those from which they came and in which they were supported have lost their meaning. Indeed, is it possible to speak of the continuity or infinity of Time when the meaning of an individualized "now" in a "present" has disappeared?

But with *nihilation* or *deep sleep*, as we have said, Time does not *disappear*. Time is still there and we have a certain understanding of it. But how is Time still there? What "is" Time viewed from Nothing? This question is meaningless. From the Nothing, Time "is" not. And not in the sense of a Non-Being, but because Time reveals itself and then "appears" as Nothingness itself. And just as it is only possible to say "*there is Nothing*," it is only possible to say also: "*there is Time*." Both expressions, however, reveal the factum of an *understanding*.[40]

In effect, in saying "*there is Nothing*," the Nothing is opened up to Existence under the perfectly defined face of its nihilating phenomena. A crucial phenomenon of the revelation of Nothing is the unveiling of *finitude*. Time too, at one with Nothingness, reveals itself in such finitude as *finite*. The finitude of Time is uncovered in the finitude of Existing. Only from this unconcealed and comprehended finitude—made possible in turn by the revelation of Nothing—is it recognized that Time, by taking root in a radically finite Existence,[41] is also finite. In this sense, the understanding of the finitude of Time that is revealed in saying "*there is Time*" testifies that Existence has understood the Nothing as it manifests itself in finitude.

The description given does not pretend to exhaust all the features of finite Temporality that are revealed in Existence. What has been attempted is only to show a path for the possible apprehension of the phenomena in which it manifests itself. As an initial approach, it is necessarily provisional.

With the same character it is indicated that only from that basis—having clear the "meaning" of Temporality that springs and originates from Nothing—would we be able to "temporally" interpret the "meaning" of that Nothing. In this regard, it is worth noting the fact that the loss of all the topological and metaphysical properties that are usually ascribed to ontological Time unquestionably derives from the finitude of that Temporality. Now, if Time is the "meaning" of Nothing, only from a Time thus understood—in which those properties no longer have validity—can one try to think of the true "meaning" of it. And only from such a "temporal meaning" of Nothing can the validity of the insights already gained by attempting the siege of the "essence" of non-ontological Time be reaffirmed.

Although what is indicated in this way does not go beyond a provisional sketch, in it the *circle* so often highlighted throughout our investigation is reliably confirmed. Addressing that *circle*, making the circular march that its meaning imposes, has been one of our main intentions in this chapter. Although all the obstacles have not yet been cleared, and enormous difficulties prevent the complete freeing of the problem, the steps that we have taken have some importance for preparing the ground. Perhaps now, having clarified how the nexus of the mutual illumination between Time and Nothing remains, the investigation can advance toward new perspectives. However, first it is necessary to complete the historical and systematic panorama that the notion of Nothingness in the Kantian conception assumes, in order to have a broader horizon that allows us to attempt a more complete trial of the problem posed.

3

Nothingness and the Ens Imaginarium

§10 Nothingness as Ens Imaginarium

If any reader accustomed to handling the common concepts taught about Kantian philosophy unexpectedly stumbled upon the third determination of *Nothingness* in the *Critique of Pure Reason*, he would no doubt think that he was dealing with gibberish, or, at least, that it expressed no agreement with the "spirit" or "general lines" of generally accepted Kantian thought. In effect, Nothingness is identified with an *ens imaginarium* and this is explained as an "*empty intuition without object.*"[1] In determining such a notion, Kant writes verbatim that "*The mere form of intuition, without substance [that is: that empty intuition], is in itself not an object, but the merely formal condition of one (as appearance), like pure space and pure time, which are to be sure something, as the forms for intuiting, but are not in themselves objects that are intuited.*"[2]

But what does all this mean? Perhaps the "pure forms" of intuition—ingredients of knowledge—are then reduced to pure chimeras? This seems to be the case, since the *ens imaginarium* is a *Nothing*. However, when attending to what Kant himself expresses, we note that that *Nothing* is a *Something* (Etwas). But how can *Something* be a *Nothing*, or how can *Nothing* be a *Something*? That *Something*, we are finally told, despite being such, is not an *object*. How then can *Something* exist that is not an *object*? Isn't everything that is, even *Nothing* as *Something*, an *object* of Knowledge?

From this set of enumerative characteristics—which, undoubtedly, can cause some confusion at first—it is necessary to slowly extract the indispensable details in order to understand the precise meaning of Kant's thought and to avoid alleged confusions. In this respect, the following points should be clarified:

(1.) Why the mere forms of intuition are Something, although not an object; (2.) The mode of being or existing of that Something; (3.) The relation of that Something with the Imagination and its status as *ens imaginarium*; (4.) The reason why that *ens imaginarium* is truly a Nothing; and (5.) The strict meaning of that Nothingness.

Only on the basis of these prior ontological clarifications will it be possible to address the issue of the Temporality proper to that Nothingness. However, due to the prime importance that the Imagination plays here—the soil from which the *ens imaginarium* springs—and the close connection that this faculty has with Temporality (schemata), the rich fabric of relationships that we will stumble upon is already itself guessed or hinted at.

§11 The Ontological Structure of the *Ens Imaginarium*

The distinction that Kant establishes—at the level of Sensibility—between the components of *matter* and *form* in the phenomenal object is well known. Sensations correspond to the former, as empirical data, and the pure forms of Sensibility, Space and Time, correspond to the latter as pure and *a priori* intuitions. While sensation contributes the real of the phenomenon (*realitas phaenomenon*),[3] Space and Time have the exclusive function of ordering that manifold of empirical data in certain and determined relations.[4]

Now, if the *object* is composed by the conjunction of both components, it is important for our task to ask the following: are these pure forms of Sensibility—Space and Time—also *objects* (Gegenstand)? Kant's answer, in this regard, is clear and unequivocal: neither Space nor Time can be perceived, and therefore, they are not *objects* in the strict sense.[5] But, if they are not *objects*, what then can Space and Time be? Kant says that they constitute the "conditions of possibility" of appearances and as such—he adds—they exist in themselves "*objectively*."[6] What, then, are these "conditions of possibility" of phenomenal objects, which, without being *objects* themselves, nevertheless exist "*objectively*"? In a strict sense, Space and Time are "*Something*"—which, however, cannot be perceived as a real-object—and on whose "existence" even the possibility of real-objects depends.[7]

Such a question clears up one of the difficulties that we mentioned in the previous paragraph. The pure forms of Sensibility—pure intuitions—are not *objects*, although they are "Something" whose "existence" cannot be doubted, since they are imposed "objectively" as "principles" to any transcendental analysis that tries to demonstrate the possibility of *a priori* knowledge in geometry and arithmetic. In this sense, not every "Something" is an *object*, although at the same time this allows us to affirm now that modes of existing cannot be restricted to the mode of being of *objects*. The knot of the difficulty then lies in specifying the mode of being of that "Something" that "exists" without being an *object*.

Despite not being *real-objects*, nor being able to be perceived, we can perfectly well have knowledge of Space and Time, as "mere forms," or as "empty intuitions without an object." This is attested to, without further ado, by Kant's own attempt, having determined through a transcendental examination the precise character [*textura*] of them as "*conditions of possibility*" of Experience. Faced with the merely real and empirical data provided by sensation or perception, the pure forms of Sensibility are those that introduce the relations and order within which these data are intuitively inserted and shaped. It would be an error—as Kant himself rightly points out—to deduce, from the fact that Space and Time are pure intuitions, the conclusion that they lack "existence." While it is true that they do not have an empirical content—as this would deny even their status as "pure"—nevertheless, it is also undoubted that these forms are capable of exhibiting a perfectly connotable entity. If this were not so, its own status as transcendental cognition would be denied. "**Spatium Absolutum, this riddle of philosophers,** is certainly something correct (but not *reale*, rather *ideale*), otherwise one could not assert anything about it *a priori*."[8] In such a way, just as I can say that perception is the representation of a reality, of Space I can say that it "is the representation of a mere possibility of coexistence," and, although Time itself cannot be perceived and therefore "is not a real object," I can however know of it that it precedes all real things and that it is the *a priori* condition of the possibility of objects,[9] including myself, since it is "the way of representing myself as object."[10]

Now: is this not giving us the general ontological structure that a transcendental examination reveals in those pure intuitions as "mere forms of intuition" or "conditions of possibility" of Experience? Indeed, having discarded their empirical and real aspects, what the transcendental examination reveals in them is their condition of being *pure* and *a priori forms*. As such, they "exist" as *mere possibilities*, and, under that condition, they are perfectly distinguished from any *object* whose mode of being (as opposed to *possible-being*) is *real*. In this sense, what differentiates *possible-being* from *real-being* is that while the latter needs to have a *real presence* in order to exist (which can only be conferred by empirical data from sensation or perception), the former, on the contrary, does not need or require such a *real presence* in order to "exist."[11]

But as mere *possibilities*, the "conditions of possibility" of Experience (i.e., those "empty intuitions without object"), they are extraordinarily similar in their way of being to that of an imaginary entity (*ens imaginarium*), that is, to a "Something" (*ens*) that "exists," but without requiring the *presence* of a *reality* in order to attest to it as an entity. Hence Kant's reason for identifying the ontological structure of pure *a priori* forms with that of such imaginary entities.

But any *ens imaginarium*—just as its name indicates—has the *Imagination* as its place of origin. In this sense, Space and Time, as such, seem to also have their origin in such a faculty.[12] Now, if this thesis is accepted, there is a serious temptation to take the fact of those pure forms having their *origin* in the Imagination as a reason for identifying Space and Time with the *schemata*, which are the typical products of such an imaginative faculty. But this, in truth, would represent a serious confusion of incalculable consequences.

In this sense, to try to correctly interpret the authentic Kantian thought, we must arm ourselves with the greatest precautions. If it is true that, as pure intuitions, or empty intuitions without an object, Space and Time can be traced back to the imaginative faculty, it is no less true that Kant himself does not believe that he can restrict the total function of Imagination to the role of the schematism. Aside from true *schemata*, Kant distinguishes *pure images* as products of the Imagination, and with exactitude indicates—distinguishing strictly between *image* and *schema*—that Space and Time are *pure images*.[13]

Without going into a detailed analysis of the differences between a *pure image* and a *schema*—an issue that will occupy us at length in the next section—let us simply indicate that the distinction given by Kant himself now allows us to better understand the reason why Space and Time, as pure forms, are identified with an *ens imaginarium*. Having their origin in the *Imagination*—in which, as *pure images*, they provide the *pure presentation* [*aspecto*] of *objects*, without being, on the other hand, themselves *objects*—Space and Time exhibit a character [*textura*] similar to that of any *ens imaginarium*, that is, "they exist" without requiring a *real-presence* in order to be what they are: *mere possibilities*. Now, as such, Space and Time show a lack or privation of *reality*. Due to this—by having the character [*textura*] of "Something" that does not *really* exist but as a mere *possibility*, to which the empirical data should be added so that it *really* exists as an *object* of Experience—empty intuitions are identified with a form of Nothingness.

But any *ens imaginarium*—despite not really existing—is the product of a *synthesis*. While its real existence is not given, nor empirically knowable, its character [*textura*] of "Something" *ideal*, merely *possible*, requires clarification. This leads us directly to the study of the constitution of the *ens imaginarium* as such. Having identified Space and Time as retaining the ontological character [*textura*] of this *ens imaginarium* as *pure images*, it is now necessary for our investigation to be applied to unraveling the relation that mediates between them and the schemata. With this, we will approach the study of the Temporality of Nothingness as *ens imaginarium*.

§12 Nothingness and the Imagination

It is almost unnecessary to declare that our investigation finds itself before a point surrounded by difficulties of all kinds. In effect: we have seen that Nothingness, as "empty intuition without object,"[14] is identified by Kant with the pure forms of Sensibility (pure Space and Time), and, as such, he ascribes to it the character [*textura*] of an *ens imaginarium*. In this sense, the Nothing having a character like that of Space and Time, it would be a *pure image*. But *pure images*, by virtue of their origin, belong to the *Imagination*.

But, on the other hand, as it is well known, the Imagination has *schematism* as its primary function. Moreover: *schematism*, in its essential aspect, is defined as a determination of *Inner Sense* and this is identified with *Time*. It would seem, then, that *Time* (and therefore *Space*)—as *pure images*—were constitutive ingredients of *schematism*. The Nothing, as a *pure image*, should therefore have a special relation with such *schematism*. What can this be?

That *images*—and in a very particular way Time—have an indissoluble connection with *schematism* is something beyond any doubt.[15] However, despite this indissoluble connection, Kant himself seems to warn us of the dangers of possible confusion when he explicitly declares that a *schema* cannot be identified with an *image*,[16] nor even reduced to it.[17] This clearly indicates that there must be a precise difference between an *image* and a *schema* and that although some terms (especially Time) may be subject to certain confusions due to this circumstance, it is necessary that their true condition be carefully specified in order to avoid ambiguities. In this regard—and motivated as we are to determine the true character [*textura*] of Nothingness as *ens imaginarium*—our investigation will be occupied with the following: a) clarifying Space and Time as *pure images* (§12-A); b) specifying the function of Time—as *Inner Sense*—in its role as *schema* (§12-B), and c) establishing the function of Time, as *schema*, in relation to the Nothing as a *pure image* (§12-C).

§12-A Time and Space as Pure Images

Images have their origin in the Imagination: a faculty that has as an essential feature the ability to form that peculiar kind of representation by means of which, even without the real-presence of the object corresponding to it, the *presentation* (species, aspectus) of that object is originally exhibited (exhibitio originaria) or reproduced (exhibitio derivativa) in it.[18] However, it is extremely difficult to determine what this *presentation* consists of, and, in such a way, under the name *image* the most various and even contradictory meanings are understood and comprehended (copy, effigy, appearance, simile, shadow, phantom, appearance, simulation, etc.). However, leaving aside the question of whether the Imagination *produces* or simply *reproduces* the features of the object in the images, it is to be observed that—as the generating faculty of images and whatever the modality or nature of the *presentation* [*aspecto*] may be—it is necessary to assign to it a *formative* capacity, since the image as such has in itself, as the representation that it is, the ontological character [*textura*] of a product formed by the mind. In this sense, what the Imagination creates, forms, or generates—producing or re-producing—is something that becomes present in the representation (the *presentation*) and through which the object corresponding to the image becomes visible. Now, this *presentation* [*aspecto*]—that is to say, that under which the object is present or visible in its image—may simply be the *presentation* which this entity offers in its presence-to-hand [*ante los ojos*] (the intuitive image of an object), or one that reproduces the features of something that is no longer present-at-hand (mnemic image), or it may even be a *presentation* that prefigures[19] the presence of an "object" created by the image itself (creative image).

But this initial way in which we have referred to images—which is no more than a crude characterization, with no other pretensions than that of serving as an introductory way in—already presents us with a serious problem when we try to apply it to our theme and study through its schema the structure of Space and of Time as *images*. In effect, in speaking of images, we have referred always and necessarily to an *object*, as their correlative term. An image, in this sense, would seem to be always the image "of" an object. Now, when saying above that Space and Time are also *images*, it would seem that they have the character of *objects* about which there was the possibility of forming *images* that would come to produce or reproduce their features in a *presentation* [*aspecto*]. But if anything has been firmly established in the previous paragraph, it is the affirmation that neither Space nor Time are *objects*. How, then, is there the possibility of speaking about *images* with respect to them? Isn't there an unfortunate confusion in all of this?

In this way, to correctly understand Kant, we must first of all stick to his own words. Kant calls Space and Time "*pure images*,"[20] and this already, per se, introduces a distinction which we must respect. In effect, a *pure image* must be carefully distinguished from an *empirical image*. An empirical image requires, necessarily, also an empirical object to which it can refer. In this sense, what the image (in its *presentation*) does is copy or reproduce the empirical appearance of the respective entity or object of which it is a correlate. A pure image, by contrast, while having a necessary *presentation* [*aspecto*], does not reproduce but rather pre-figures or draws, as the condition of possibility, certain rules under which the empirical appearances of possible objects to which are referred are ordered. Its *presentation* [*aspecto*], instead of being derived from the empirical appearance that grants the real-presence of the reproduced object in the image, creates the conditions under which the empirical objects must appear or be exhibited. In this sense, when Kant calls Time and Space *pure images*, he thereby indicates that they draw or order in an *image* (whose ontological structure we must study in more detail) the horizon of presentation under which all possible empirical entities or objects appear insofar as they are spatially or temporally formed. Time and Space are *images*, not because they *reproduce* an *object*, but rather because they *produce, create,* or *prefigure* the conditions under which sensations and perceptions have to be synthesized in order to be apprehended in Sensibility (intuition). And Time and Space are called *images* because they, in a strict sense, exercise this particular function of the *image* that is to give a *presentation* to all possible entities that can fall under their jurisdiction as pure intuitions. As such, instead of reproducing an *empirical presentation*, they give the *pure presentation*—the pure Form—under which empirical entities or objects are ordered and presented. Time and Space are not, thereby, *objects*, but strict *conditions of possibility* of *objects*. If as *images* they are images "of" objects, the nexus that is expressed in this "of" is not that of an *exhibitio derivativa*, but rather that of an *exhibitio originaria*.

However, to understand concretely what is thereby exposed only in an abstract and general way, it is necessary to turn to Kant himself and sketch—although in a narrow glimpse—the function which he assigns to the *Imagination* within the total process of Experience. Through this, by specifying its synthetic function in relation to other faculties (Understanding and Sensibility), not only the character [*textura*] of Time and Space as *images* will be highlighted with greater clarity, but at the same time, the connective and intermediary function that it exercises in the total production of knowledge. Apart from that, it is absolutely necessary to advance in this direction if we want to prepare the ground which will allow us to discern more clearly the role of *schemata* in this functional Whole that is *Experience*.

In the *Deduction of the Pure Concepts of the Understanding*—which is the core site of the *Critique* in which the complex scheme of the cognitive process is specified with the greatest rigor and clarity—Kant assigns to this process three major *synthetic* moments, which he distinguishes by the names *Synthesis of Apprehension*, of *Reproduction*, and of *Recognition*. Each one of these *syntheses* is ascribed—in a systematic effort and with the aim of making its initial comprehension clearer—to a different cognitive source (to Sensibility, Imagination, and Apperception respectively), although in the end, when knowledge is conceived as an undivided Whole, these three subjective sources are indissolubly mixed and interlinked in a unified activity. In this respect, although the *Synthesis of Apprehension* has its beginning in the Sensibility (Sinn), nevertheless the synthetic function of the Imagination becomes part of it as an indistinguishable ingredient. Indeed—as Kant explains—although the first thing given to us of the appearance is a perception of manifold sensations, and consequently this first encounter would make "different perceptions ... dispersed and separate" exist only in the mind [*Gemüt, espíritu*] and "a combination (Verbindung) of them, which they cannot have in Sense itself" therefore necessary, he concludes that it is essential that there exists in us "an active faculty of the synthesis of this manifold in us, which we call imagination, and whose action exercised immediately upon perceptions I call Apprehension."[21] As such, the Imagination, as a synthesizing faculty, intervenes in Sensibility and actively merges into the Synthesis of Apprehension. The product of this—as Imagination gathers the manifold of Sensibility into a primitive synthetic unity—is the *image*. To gather and synthesize the manifold does not mean, as such, to reproduce it, but precisely to confer upon it the *presentation* [*aspecto*] under which that manifold of sensory data enters as a material element in the cognitive process. Thus Kant says: "[…] the imagination is to bring the manifold of intuition into an **image**; it must therefore antecedently take up the impressions into its activity, i.e., apprehend them."[22]

It is clear—and Kant was perfectly conscious of this—that, at first, such an act of Imagination upon Sensibility might seem strange. However, this is due, in part, to the fact that Imagination is considered by some to be only a *reproductive* faculty, and, in part also because an active and spontaneous function is assigned to Sensibility which, in truth, does not possess. Sensibility, in general, is only the capacity for receiving impressions, for whose organization is required—as we have said—the *synthesis* operated by the Imagination. But, at the same time, such *synthesis* cannot be identified with the mere *reproduction of images* established through their *association*—if it is understood that such *association* is realized on the basis of a merely subjective and therefore empirical foundation—since "then it would also be entirely contingent whether appearances fit into a connection of human cognitions"[23] and there could be a multitude of perceptions and, therefore, manifold separate empirical consciousnesses "without belonging to **one** consciousness of myself,"[24] which, as is evident and reflected in the total phenomenon of human cognition, is impossible. Thus, on the basis of the mere *association* regulating the *Reproductive Imagination*, it is necessary to assume an *objective principle*

("I call this objective ground of all association of appearances their **affinity**"),[25] which on the one hand is made possible by the unity of Apperception[26] and which, on the other hand, is the product of a synthesis previously operated by the *Productive Imagination*.[27] "The objective unity of all (empirical) consciousness in one consciousness (of original Apperception)"—Kant concludes—"is thus the necessary condition even of all possible perception, and the affinity of all appearances (near or remote) is a necessary consequence of a synthesis in the Imagination that is grounded *a priori* on rules."[28] "The Imagination is therefore *also* a faculty of a synthesis *a priori*, on account of which we give it the name of *productive imagination*, and, insofar as its aim in regard to all the manifold of appearance is nothing further than the necessary unity in their synthesis, this can be called the transcendental function of the Imagination."[29] As the original unity of Apperception serves as the ground of the possibility of all cognition—and this *apperceptive unity* presupposes or includes the transcendental function of Imagination[30]—"the transcendental unity of the synthesis of the Imagination is the *pure form* of all possible cognition, through which, therefore, all objects of possible Experience must be represented *a priori*."[31] This *Pure Form*—which in the manner of a synthetic unity is the particular and direct product of the imaginative function—is the *image*. By means of this image a *pure presentation* [*aspecto*] is conferred upon "all objects of possible Experience," insofar as they are apprehended and assimilated in the cognitive process. Space and Time—as Pure Forms, i.e., as *pure images*—are those which exercise such a function. And it is through this—thanks to their dual *synthetic* and *explanatory* nature—that a connection is established between Understanding and Sensibility. The Imagination is not credited simply as one of the cognitive faculties, but it is highlighted as fundamentally preeminent among them all. Hence the extraordinary standing that Kant ascribes to it:

> We therefore have a pure imagination, as a fundamental faculty of the human soul, that grounds all cognition *a priori*. By its means we bring into combination the manifold of intuition on the one side and the condition of the necessary unity of apperception on the other. Both extremes, namely sensibility and understanding, must necessarily be connected by means of this transcendental function of the imagination, since otherwise the former would to be sure yield appearances but no objects of an empirical cognition, hence there would be no experience.[32]

§12-B Time as Schema

But by ascribing to pure Imagination that fundamental hierarchical position between the faculties of the human soul and by highlighting the role that *pure images* play in the elaboration of the cognitive process, two serious dangers lie in wait for us. One of them lies in the temptation to confuse these *pure images* with *schemata*—since the intermediary function that we have seen develop in the Imagination is very similar to the one that Kant specifically assigns to *schemata*[33]—and the other danger lies in not discerning, within the schematism, the preeminent function that Time has. Indeed, if we stick to what has been said so far, Space and Time, as *pure images*, would seem to have a parallel function.

Hence, if we want to explain Kant's thinking with total precision, we need to clarify the function of *schemata* vis-à-vis *images* and, in tandem with this, highlight the reason why Time (and not Space) is the root of the schematism.

The quintessential and most fundamental problem of the *Critique of Pure Reason*—insofar as it attempts to explain the factum of human knowledge—lies in clarifying the possibility of applying categories to appearances.[34] It is precisely this problem which fully occupies Kant's attention when approaching the chapter on the *schematism*.

The possible application of the categories to appearances—given the manifest heterogeneity remaining between the two—implies the discovery of a "third term" that acts as a mediator between them. To adequately fulfill its functions, such a term would need to be, on the one hand, a representation of an *intellectual* nature (like the categories), but on the other hand, also capable of participating in the *sensible* kind (characteristic of appearances). Such would be, in Kant's opinion, the *transcendental schema*.[35] Through it—*roughly speaking*—it would be able to *sensibilize* the concept, and *intellectualize* the intuition. The former would be obtained by giving a *sensible presentation* to the concept, while the latter would be achieved by conferring *generality* (Allgemeinheit) onto the *individual* character [*textura*] that every sensible representation would seem to have. "Now this representation of a general procedure of the imagination for providing a concept with its image is what I call the *schema* for this concept."[36] Or—as he also says referring to the second function—the schema is "a rule for the determination of our intuition in accordance with a certain general concept."[37] In such a way, "the schemata of the concepts of pure understanding are the true and sole conditions for providing them with a relation to objects, thus with **significance**."[38]

But just this dual function assigned to *schemata*—that of *sensibilizing* concepts and conferring a *generality* to sensible representations—raises the crucial problem at hand. Is it not a similar function which images fulfill? Indeed, as we have seen, images (and among them even *pure images*) are a product through which Sensibility, by synthetically bringing together the manifold of Sense, gives the possibility of offering a *pure presentation* [*aspecto*] to concepts, at the same time that, as Space and Time are a priori intuitions, they seem to offer the *generality* sought.

Raising the question in such terms—and they are, indeed, the ones which must prevail when approaching such a crucial problem of the *Critique* as that of the *schematism*—it is not easy, without extensive elucidation,[39] to find and explicate the precise criteria that allow for clarity about the fine nuances that should be taken into account for attaining the desired distinctions between an *image* and a *schema*. However, although the exposition suffers from its generality, there is no alternative but to approach the question in such a way, trying to point out the fundamentals of the case.

The *image*, certainly, provides a *sensible presentation* [*aspecto*]. But this mere *presentation*, considered in itself through the cognitive process, does not in itself constitute a *cognition* of the *object* as such. What Time and Space do, as pure Forms, is synthetically bring together the manifold data that are received through the senses, incorporating them into a temporally and spatially formed character [*textura*]. Through this function of Space and Time, the sensory data are organized into a nexus of *external juxtaposition* and subjected, ultimately, to a relation of *successivity*, under which—as we will see—the mere *external juxtaposition* that comes from spatial arrangement is finally integrated. But this *pure presentation* [*aspecto*] of the appearances—the *presentation of pure successivity* under which all sensory data must be integrated upon being received and apprehended by the cognitive subject—does not in itself constitute a *cognition*, as is emphasized when we analyze in greater detail what this implies.

In effect, subjective and empirical apprehension of appearances is always *successive*, that is, in order to apprehend an appearance I must, necessarily, run through and successively combine its parts, which occurs in Time. Now, this mere *succession* that is essential to my apprehension of the appearance is not capable (for two basic reasons) of representing by itself any determinate object, nor of serving, therefore, as an indication of an authentic cognition of it. Indeed, as this *succession* is common to and identical in every process of apprehension, through it (as pure *succession*) it would be impossible to distinguish one process from another, and all appearances, as merely *successive*, would be identical to each other.[40] But, moreover, insofar as the succession is a merely subjective connection, there is nothing that determines it in such a way as to make it—in relation to a given appearance—a truly *objective* connection. "I would therefore not say that in appearance two states follow one another, but rather only that one apprehension follows the other, which is something merely **subjective,** and determines no object, and thus cannot count as the cognition of any object (not even in the appearance)."[41]

But the truth is that in Experience—as I cognize an object—something different happens. In effect, I observe that the perceptions I have of things, and therefore of the states of the appearance, are gathered together, apparently always following an objective connection and excluding any subjectively whimsical play. Now, this is possible—and revealed by a transcendental examination—only because apprehension, in each particular case, is subject to a *rule* that makes absolutely necessary that its operation or synthesis be carried out in such a way as to draw an objective connection upon receiving the manifold of sensory data. But since such a rule of synthesis cannot come either from the senses or from intuition itself, it is necessary to conclude that it must originate from a synthetic faculty of Understanding, carried out through Imagination, which determines Inner Sense with respect to Temporal relations.[42] The subsequent synthetic process that organizes this pure successivity into unities generated according to conceptual *rules* falls upon the data of the pure image which are marked by a mere successivity. Such synthetic organizations of pure successivity (pure presentation) according to concepts of Understanding are *schemata*. "The schemata are therefore nothing but a priori **time-determinations** in accordance with rules, and these concern, according to the order of the categories, the **time-series,** the **content of time,** the **order of time,** and finally the **sum total of time** in regard to all possible objects."[43]

Thanks to this function of Understanding, which brings the sensible data together with the categories, the schematism fulfills its specific mission in the application of them [the categories] to the appearances. Because, in effect, a *"transcendental time-determination"* is, on the one hand, similar to the category insofar as it is *general*, since it rests on an *a priori rule* that draws the temporal synthesis, and, on the other hand, it is homogeneous with the appearance, insofar as Time is included in all empirical representations of such appearances.⁴⁴ Faced with every possible *image* (be it empirical or pure)—which in its realization is restricted to an individual sphere of application—the *schema* is rather a *general procedure* that, according to the *rule* provided by the Understanding, serves to determine our intuition according to a certain general concept.⁴⁵ In this sense, at the basis of *concepts*, when they are applied to the appearances, there are no *images* but *schemata*, and it is through the latter—as they regulate the concrete construction of each *image*—that these are provided to *concepts*.

> Thus, if I place five points in a row, ….., this is an image of the number five. On the contrary, if I only think a number in general, which could be five or a hundred, this thinking is more the representation of a method for representing a multitude (e.g., a thousand) in an image in accordance with a certain concept than the image itself, which in this case I could survey and compare with the concept only with difficulty.⁴⁶

This representation of a general procedure, i.e., of a *method*—which as such is based on a principle (the one supplied by concepts)—through which the configuration of Inner Sense (Time) is established in the constitution of the *pure presentation* [*aspecto*] inherent in every *image*, is what Kant calls the *schematism* of the pure concepts of the Understanding. Its operation in the Imagination—as an intermediary faculty—is "a transcendental product of the Imagination, which concerns the determination of the Inner Sense in general, in accordance with conditions of its form (Time) in regard to all representations, insofar as these are to be connected together a priori in one concept in accord with the unity of Apperception."⁴⁷

But from the perspective achieved, the preeminent function that *Time* has in relation to the *schematism* is already clearly highlighted. In effect, although Space and Time are equally original intuitive sources and both have a different function as Forms of outer and inner intuition, it is unquestionable that every *image*, insofar as it is a *representation* of our mind and therefore a modification of *Inner Sense*, is subject to Time. Every *pure presentation* [*aspecto*] (whether or not it refers to outer appearances) must therefore be reduced to a *temporal relation*. Although Space is the pure Form of all outer appearances, the factum that representations are to be ordered in *Inner Sense* determines that Time *eo ipso* acquires the preeminent function of being "*the a priori formal condition of all appearances in general*,"[48] and therefore plays, as such, a role of fundamental and singular importance in the development of the cognitive process. The subsequent process of the synthesis brought by the Understanding, and by means of which the drawing of this temporal manifold is ordered through the schemata, must be exercised upon its contents—i.e., the data of the *pure image* marked by a pure *successivity*. These *schemata* are—as we have repeatedly pointed out—nothing more than determinations of Inner Sense in general, by means of which the temporal elements, in accordance with the corresponding *concept* that modulates the synthesis, acquire in each case a different organization in their function of constituting appearances ("*pure presentation* [*aspecto*]" or "*temporality*").

Without going into further details—whose study would make this point extremely long—with what has been said already, the issues that we were interested in highlighting in reference to our theme are perfectly outlined. We can now see with complete clarity not only the specific function of *schemata* in relation to *images*, but also the preeminent hierarchical position that Time occupies in all of this. As *Inner Sense*—i.e., as that into which the *pure presentation* [*aspecto*] of all appearances in general is integrated and reworked—Time is the *Pure Form* (pure image) of all possible objects. While the *Nothing*—as *ens imaginarium*—has been identified with the character [*textura*] of an empty intuition (pure Form),[49] *eo ipso* it would have a structure similar to that of this *pure image*. Or, said more precisely: it would have to possess a character [*textura*] similar to that of this pure manifold of merely *successive* temporal data that constitute the fabric of Inner Sense as pure Temporality.

But this formulation, as it is easy to see right away, presents a dangerous ambiguity. Thus described, the *Nothing* would also be the *pure presentation* of every possible *real* entity. It is necessary then that if the *ens imaginarium* wants to be considered an authentic *Nothing*, the pure successiveness of Time will be determined by a *concept* whose *schema*—clearly—cannot be identical to that which comes into play and determines Time when it intervenes in the structure of actually existing entities. It is therefore necessary to shed light on the function that must be assigned to the *schematism*, and hence to Time, in relation to the *Nothing* as *pure image*.

§12-C The Schematism of the Nothing as Pure Image

The general procedure for providing to a concept its corresponding image—in accordance with the *rule* that this concept gives—is what Kant calls its *schematism*. The *schematism* works on the manifold of temporal sensible data and brings about the connection between them according to the dictates of that *rule*, thus drawing the corresponding *pure temporal presentation* [*aspecto*] that, as such, exhibits the image of the appearance. Applying this procedure to the *categories of relation* (which are those that should be treated according to the general order in which the notion of Nothingness is studied in the Kantian table), our proposal cannot be but to indicate how such categories govern the generation of time in its *order* (Zeitordnung), imposing upon it a "transcendental determination" by means of which its *pure presentation* [*aspecto*] is organized in this sense. But, in contrast to what can be the *schematism* of the *categories of relation* referring to *real entities*—i.e., in their *ontological use*—those categories must be studied or considered in reference to the *Nothing* as *ens imaginarium*, since, as it can be concluded from its own definition, its structure is that of a "Something" (Etwas), though lacking *substance*.[50] In this sense, acknowledging this lack of *substance* in the *ens imaginarium*, the study of its *schematism* implies the clarification of the possible connection that the *categories of relation* maintain with the generation of their corresponding *pure presentation* [*aspecto*]. With such a pure form constituting the temporiform character [textura] of the Nothing as *image*, we must inquire into what the structure of such a Temporality could be in which the *substance's* lack or emptiness of determination prevails.

But, to better understand what this means, we must contrast such a situation with the one presented when the *categories of relation* intervene in the generation of the *pure presentation* [*aspecto*] that the objects exhibit as *real*, imposing upon them the corresponding temporal order. Fully understanding this, whatever is the *non-ontological* function of Understanding and the generation of the respective Temporality of the Nothing shall be seen with greater clarity from such a perspective.

The specific function of the *categories of relation*—just like that of the *Principles* (Grundsätze) that regulate their objective use (*Analogies of Experience*)—is not aimed at determining the aspects of empirical synthesis through which appearances are constituted, but rather their *existence* (Dasein) and their *relationship* to each other with respect to this existence.[51] In this sense, the function of such categories and Principles is not *constitutive*, but merely *regulative*.[52] What they regulate are the *temporal relations* of appearances, according to which the latter's *existence* can be determined in reference to the unity of the whole of Time. Thus, the categories of relation determine the *temporal order* in reference to the existence of appearances and express—through the Principles and corresponding schematism—the modes that Time can exhibit in its *pure presentation* [*aspecto*] in regard to their *order* and, therefore, to the *temporal order* in which the appearances themselves are inserted into the general context of Experience. Such modes of temporal order are those of *Permanence* (Beharrlichkeit), *Succession* (Folge), and *Simultaneity* (Zugleichsein).[53] The categories regulate these modes of temporal order and their expression is given by the corresponding *schemata*, according to which the *pure presentation* [*aspecto*] of the temporal image is, in each case, generated according to the *rule* of the corresponding concept. Thus, e.g., the *schema* of *substance* is *permanence*, that of *cause* is *succession*, and that of *reciprocity* is *simultaneity*.[54] Such *schemata* express the temporal relation in which appearances occur and the modes of their mutual involvement with respect to their existence. That an appearance is a substance means, according to this, that its existence exhibits a certain *permanence* in Time (which differentiates it from *accidental existence*, which is *changeable*); that an appearance is a cause with respect to another means that it *precedes it* in the order of Time as its antecedent; and that an appearance is in *community* with respect to another means that its existence is in a relation of reciprocal causal dependence with it, i.e., they are *simultaneous* with respect to each other.

Now, of whatever Time is in itself—of its self-consistency—we cannot know anything, since (as Kant expresses it) it does not subsist by itself, nor does it belong to things in themselves.[55] Otherwise, not being an *object*—but a condition of the possibility of *objects* themselves—Time cannot be perceived by itself.⁵⁶ Time is given, and from it we are capable of having a representation, only insofar as it is a subjective condition under which intuitions are possible in us.⁵⁷ But as the a priori Form of all appearances—that is, as Inner Sense—Time, insofar as through it we apprehend all appearances, is only a pure succession of consecutive *nows*.

But appealing to this pure *succession of nows*, that is, based on pure Time itself, we would never manage to determine in the existence of appearances those *modes*—of permanence, succession, and simultaneity—which allow us to objectify that existence as a *substance*, as a *cause* in relation with its *effect*, or as subject to an order of causal *interdependence*. In this sense, for that to occur—as it in fact occurs in Experience—the Understanding's regulative act upon this pure Form that is Time is necessary (i.e., an act of the categories, via the schemata).

Indeed, upon the pure succession of *consecutive nows* given in the apprehensive act, the category of *substance* executes its synthetic act by organizing that pure succession as something *permanent* and *constant* through all possible *change*. In this way, the substance of appearances—i.e., the substrate that permits their identification despite any possible *change* in their accidents and through which, moreover, it is possible to establish that *change*—is that to which their *permanence* in Time corresponds. "Our **apprehension** of the manifold of appearance"—Kant writes with respect to this point—

> is always successive, and is therefore always changing. We can therefore never determine from this alone whether this manifold, as object of experience, is simultaneous or successive, if something does not ground it **which always exists,** i.e., something **lasting** and **persisting,** of which all change and simultaneity are nothing but so many ways (modi of time) in which that which persists exists.⁵⁸

In this sense, all appearances contain something *permanent*—i.e., *substance*—on the basis of which, as identical substrate, it is possible for us to represent in them the process of change. "Consequently that which persists, in relation to which alone all temporal relations of appearances can be determined, is substance in the appearance, i.e., the real in the appearance, which as the substratum of all change always remains the same."⁵⁹ *Permanence* is, thus, the *schema* of *substance* in appearances; that is: a transcendental determination of its temporal structure by means of which its *pure presentation* [*aspecto*] is represented as a constant substrate amidst change. "Therefore in all appearances that which persists is the object itself, i.e., the substance (phaenomenon), but everything that changes or that can change belongs only to the way in which this substance or substances exist, thus to their determinations."[60] The permanent—substance—is thus "the identity of the substratum in which alone all change has its thoroughgoing unity."[61] As a representation of the pure temporal presentation [*aspecto*] of the appearance—i.e., of its image—the *schema* of substance is that which organizes the manifold data of succession in a substrate that persists and doesn't change, which is fixed, constant and immutable, in the midst of the changing flow in which the apprehension of the appearance develops ("the everlasting existence of the proper subject in the appearances").[62] In this sense, as *permanent*—i.e., as transcendentally determined by the category of *substance* as substrate or subsistent pure presentation [*aspecto*]—"that which is unchangeable in existence, i.e., substance" corresponds to Time in the appearances.[63] *Substance* is thus the ontological determination of permanence in the appearances; *permanence* is the temporal sense (*schema*) of that substance as a determination of appearances as the representations of Inner Sense.

But if in this way we clarify the function of the category of substance in the determination of Time as constitutive of real entities, it must be remembered that our concern points rather to the elucidation of the transcendental schematism of the categories when it is referred to the Nothing as *ens imaginarium*. In this respect, it should be noted that this *ens imaginarium* is defined by Kant himself as "*the mere form of intuition, without substance.*"[64] What is being said here?

First of all, a fact expressed by the definition itself must be determined. In effect, we find ourselves before a structure in which the organizing function of the category of substance and, therefore, that of its corresponding schematism seems to be excluded. As such a function is not exercised, and as the *pure presentation* [*aspecto*] of Time lacks this synthetic and productive act, it exhibits only what is proper to it, that is, a merely formal *successivity*. In this sense, as *pure successivity*, Time itself is only a succession of *nows* which, by lacking all determination (empirical as well as transcendental), are *identical* to one another with reference to their pure temporal structure. As a *pure successivity of identical nows*, Time is always the *now* and thus reveals a self-constancy through its uninterrupted identity. Seen from the *now*—being always *now*—Time would appear not to elapse, to be immutable and, therefore, persistently *now*.⁶⁵

In the pure successivity of its always-identical *nows*—as pure Form lacking all content and categorial determination—Time (this "pure form" that we must imagine without the corresponding organization upon which the category of *substance* is exercised when it refers to the appearances of Experience) is not in itself any *object*, nor is it possible—through it—to determine any *object* as such. Indeed, through its pure successivity—that being *identical nows*—it is impossible to distinguish anything from anything else, or to represent in this *now* any objective nexus that orders the pure successivity and makes appearances appear as substances, causes, etc.⁶⁶ In the pure successivity of this Temporality, that which "appears" (the Nothing) lacks *substance*, that is, *reality*, and is, so to speak, the pure specter of a mere form that doesn't contain any determination through which it could be distinguished. The structure of Time that exhibits the *ens imaginarium* is thus a pure *now* and nothing more. As such, being always *now*, this Time—"pure form" of Nothingness—would appear not to elapse, to be constantly self-identical, immutable, as if it were a single and pure *static now* (nunc stans) that symbolized *eternity*.⁶⁷

Now it is a matter of noticing that with what we say we don't commit the contradiction of affirming, on the one hand, that the succession of the apprehension of appearances is always *changing*, and, on the other hand, that the succession of pure Time gives the presentation [*aspecto*] of being a succession of always *identical nows*. If what is expressed thusly is understood correctly, it will have been seen that the description refers to two completely distinct levels. Indeed, the successivity of pure Time is *identical* with respect to the mere temporal structure of the *now*. On the other hand, the fact that this successivity is *changing*⁶⁸ comes from the fact that the pure temporal structure of the *now*, by referring Time to the empirical appearances as the form of their intuitive apprehension, is at each instant filled with various empirical elements that must be organized subsequently by the categorial synthesis in order to give them the form required by their objectivity. With regard to the Temporality of the *ens imaginarium*—by contrast—having seen that it is "pure form," and that, furthermore, the categorial function is not exercised upon it, the structure of the *now* is always identical, and, on the basis of it, even the passage of Time apparently ceases. "Time itself"—as Kant says—"does not elapse, but the existence of that which is changeable elapses in it."[69]

But this initial characterization of the Temporality of Nothingness—in which it stands out as the uninterrupted sequence of *identical nows*—cannot fully satisfy us. If the procedure we have followed to attain it is thoroughly understood, it will be easily noticed that it has been derived following the common thread that provides a "de-ontologization" of categorial Time. The Time of Nothingness—the pure successivity of *identical nows*—is, thus, the negative residue that remains when the constitutive and organizing function of the categories of relation—and its corresponding schematism—ceases acting upon the *pure presentation* [*aspecto*] of the temporal stream characteristic of Inner Sense. The Temporality of the *ens imaginarium* is, thus, a *pure image* deprived of ontological characteristics, or de-substantialized. But does Nothingness, as such, respond to these characteristics? Or is it necessary, on the contrary, to think it as a *pure image*, though not simply "*deprived*" of ontological elements, but as "*pure image*" *of the Nothing itself* and, therefore, modalized through its own categories and schemata? What does this mean? And what consequence does this new perspective bring for the Temporality proper to it and to Time in general?

§13 The Temporality of the *Ens Imaginarium*

When orienting himself in accordance with the *ontological* function of the Categories and Principles of the Understanding, Kant conceives of Nothingness as the product of that function's absence, or of its action exercised under the modality of privation or negation. In the case of the *ens imaginarium* this procedure is manifest. Being conceived as "Something" lacking *substance*, its pure temporal presentation [*aspecto*] displays the lack or absence of *permanence*, i.e., is reduced to a mere *successivity*.

But the greatest objection that could be formulated against this conception would be the radical indifference that pure *successivity* shows in its role as a constitutive ingredient with respect to Being or Nothingness. Indeed, the *successivity* of the pure temporal presentation [*aspecto*] corresponds equally (apart from its categorial determination) to both Being and Nothingness. That is: the Temporality in both instances is identical with and clearly guided by a prior *understanding of Being*, which exerts a decisive influence on the final determination that is given to such Temporality. It is precisely in this that its greatest deficiency is manifested, since, as the *Temporality of Nothingness* is variegated in its ontological background, it could hardly serve as a *way* of achieving an authentic understanding of the features of Nothingness itself. To the contrary, that Temporality being a mere negative ontological residue (attained via the process of a *privation* or imagining the lack of all categorial determination) serves only for thinking the "Nothing" under the aspect of a mere Non-Being, lacking substance or reality, as the *ens imaginarium* turns out to be (in the Kantian conception). Because this lack of *substance* is apparent in it, and being precisely this that determines its presumed temporal character [*textura*]—as it is possible to prove by analyzing Kant's attempt to conceive *substance* (Being) as a substratum of permanence which is indispensable for representing *change* (Non-Being)—we must examine its assertions in this respect (developed principally in the *First Analogy*), in order to critically evaluate the *presuppositions* that support them and attempt to set the limits of their legitimacy in relation to the authentic Temporality of Nothingness itself.

In doing this—as we will see—a *circle* will be revealed once more, like the one that we have acknowledged so many times throughout this investigation and whose reiteration demonstrates again the intimate coupling of Temporality with Being. It is now a matter of seeing whether this Being—under its guise of *substance*—is capable of serving as the ground of the *temporal meaning* that is patently revealed by Nothingness.

The Kantian line of argument attempting to establish the relationship between *change* and *substance* is clear and conclusive: in effect, all *change*, in order to be perceived, requires a *substance* (i.e., a *permanent substratum*) that makes its perception possible. If by *change*—in its quintessential meaning—one understands the emergence or disappearance of something, "arising or perishing per se cannot be a possible perception unless it concerns merely a determination of that which persists, for it is this very thing that persists that makes possible the representation of the transition from one state into another, and from non-being into being, which can therefore be empirically cognized only as changing determinations of that which lasts."[70] Hence, if this *substance* did not exist, we could not even think about *change*.

Now, this schema—which represents an *ontological* occurrence—can and must be transposed to the very *temporal structure* that gives it meaning. Indeed, just as it is necessary to presuppose a *substance* at the center of all possible *change*, so it is essential to represent a "substantial" Time—i.e., an immutable, fixed, and eternal Time—that serves to establish a *permanent substratum* at the center of the phenomenal succession and thanks to which the course of those appearances can be fixed. Indeed, says Kant, suppose something begins to be absolutely. For this it is necessary to admit a moment of Time in which that something did not exist. But to what can we attach that moment of Time if not with what existed previously? For is it possible, perhaps, to represent an empty Time? By no means, he replies: "For an empty time that would precede is not an object of perception."[71] As we have already seen,[72] an *empty Time*, i.e., devoid of reality, is impossible to conceive. Reality, the substance of appearances, must exist *permanently* in Time and this *substantial permanence* eo ipso guarantees the *permanence* of Time itself, i.e., its "substantial" structure. If this weren't the case and it were admitted that the substance of appearances could suddenly arise or disappear, then "everything would disappear that alone can represent the unity of time, namely the identity of the substratum in which alone all change has its thoroughgoing unity."[73] "Consequently"—he adds—"that which persists, in relation to which alone all temporal relations of appearances can be determined, is substance in the appearance, i.e., the real in the appearance, which as the substratum of all change always remains the same."[74] In this sense, clearly and definitively establishing the link that we are interested in highlighting, Kant concludes:

> Substances (in appearance) are the substrata of all time-determinations. The arising of some of them and the perishing of others *would itself remove the sole condition of the empirical unity of Time*, and the appearances would then be related to two different times, in which existence flowed side by side, which is absurd. For there is **only one** time, in which all different times must not be placed simultaneously but only one after another.[75]

Now, what does all this reveal? In our judgment, by means of the above, the *ontological grounds* of Kant's conception of Time are clearly and evidently established. Its roots reveal how, from the notion of a *substance* (which in turn implies a prior *understanding of Being* of which *substance* is a determinative mark), the characteristics of Time are fixed, and how—in a complementary way—from this conception of Time, the *substance* is defined by a temporal meaning (*permanence*) extracted from that previous "substantialization" of Time. As such, the *permanence* of Time is nothing other than its entitative determination as *substance* and, from the determination of Time as *permanent*, the *substance* is that which bears such marks of *permanence*. The twofold determinative influence of these two poles reveals once again the *circle* that we have repeatedly tried to point out throughout our investigation.

And now, when the characteristics of Time are fixed under the archetype of *substance*, it clearly reveals that this determination conforms to the previous fact that its "Being," as such, has been understood as that of an entity "*present at hand*" (Vorhandene, [*ante los ojos*]). In this sense, i.e., even serving as a *horizon* for other beings (being their "condition of possibility"), Time itself is the bearer of a real ontological structure, and, therefore, like that of any entity "present at hand."[76] In attempting to achieve its entitative determination, needing to have the character [*textura*] of a substratum from which the *change* proper to those merely *accidental* entitative determinations can be made intelligible, all the characteristics distinguishing a *substance* are ascribed to it, and among them primarily its *permanence*. As a condition of the possibility of real appearances, and a constitutive ingredient of them, Time is then objectified as something bearing all the characteristics of a *substance* which is also "present at hand." *Permanence*, as such, is the *schema* (i.e., the connotation effected in temporal language) of that *substantial* characteristic imputed to it. And it is from such a mark of *permanence*—as we have said—that *substance* is re-interpreted with a temporal meaning, hence the establishing of the *circle*.

But the *ens imaginarium*—as we have seen—is a "Something" deprived of *substance*. Now: does this mean that the Temporality of its structure is that of an "*empty*" Time? Not at all. The temporal structure of the *ens imaginarium* is that of *Pure Time*,[77] but this *purity* of Time is not synonymous with "empty" Time, which in principle would be unrepresentable and conceptually unsustainable. The Temporality of the *ens imaginarium*—this being a "Something" deprived of substance—responds to the same structure exhibited by that of real appearances, with the sole exception that it has been stripped (through a privation) of the character of empirical existence (permanence) that distinguishes it as a real-substance. In this sense, the *negation* (privation) that is inflicted upon the Temporality of the *ens imaginarium* is not enough to distort its radical ontological condition (because it continues to maintain the formal structure of a *substance*) although it does not acknowledge any corresponding empirical marks. The *successivity* that it exhibits is thus the subject of a substantial Form simply deprived of empirical reality. In this sense, the *ecstatic now* (nunc stans)—which the *ens imaginarium* bears as its character— is certainly a *now* abstracted from the flow of *real-nows* and hypostatized as *supratemporal*. But both because of the temporal structure from which it originates (Time conceived as a *substance*), and because of its own merely privative characteristics, that *nunc stans* (despite the *privation* it exhibits) continues to maintain the ontological marks (now expressed abstractly) that characterize the *substance* (infinity, uniqueness, immutability, etc.). In order for the pure *successivity* outlined here to be filled with real contents, it would be sufficient for it to have the structure of a *real-substance*. Otherwise, as Kant says, if the Temporality of the *ens imaginarium* were ontologically distinct from that of the *ens real*, one would need to suppose two different species of Time. On the contrary, Time is one and the same: filled with real contents (therefore existing as a substance marked by permanence), and once considered in its purity, as a pure (substantial) Form. In both cases the prior *understanding of Being* that guides its possible determination is one and the same. That is why, on such a path, it becomes impossible to understand the Temporality of Nothingness.

But what would happen if instead of following the Kantian path—which ultimately, as we have seen, is nothing more than a *de-ontologizing* path by which, by *ontological negation*, one arrives at the conception of a Time deprived of reality—we were trying to attain a determination of Temporality by starting from our own *understanding of Being*? In this respect, it should first be recalled that this Nothing is not manifested through the simple negation of real contents, but that it, on its own, exhibits a positive and radical *negativity*, viz., it manifests itself through *its own negative qualities* (absolute negativity). Such is what occurs—as we have had occasion to note[78]—in phenomena such as *nihilation* and also (within the oneiric dimension) in *deep sleep*. In these there is a fading of the *real world* and with it, at once, comes the loss of the *meaningfulness of Time* with all the consequences that this implies (emergence of the non-presentative Temporality, disappearance of the *now*, of the "direction" of the course of time, etc.). Moreover, along with this, the openness [*la patencia*] of Nothingness enables—as a crucial and decisive occurrence—the revelation of the radical *finitude* of Existence. Starting from such an understanding of *finitude*—as already indicated—a new and radical understanding of Temporality is revealed, *eo ipso*. Is it not only on the basis of this—and of the horizon of "meaning" that it offers—that one would be able to assign an adequate temporal character [*textura*] to the phenomena of Nothingness itself?

It is important to see that following the path proposed by Kant—which leads him to extract the axioms of Time from its mere structure as a Form of pure intuition—by preserving Time's character [*textura*] of an entity "present to hand" (although it is conceived as a mere "condition of possibility" and not as an *object*), Time exhibits infinity as a constitutive property.[79] Now, can this *infinity* be supported as a characteristic of Temporality when it is manifested as *finite* in our very understanding of Existence? Enclosed in this *infinity*—and in the ontological conception sustaining it—is one of the greatest obstacles to arise when we desire an adequate temporal interpretation of the phenomena of Nothingness, isn't it? Indeed. However: does this mean, perhaps, that the property of *infinity* is a capricious attribute assigned to Time? Absolutely not. For this reason, when confronted with this problem, and when observing that both properties seem to negate one another, we would be wrong if we dedicated ourselves to discussing which of the two is correct, or what rights each one has to define the essence of Time—when, in truth, both are perfectly legitimate—without first attempting to clarify the fact itself and the roots that make it possible. In keeping with such a purpose, what has already been said will be repeated: even manifesting itself as *finite* to the very understanding of Existence, Time is objectified—commonly and generally—as *infinite*. Where does this come from? What is the factum of such a "*concealment*" based upon?

When speaking of "concealment" there is firstly a need to avoid any moral resonances that this term could evoke, and second, any sense of conscious behavior or self-deception inflicted by man upon himself in the interpretation of Time. "Concealment" (Verdeckung)—by contrast—obeys the phenomenal structure itself and is, so to speak, an essential property of the phenomenon of "concealing" itself. In this sense, the "concealment" of the finitude of Time occurs when, starting from the natural understanding of its Being as that of an entity "present at hand" (which already supposes that Temporality may be extracted from Existence itself and is "objective" in Nature), the course of Time is "objectified" as an uninterrupted sequence of *nows* (also "present at hand"). In this sense, if the characterization of Time keeps primarily to this *sequence*, it is not possible to find in it a beginning or an end, since every *now* is inserted into a Time that, as such, neither arises nor disappears, but has always existed.[80] Due to this—considering Time as that "present at hand" course of *nows* floating in the void—it is seen as endless on both sides, since each *now* presupposes the previous one and so an *ad infinitum*. Hence, in trying to think this Time to the end, there is a need to think always more Time, from which it follows, as a consequence, that Time is *in-finite*, i.e., without end.

But what is being expressed here? First of all we have to see that, in addition to the supportive basis that exhibits Time, and which makes possible the representation of its *infinitude* (its condition as a "present at hand" entity), this same *in-finity* signifies only a *negation*—as is manifested even in the particle "*in*" that composes it—which is and can be exercised precisely because Time has previously appeared under the guise of that which aims to negate itself. In such a way, the *in-finity* of Time, in its own negative structure, attests that what is negated originally appears bearing opposing properties. And, in fact, within Existence—Nothingness manifested, and with it the *finitude* of Existence itself—Time (as the "meaning" of this Existence) reveals *eo ipso* its own *finite* condition. Faced with this *finitude of Time* so revealed, its "objectification" as something *in-finite*, represents a flight and a concealment that, as such, are the expression of an *understanding of Being* realized from that mode of Existence that Heidegger designates with the generic title of "*inauthentic*" (Uneigentliche).[81] On this basis, as the *understanding of Being* is projected from the alienated "being-in-the-world" in which it rests and becomes attached to the domain of entities, not only is the *understanding of Being* qua Being lost, but the diminished "understanding" of it begins with the "present at hand" aspect of the entities themselves. The "objectification" of Time as an entity "present at hand" and the ascription of the property "real" to the same—until elevating it, due to its rank, to the category of a *substance*—is thus explained by this factum.[82]

But this is not a question here—because it is not our purpose to pursue the epigenetic-existential development of this conception of Time, but to show the conditions of its possibility and the existential *factum* that sustains it.[83] For this at once opens the understanding for grasping its *finitude* and that terrain in which it originally manifests itself. Indeed, apart from the distinct and radical differences that Temporality can exhibit across both cases, it is a matter of seeing that—fundamentally—Temporality can exhibit and present itself in Existence as something that in principle does not have a "present at hand" structure. So, although it is true that the course of Time, to the extent that it is "objectified" as a sequence of "present at hand" *nows* (as occurs, e.g., in the Natural Sciences), can be an entity which may rightly be understood from the perspective of the dominant sense of "Being" in that case (in which an unquestionable domain of the "entitative" prevails), it is at the same time no less true that Time itself can offer itself as that which resists being apprehended as an entity "present at hand," since what is made manifest to Existence—when it is exhibited in terms of "meaning" in this case—is not *Being* but precisely *Nothingness*. In this way, within the phenomena named (nihilation, deep sleep, etc.) Nothingness is manifested and realized—"there is Nothing," it is said—and, together with this, the Time that confers "meaning" on them is exhibited as something impossible to be apprehended as something "present at hand" since, in principle, it refuses the ascription of any real or positive property, as well as any nexus of meaning or reference, etc., which are possible only within the framework of the *understanding of Being* and the emergence of "present at hand" entities that is correlative to it.

Now, from this point of view—although it is true that a positive characterization of the Temporality of Nothingness has not yet been given—the reason why this third notion of Nothingness qua *ens imaginarium* obstructs a possible understanding of such Temporality is at least clear. Since the temporal structure of the *ens imaginarium* has a hidden *ontological* character [*textura*], it can serve only as configuring a mere *successivity* that, as a "condition of possibility" deprived of "reality," is indifferent to whether it is used in the constitution of real entities or is, in itself, a mere "possibility" of the real. It is precisely as a merely "possible Something"—as opposed to the real or existing empirical appearances—that the "Nothing" represented by the *ens imaginarium* constitutes a "privation." Or put another way: the "Nothing" of the *ens imaginarium* is only a *privation of the real*.[84] But the mere *ontological privation* qua *negation*, or as a mere "*condition of possibility*" *of the real* in the face of already-constituted empirical reality, is not on its own, or in itself, an authentic *Nothing*. On the contrary, as Kant himself says, "negations are merely determinations that express the non-being of something in the substance"—but as "determinations" that affect the existence of this *substance* they are always *real*[85]—thus, in being the "conditions of possibility" and "conditions of the possibility of Experience," they are always and necessarily of the real.[86] This means that, in their being *privative* modalities, they leave Being itself unscathed and only manage to express, always in a deficient way, its presumed and not total absence.[87] For this reason—as we have indicated in the previous chapter—it would be necessary to view the *Nothing* on the basis of *absolute negativity* in order to comprehend its corresponding temporal structure. Only in this way would we be able to "apprehend" a Time that, without losing its character of a "pure image," could show us in its "appearance" the realization of Nothingness itself and not that of a mere privation of Being. Otherwise—as we have said—only on the basis of this Time (as the "meaning" of Nothingness) could we properly understand and interpret its phenomena, without the risk of getting lost and confused by the use of that other horizon of "meaning"—the one offered by ontological Temporality—which, because it refers to Being and is introduced in its "understanding," would be inappropriate in this case.

The path for this is sketched—even if only in a preliminary outline—through the previous reflections. Abolishing the ontological categories—and therefore their corresponding schematism—it is necessary to investigate, and then transcendentally deduce, the possibility of the categories of Nothingness and their respective schematism, since this would come to be like a kind of expository key to its Temporality.

But a fundamental and prior question with respect to all this—since the results that can be achieved depend on it—would be to ask whether such categories of Nothingness would have a *structure* and *function* similar to what Kant assigns to the *ontological categories*, or whether, on the contrary, they should be conceived in a radically different way. In this respect, it is not only possible to ask whether one can speak in general of "categories" of Nothingness—or of "anti-categories," as we have called them elsewhere—but, more radically, if Nothingness is constituted by such "categories," or if, on the contrary, all possible *idealistic* perspectives—however nuanced or subtle—should be abandoned when trying to think about this problem. But for now, this is only formulated in its bare-bones plan.

4

Nothingness and the *Nihil Negativum*

§14 Problems of the *Nihil Negativum*

The indicators Kant provides when referring to the *nihil negativum* as the fourth example of Nothingness are brief and succinct. In succession—as they are exhibited in the *Critique of Pure Reason* (B348-9)—these indicators are, in summary, of three types:

(1) A statement. Succinctly, it says: "The object of a concept that contradicts itself is nothing because the concept is nothing, the impossible, like a rectilinear figure with two sides (*nihil negativum*)"[1];
(2) A definition. In it the *nihil negativum* is characterized as "an empty object without concept"[2]; and
(3) A comparison. Here it is stated that the *nihil negativum* is distinguished from the *ens rationis* because, unlike the latter, as the object of a concept that contradicts itself, it is opposed (entgegengesetzt) to possibility.[3]

Now, despite the fact that such indicators may seem exaggeratedly simple—and, undoubtedly, less explicit than those devoted to the other three notions—it is anyway possible to extract and raise from them the rich and intricate problematic that lies hidden behind this notion of Nothing as *nihil negativum*. Doing so and highlighting its connection with the fundamental question which occupies us—the relation between Temporality and Nothingness—is the principal aim that has to guide us throughout our journey.

According to the statement Kant offers about the *nihil negativum*—and insofar as this is the expression of a Nothing—it is necessary to see that the Nothing that it expresses turns out to be the *object* of a *concept*, viz., its objective correlate. Now, as this *concept* (according to what is said about it) contradicts itself, and in fact cancels itself, it is itself a Nothing, viz., "*the impossible.*" In this sense—Kant himself says, leaving room for an apparent contradiction—that *object* is not simply the correlate of a *concept* (such as an *object* corresponding to the *nihil privativum* could be),[4] but rather, strictly speaking, turns out to be an "*object without concept.*" But this "*object without concept,*" moreover, is not only a contradictory *object*,[5] but also must be qualified as "*empty.*" The Nothing, as *nihil negativum*, is therefore characterized as an "*empty object without concept,*" as stated in the definition we highlighted above in (2).

Now, this "*empty object without concept*" is not, as the *ens rationis* could be, a simple chimera or a rational noumenal construction—which as an invention or creation of Reason (Erdichtung) is not, even while being impossible, contradictory in itself—but is rather, in itself, something *im-possible*, since it opposes and contradicts itself, and, as such, is an absurdity, a contradiction (Unding) incapable of being counted or taken as being among the possibilities. In this way, while the *ens rationis* is not possible because it cannot be real—viz., because it lacks the power of being real which is required for being possible—the *nihil negativum* is not possible because it is radically opposed to all possibility, since in principle it is "*the im-possible,*" being the expression of a concept which, as contradictory, cancels itself.

But in addition to being "impossible," and precisely because of this, the *object* that corresponds to the *nihil negativum* is "empty." And this emptiness is not synonymous with an absence, deficiency, or lack of content—like that which registers the merely possible in the *nihil privativum* or the *ens imaginarium* in the face of reality—but rather expresses that the *nihil negativum* is empty of possibility. For this reason, the *nihil negativum* is not a mere empty possibility—as the *ens imaginarium* or the *nihil privativum* can be—but the expression of an *object empty of possibility*, viz., something im-possible, absurd, lacking meaning, since that of which it turns out to be an objective correlate is, in turn, a concept that, by contradicting itself, annuls all possibility and cancels itself.

Now, let us reflect on the above. First of all, there is the issue of seeing that the "*empty object*" that represents the *nihil negativum* is Nothing—but a Nothing that exhibits the character of *the negative (nihil negativum)*—because that which corresponds to it as *concept* is, in turn, a structure or notion that is *Nothing*, since, given its contradictory character, this *concept* cancels itself.[6] In this sense, the *Principle of Non-contradiction* plays a decisive role here in the determination of such a character. The *concept* that corresponds to the *object* is *Nothing* (and the *object* eo ipso is *Nothing*), viz., it is "*the im-possible*," because that *concept* violates the *Principle of Non-contradiction* and, by doing so, must be excluded from the possibilities in order to become ipso facto an absurdity due to the contradiction that envelops it. In this way, the im-possible is Nothing because this im-possibility violates the *Principle of Non-contradiction*. Only what is in agreement or does not transgress such a Principle is possible; whatever opposes it, or violates its dictates, is im-possible, viz., turns out to be Nothing at all.

It is made clear in such a way that the *Principle of Non-contradiction* is manifestly an essential criterion for judging about Nothing. But, about what "Nothing"? Well, as we have seen, even without transgressing the Principle of Non-contradiction, both the *ens rationis* as well as the *nihil privativum* and the *ens imaginarium* are expressions of Nothingness. For what reason, then, does this *nihil negativum* become a Nothing simply by violating the Principle of Non-contradiction? What structure does this Nothing have, which arises from the Principle of Non-contradiction, compared with the Nothing of the *ens rationis*, or with that of the *nihil privativum* and the *ens imaginarium*?

But at this point we must ask certain questions that, due to how strange and unusual they seem to be—and especially because they question what is apparently obvious and comprehensible—may seem idle or arouse perplexity. Indeed, supposing that the Nothing of the *nihil negativum* arises from a violation of the Principle of Non-contradiction ... is this *alone* sufficient for a Nothing to automatically and necessarily manifest in the form of the *nihil negativum*? Or, asked the other way around: is the non-violation of the Principle of Non-contradiction sufficient for something to be *possible* and to have in itself the ability of becoming *real*? Or does the possible, in order to be such, need not only not to violate the Principle of Non-contradiction, but to agree with and meet other conditions that make possible "the possible"? But what can these other "conditions" be—concomitant with the merely logical ones stated by the Principle of Non-contradiction—which would make possible the emergence of "the possible" and on which it would even depend, such that if they are transgressed, there would arise the "impossible" in the sense of the *nihil negativum*? But in what sense do we use the terms "*possible*" and "*im-possible*" here? Are they synonymous with merely logical conditions (such as those that seem to persist in the domain where the Principle of Non-contradiction is developed), or do "*possibility*" and "*im-possibility*" refer to the *possibility* of the objects of Experience? Is it not fair, then, for us to separate mere *logical possibility* from the *possibility of the real*? Does the *Principle of Non-contradiction* govern in both cases, with the same sufficiency, and as the sole determining ground?

Not intending to answer these questions—which merit the most careful consideration—let us observe, nevertheless, that we have spoken of a *concept* that contradicts itself, viz., of a contradiction, of something absurd and impossible, without giving an example of it. Kant, on the contrary, exemplifies such a *concept* and as his example he offers that of a rectilinear figure with two sides. Now: why does such a *concept* (or what it signifies) run against the Principle of Non-contradiction? A rectilinear figure, as a geometric object, would seem to be a real object, endowed with objective reality, as all geometric objects have to be. Now: the impossibility of having an objective reality which that concept seems to indicate … does it only come from the fact that it opposes the Principle of Non-contradiction—which, according to Kant, is the principle that governs all analytic a priori knowledge—or is its impossibility rooted in the fact that, in addition to that Principle, it transgresses all the laws of Experience and with it the *Principle of the Possibility of Experience*, which is the supreme Principle of all knowledge that makes a claim to objective reality? Along these lines, it is now worth reiterating this question: is the *nihil negativum* a merely logical Nothing, which is simply opposed to the Principle of Non-contradiction, or is the impossibility it expresses a real impossibility? And, at the same time, it is worth asking this other crucial question: is the *nihil negativum* logically impossible *because* it really is, or is it really impossible *because* it doesn't even admit to being thought as "possible"? This question—which apparently could receive a simple and obvious answer—is not, however, as easy to answer as it seemed at first. Kant himself seems to have understood this.

With what is merely announced in this series of questions—whose intention has been none other than to raise the problems that will occupy us when attempting to clarify the structure of the *nihil negativum*—certain areas bristling with difficulties can already be seen. The mere fact of relativizing the Principle of Non-contradiction in order to determine *impossibility* already signifies that the *nihil negativum* seems to go beyond the sphere of the merely logical and that its problematic transcends into the domain of what is properly ontological. On what does ontological impossibility rest? We have called it the *Principle of the Possibility of Experience*. What does such a Principle express? The *possibility*, the *actuality*, and the *necessity* of knowledge in the sphere of Experience are issues with which Kant deals when analyzing the *Postulates of Empirical Thought in general*. These *Postulates* refer to the objective use of the *categories of modality*. For this reason it cannot now seem very strange that these *categories* are also those that, according to Kant's own rigorous indication, should be considered in strict correspondence with the *nihil negativum*.

These categories of modality, as well as the Postulates of Empirical Thought in general, are examples from an ontological origin and structure, viz., they are significations of Being as such and of the entities that participate and acquire dimension in such a region. Instead, it is now a matter of studying those categories in relation to Nothingness and what is manifested by that Nothingness. As categories of Being, they gain their significance and sense from Time. *Possibility*, *actuality*, and *necessity* have, in this regard, their corresponding *schematism*. Is this *ontological schematism* adequate—as a temporal horizon of the categories of Being—for achieving the understanding and development of the Temporality of Nothingness? It seems right, then, that we should investigate in depth what is thus posed.

In order not to lose our orientation through the tangled path and multitude of problems that arise from the brief indicators that Kant provides, it is convenient to signify in advance the meaning of the steps that we propose taking in the following paragraphs. It will then be possible to understand their necessary implication and coherence, while not losing sight of the goal that we aspire to through them.

In successive order, the steps are the following:

(1) *The principle of non-contradiction and the possible* (§15). Through this, an attempt will be made to highlight the connections that exist between both issues, while at the same time specifying the meaning of *logical* and *ontological* possibility, showing the foundational nexus that governs among them.

(2) *The roots of ontological possibility* (§16). The aim of this section will consist in showing the lawful structure exhibited by consciousness, in its temporal aspect, as far as *possibility* is concerned. *Possibility*, in its *ontological* sense, will in this way remain rooted in Time.

(3) *The ontological-temporal structure of the possible and the im-possible* (§17). Since there is a mutual illumination of meaning between Being and Time, it is necessary to clarify this circle in order to apprehend the meaning of *the possible* and *the im-possible*. The Time of *ontological schematism* thus reveals its limitations in reference to *the impossible*. Faced with *ontological im-possibility*—Non-Being or "Nothing"—the meaning of the *im-possible* will be emphasized as *ens extramundanum* as an expression of authentic *Nothingness*. And from its own "comprehension" the meaning of the respective "Temporality" of that *Nothingness* will be delineated.

§15 The Principle of Non-contradiction and the Possible

Almost from the very origin of philosophy, and from its first formulations, the *Principle of Non-contradiction* has been thought in close connection with the problem of *possibility*. In Aristotle's own statement of it—and in which that Principle is depicted for the first time in an explicit and thematic way—the relationship between both questions is clear and evident. Referring to it, Aristotle says τὸ γὰρ αὐτὸ ἅμα ὑπάρχειν τε καὶ μὴ ὑπάρχειν ἀδύνατον τῷ αὐτῷ καὶ κατὰ τὸ αὐτό ("*the same attribute cannot at the same time belong and not belong to the same subject in the same respect*").[7]

In light of such a statement, it is easy to notice, "*impossible*" (ἀδύνατον) turns out to be that which, as a consequence of the Principle itself and due to the very structure of reality (be it that of appearances, or of one's own thinking about those appearances), demonstrates a self-contradiction. This contra-diction concerns the λόγος, which when manifesting itself in such a manner hides or conceals (rather than unconcealing = ἀλήθεια) that of which it can or should be a manifestation (λόγος ἀποφαντικός) and it turns out to be un-thinkable because it is un-true, since Being, Truth, and Logos mutually imply one another. The im-possible (ἀδύνατον) is therefore the contradictory structure of λόγος itself and is rooted, as such, in what the λόγος is or should be the manifestation of: the Truth of Being.[8]

However, our intention is not to pursue this connection, but simply to let it reveal itself. Whether historically this connection has persisted, or if, losing all its ontological roots, the *Principle of Non-contradiction* has come to be the mere exteriorization of a logical structure, is a problem that has to be seen for itself. What follows—in which a manifestation of "*the impossible*" is studied in close connection with the Principle of Non-contradiction—could shed some light.

As an expression of the *nihil negativum*—and as indicated by the Kantian claim itself—the Nothing is the *object* (Gegenstand) of a *concept*. Now, that *object* has the character [*textura*] of Nothingness (and, therefore, is opposed to that of a Something) because the *concept* to which it corresponds contradicts itself and, as such, is "*the im-possible.*" The Nothing—"*the im-possible*"— therefore has its origin in a *contra-diction*.

Now, there are at least three issues following from the above that need to be noted: 1.) The ground of Nothingness, as *nihil negativum*, seems to rest on a structure of intelligible nature (concept, thought, λόγος); 2.) Only insofar as this structure is affected by un-intelligibility does the *factum* of being negated as Something (Something-possible) overcome it, making it automatically "the im-possible," viz., a Nothing; 3.) That intelligible structure is affected by un-intelligibility (it is "the im-possible") by the fact that it violates the *Principle of Non-contradiction*.

Formally speaking, then, the Nothing—as *nihil negativum*—has its origin in the transgression of one of the supreme Principles governing the intelligibility of Thought and that constitutes one of the highest laws that guarantees its Truth, viz., its adequacy to Being and, therefore, its capacity to manifest it (λόγος ἀποφαντικός). Insofar as that intelligibility of Thought only exists as it is supported by the Principle of Non-contradiction, the Nothing is the expression of an annihilation of that intelligibility by the very destruction of the Principle sustaining it. As such, the Nothing is the expression of an absurdity, of a contradiction, of something il-logical or a-logical, that is, of something unintelligible, since only Thought governed or oriented by Truth (guaranteed by the Principle of Non-contradiction) exhibits an intelligible meaning and conforms to Logic (doctrine of the Truth of λόγος). The im-possible, the

Nothing, as *nihil negativum*, is thus the externalization of the im-possibility of Thought ("the concept cancels itself," Kant would say) and, as such, is both an expression of the contra-dictory (viz., what contradicts the logical voice of λόγος) and a *negation* (*im*-possibility, *nihil negativum*) in relation to what Being is in its *possibility* (Something).

But, if all of the above is true, and from the transgression of the Principle of Non-contradiction the externalization of "*the im-possible*" becomes manifest, it does not seem just that a matter of such importance should be reduced to being treated only from this perspective we have sketched. Indeed: can "*the impossible*" be restricted only to what violates the *Principle of Non-contradiction*? Or, asked the other way around: is the "*possible*" that which does not attempt to violate such a Principle? The answer to these questions—which have to be negative—reveals another aspect of the problem.

In effect, we have seen that, even without violating the Principle of Non-contradiction, viz., being perfectly coherent intelligible structures in themselves, the *noumena*—whose expression we find in the *ens rationis*—cannot be counted among the *possibilities*.[9] The *noumena*, not being contradictory in themselves, do not belong to the sphere of "*the possible*" as such, since they are not counted at all as *objects* of our sensible intuition[10] and, as such, as having any phenomenal reality.

But what is being said in the above? Are *noumena* not intelligible realities and, therefore, structures whose possibility is confirmed in this very factum? Indeed, if "the possible" were restricted to "the intelligible," the *noumena* would be "possible," but if "the intelligible" does not set limits to or fully cover "the possible," then the *noumena*—as Kant puts it—cannot be counted among the possibilities. In this way, the Kantian doctrine itself forces us to establish two senses, and therefore two criteria, for examining "the possible" as such. Kant himself was conscious of this when he expressed the following: "For the deception of substituting the logical possibility of the concept (since it does not contradict itself) for the transcendental possibility of things (where an object corresponds to the concept) can deceive and satisfy only the inexperienced."[11] In this manner, relying on Kant himself, we can now say that although the *noumenon*—the *ens rationis*—has a *logical possibility*, it nevertheless lacks a *transcendental*, that is, a *real possibility*.[12] We have called this *real possibility*—and will henceforth designate it—"*ontological possibility*."

But the issue is not simply to distinguish these two classes or species of *possibilities*, but to reveal the relations between them. Indeed, it is fair to ask: do both *possibilities* subsist alongside one another, do they imply one another, or are they distinct and independent from each other? To this it is possible to respond categorically: all *ontological possibility* presupposes and requires compliance with a *logical possibility*—that is to say, everything that is *ontologically* possible must be *logically* possible—but not everything that is *logically* possible must be *ontologically* possible. In another way—but in a context of issues closely related with this problem—Kant expresses a similar idea when he states:

> Hence we must also allow the principle of contradiction (Satz des Widerspruchs) to count as the universal and completely sufficient principle of all analytic cognition; but its authority and usefulness does not extend beyond this, as a sufficient criterion of truth. For that no cognition can be opposed to it without annihilating itself certainly makes this principle into a *conditio sine qua non*, but not into a determining ground (Bestimmungsgrunde) of the truth of our cognition.[13]

Or, said another way: if the Principle of Non-contradiction is truly the criterion that allows us to secure *logical possibility*, it is nevertheless not a *sufficient determination* for *ontological possibility*. And although this is presupposed—for which reason no violation of the Principle of Non-contradiction is permitted—not everything that complies with this Principle can be considered *ontologically possible*. Though there is a relation of dependence among both kinds of *possibilities*, the *ontologically possible* restricts, and at the same time enriches, the sphere of pure *logical possibility*.

But, then, what is the *nihil negativum*? Does its im-possibility lie in being ontologically im-possible (though logically possible), or is it ontologically im-possible because it is also logically im-possible? What would this last question reveal? To give an adequate answer, we must refer to the example that Kant himself provides regarding the *nihil negativum*. As we can recall, Kant points out as an example the "two-sided rectilinear figure." Now: wherein lies the impossibility manifested by such an example, and what is its source?

To avoid ambiguities—and though it may be somewhat superfluous to point out—let us say, first, that the im-possibility expressed by such an example does not correspond to that of a *noumenon*, for the simple and obvious reason that what is being exemplified (a two-sided figure) is not a *noumenon* at all.

Moreover: if somehow the *noumenon* turns out to be possible (i.e., *logically* possible, because non-contradictory), then by contrast what is exemplified by the above is *im-possible* because—according to Kant—it reveals a contradiction in itself.

But having said this, the problem then becomes clear: just what is the *contradiction* expressed by such an example? Is it a mere logical contradiction—and, therefore, its impossibility also logical—or does that example show an ontological contradiction? Let's examine this question carefully.

Without a doubt, the given example exhibits a *logical* contradiction. This is how Kant understands it. But, without attending to and taking into account the historical-scientific horizon from which this example arises and in which it is included, his reasons would not be fully understood and, ultimately, that contradiction would not be made clear. In effect, the source from which Kant draws the example and to which he gives all credit is Euclidean geometry. In Definition 14 of his *Elements*, Euclid asserts: "*Figure is that which is comprised (surrounded) by a limit or many limits*." As such, by definition, every *rectilinear* figure requires at least *three* sides that are its limits, since fewer sides (e.g., two) would not in any way be enough to enclose it.[14] The very definition of "*rectilinear figure*" is thus—in Kant's eyes—a subject that repels the predicate that one tries to ascribe to it (having two sides), due to its incongruence [*inconveniente*] and contradiction with the subject's own marks.[15]

But, apart from any consideration of a historical nature, and without debating whether the fact of relying on Euclid invalidates or relativizes the validity of the Kantian assertion, the fundamental issue lies in discovering whether this example can be considered as exhibiting a mere logical contradiction, or if, on the contrary, it implies a surreptitious support for other contents that exceed that formal and empty sphere of the purely logical.

For Kant, as we have already seen, that contradiction is apparently purely logical and is established by the negation of the predicate from the very marks contained in the subject. But is such an account true, without any further explanation? Does Kant really hold onto this purely *analytic* criterion when referring to an example that clearly seems to contain an element of *synthesis*? Here there is a highly delicate question to be answered. When reviewing other examples provided by Kant himself, and in which he seems to consider a similar problem more carefully and explicitly, it is fair to note that his explanation places the weight of *impossibility* not on the pure formality and abstraction of *logical contradiction*, but in the very conditions of Space and, therefore, in a first and primordial *ontological* element that transforms the pure *logical impossibility* into an authentic and original *ontological impossibility*. "Thus in the concept of a figure that is enclosed between two straight lines there is no contradiction, for the concepts of two straight lines and their intersection contain no negation of a figure; rather the impossibility rests not on the concept in itself, but on its construction in space, i.e., on the conditions of space and its determinations [...]."[16] But what is this example telling us? This example—whose similarity to the previous is evident—gives us the key for interpreting the correct line of thought in Kant. In effect, it is Space—with its conditions and determinations, viz., through its strictly ontological features—that makes *im-possibility* emerge as such. It is those "conditions of space and its determinations"—those that "in turn have their objective reality, i.e., they pertain to possible things, because they contain in themselves a priori the form of experience in general"[17]— that make it *im-possible* for that which claims to be constructed to exist as a *Something*. The *nihil negativum* is, in this way, not the product of a mere logical contradiction, but the exhibition of an *ontological* or *real* im-possibility; that is, of a *Nothing* that denies any connection with Experience since it refuses to present itself through those Forms (those of Space) that configure the horizon of manifestation of the possible "real-objects." In this sense, the Nothing— the *nihil negativum*—is an "*empty object*" (empty of "real-possibility"), and "*without concept*." Indeed, due to the indicated ontological im-possibility, that concept (e.g., of a rectilinear figure with two sides) also turns out to be logically contradictory and, as such, cancels itself out: it is Nothing.

But now we have arrived at a truly decisive point. If one fully understands what our reflection has highlighted, it will be possible to see that the notion of *possibility* has been radically transformed. Indeed, the *possibility*, as such, now reveals an *ontological nature* and it is to this character that the *nihil negativum* originally refers. The *nihil negativum* is logically im-possible because it is fundamentally ontologically im-possible.

But in what is such ontological im-possibility based? We have seen that it stems from the "conditions and determinations of Space" and that, at the same time, those conditions configure the im-possibility of the *nihil negativum* because "they contain in themselves a priori the form of experience in general." Isn't it fair, then, to shed light on the roots of the ontological im-possibility manifested by the *nihil negativum* from the context of such relations?

§16 The Roots of Ontological Possibility

Having gone beyond the sphere of purely *logical* possibility—since the *nihil negativum* transcends this and reveals itself as an *ontological im-possibility*—we must ask directly: what is *the possible*, as such, considered *ontologically*? Kant answers this question—in the *Postulates of Empirical Thinking in General*—when he says: "Whatever agrees with the formal conditions of experience (in accordance with intuition and concepts) is **possible**."[18]

So, now, the term *possible* no longer refers here only to the concept or judgment in itself—as long as they imply an inner and formal coherence or are in agreement with the Principle of Non-contradiction—but to the *object* designated by that concept of judgment, insofar as it agrees with or conforms to the *formal conditions* of Experience (just as the same *object* could be *actual* or *necessary* if it were fit to other *conditions* of the same Experience). For this reason, since this Experience is the framework wherein that *possibility* is put to the test, it is its limits, and its own conditions, that determine the *possibility of the object*.

In this sense, if the *logical* possibility or im-possibility could be drawn from and recognized by the Principle of Non-contradiction, the *ontological* possibility or im-possibility are referred to the *formal conditions* that construct and govern the *synthesis* of Experience. "The possibility of the concept"—says Kant—"rests only on the Principle of Contradiction. That of synthesis on Experience."[19] For this reason, the first *possibility* is called *analytic*, the second *synthetic*.[20] While the first belongs to analytic judgments, the second is characteristic—and represents the principal problem—of synthetic judgments. "For whence"—asks Kant—will one derive the character of the possibility of an object that is thought by means of a synthetic a priori concept, if not from the synthesis that constitutes the form of the empirical cognition of objects? That in such a concept no contradiction must be contained is, to be sure, a necessary logical condition; but it is far from sufficient for the objective reality of the concept, i.e., for the possibility of such an object as is thought through the concept.[21]

Now, by relating the problem of *ontological possibility* to synthetic judgments and by incorporating such a problem into that of *synthesis*, we have reduced ourselves to the path of taking this question to the authentic terrain in which

Kant raises and discusses it. As expressed in the very definition of *possibility*, its treatment must be seen as referring to Experience—or, said more precisely, to its *conditions*—in whose field, as it is well known, the *synthetic function* productive of objectivity is realized and implemented. *Ontological possibility* is thus referred to the *synthesis* that produces the objectivity of the object and, as such, a *modality* is designated through it that can be affirmed or denied of that object. In this sense, it can be asked: (1.) How is the *synthesis* which produces objectivity possible?; and (2.) When does this *synthesis*—once seen as possible—give modality to its objective correlate as a *Possible-Something*? The first question refers, as is easy to understand, to the very Principles of the possibility of Experience; the second, on the other hand, to the *formal conditions* that must be met in such an Experience, in order that its objective correlates are modalized as *possible* or *im-possible*. It is just this last aspect—supposing the clarity of the previous one—that we are interested in pursuing in a primordial way in our reflections.

Possibility and *im-possibility* are, within Kantian thought, *categories of modality*. Now, compared with the other categories (those of *quantity*, *quality*, and even of *relation*), they exhibit a very special characteristic that distinguishes their precise function within the field of Experience. Indeed—as Kant says—their peculiarity is that they in no way add any determination to the object itself to which they are applied, but are limited to expressing how "the object itself (together with all its determinations)" is "related to the understanding and its empirical use."[22] In this sense, when such categories are employed, "they do not augment their concept of things in general, but rather only indicate the way in which in general it is combined with the cognitive power."[23] As such, these categories are not involved in the constitution of the material predicates of the objects of Experience—"the principles of modality are not, however, objective-synthetic," Kant thus says[24]—but rather, as exhibitions of *modality*, they point to and determine the position of that object in relation to the cognitive faculty and the character exhibited by its concept (already constituted in its material predicates by the work of the other categories) within Experience. Thus, even if "the concept of a thing is already entirely complete, I can still ask about this object whether it is merely possible, or also actual, or, if it is the latter, whether it is also necessary."[25] Such asking is not an attempt to determine any new material content in the object itself, but is rather an inquiry about whether the representation or concept of it—in its relation to the cognitive faculty within which it originates—is constituted in accordance with the conditions of the possibility of Experience in general and to what extent it agrees or complies with the formal and material conditions of the same. An object is *possible*—in this sense—when it is constituted according to the "formal conditions" of Experience; *actual*, if it meets its "material conditions"; and *necessary*, if its already-constituted actuality "is determined by the general conditions of Experience."[26] It is, then, the *possibility of Experience in general*— as the sphere within which the process of cognitive synthesis occurs—which is the general and absolutely necessary condition of the *modal objectification* of any object. The specific and concrete aspect that this *modal objectification* can adopt in each case (viz., whether the object constituted by means of it is *possible, actual,* or *necessary*) depends instead on whether the constitutive process itself complies now with the *formal conditions*, now with the *material* ones, etc., which are verified in the general process of the synthesis of Experience. On the contrary, the *im-possible* is that which does not meet any of these *conditions* and, therefore, is incapable of being represented in a concept or of being an object within the sphere of the possibility of Experience in general.

Now, as correlates of an Experience—viz., by being objectified within the sphere of the possibility of Experience in general—all its possible objects (and among these, of course, those characterized as merely *possible*) must manifest or exhibit an *objective reality* (objektive Realität), otherwise they would be mere inventions or empty chimeras (blosses Hirngespinst),[27] incapable of possessing objective validity, any sense, or meaning. But isn't such an *objective reality* opposed to *possibility* as such? Or, asked another way: doesn't the necessary reference to an *Experience*—and the corresponding *objective reality* that it confers on its correlates—express that every object belonging to it is *actual*? Not at all. Experience, as such, is not merely *actual* (empirical) Experience, nor does the *objective reality* that its possible objects must exhibit express that their mode of existence is reduced to being *actual*. Just as objects can, within the possibility of Experience in general, be exhibited as *possible, actual,* or *necessary*, their *objective reality* can be that of Something limited to existing as *possible* (without being *actual* or *necessary*). In this sense, for example, without recourse to any perception (and, hence, without the respective object meeting the *material conditions* of Experience, or, therefore, being *actual*), we can know and determine completely a priori the *possibility* of an object, such *possibility* having complete *objective validity*, which is fully attested to, e.g., in the construction of geometrical objects.²⁸ In this way, Kant says "we can cognize and characterize the possibility of things solely in relation to the formal conditions under which something can be determined as an object in experience at all (understood here as a synonym of *real* or *empirical* experience), thus fully a priori but only in relation to these conditions and within their boundaries."²⁹ This doesn't mean—and one should understand this point—that in this case the Experience is completely forgotten or denied, although what is taken into consideration are its *formal conditions* and not its *empirical* or *real* aspects. Hence, *the possible* must be in agreement with the *formal conditions* of Experience, without the concept corresponding to this object thereby prescribing that it must exist as Something *actual* or *necessary*. Now, these *formal conditions* of Experience guarantee *objective reality* for their possible correlates (and thus the merely *possible* means this, viz., that it exists as a *possible-object*) since as "conditions of the possibility of Experience in general" they "are at the same time conditions of the possibility of the objects of Experience."³⁰ As such, an object is *possible* when its concept—originating in the synthetic process of Experience—is in accordance with the *formal conditions* of that Experience and these are, at the same time, those conditions that impose the corresponding modal objectification—viz., the character of being *possible*—onto the respective object constituted by that synthesis. If it contained an empirical element (e.g., a sensation), then the modal structure of the objectification would meet the *material conditions* of Experience and, *eo ipso*, the objective correlate constituted by it would appear determined as *actual*, etc.

As one can see, it has been possible from the above to outline (even if only in a formal way) the origin of *possibility* and, therefore, of *im-possibility*. It is the conditions of the possibility of Experience, viz., the conditions that govern the very *synthesis* productive of objectivity (in our case referring especially to the modal aspect exhibited by the object) that construct and determine the sphere and meaning of *the possible* and *the im-possible* in their *ontological* sense. *Possible*, then, is what is in agreement with the *formal conditions* of *synthesis* (viz., the object constituted in accordance with them).

Im-possible is that which, by not agreeing with them, is *deprived* of them, or perhaps, *excluded* from their sphere.[31]

However, our attempt cannot stop at this merely formal sketch. But, remaining faithful to its purpose of bringing to light that *ontological* sense—since only in this way can the authentic temporal structure of the *nihil negativum* be revealed as an expression of the *im-possible*[32]—it must now specify in its details the rich and complex web of relationships that make up the fabric of that Experience and its conditions of possibility.

Experience, as a sphere within which the objectifying synthesis is realized, is a process subject to precise laws, agreement with which depends on its having objective validity (that is, that its results can reveal the true profiles of objects and constitute authentic knowledge of them) or, that otherwise, everything is reduced to a mere "rhapsody of perceptions,"[33] incapable of being authentic knowledge (valid both for the subject that realizes it and for others), nor even of adjusting to the context of a possible consciousness subject to universal laws. In this way, Experience and its conditions of possibility—so long as the objectification constituting the truth of the object is verified within its sphere—demonstrates that its synthetic process "has principles of its form which ground it a priori, namely general rules of unity in the synthesis of appearances, whose objective reality, as necessary conditions, can always be shown in experience, indeed in its possibility."[34] The Postulates of Empirical Thinking, as well as the categories of modality and the intuitions to which they apply, are thus exhibited in their full necessity as conditions of *the possible* and *the im-possible*.

But what does this mean concretely? How is it that the *categories of modality*—as "general rules of the unity of the synthesis of appearances"—act or function within the general context of Experience determining that the objectifying synthesis is characterized modally in such a way that the objective correlate of it is exhibited as a *Possible-Something*?

In this respect, there is no need to reiterate what has been expressed at length elsewhere. The categories have the specific function of constituting the intelligible structure of the object. Such a function—according to the particular nature of each category—is established (in the moment that Kant designates with the name *figurative synthesis* or "*synthesis speciosa*"),[35] when the category brings a principle of pure synthetic unity over the diversity of intuition. This intuitive diversity—viz., the manifolds of sensible data of the appearance upon which the unifying and synthesizing function of the category must be carried out—is contained in Time, which as "formal condition of the manifold of inner sense,"[36] acts as a receptacle for the data of intuition. The concepts of the Understanding (the categories), by working as ordering and synthesizing principles of Experience—viz., by acting as constituents of the intelligible aspect of the phenomenal object—determine this Inner Sense (Time) by prescribing the form and disposition that must conform with the temporal structure of consciousness. Such a "transcendental time-determination"[37] is established through the *schematism*. *Schemata* are therefore nothing more than expressions of a "pure synthesis, in accord with a rule of unity according to concepts in general, which the category expresses."[38] Or, as Kant himself puts it even more clearly: "The schemata are therefore nothing but *a priori* **time-determinations** in accordance with rules, and these concern, according to the order of the categories, the **time-series**, the **content of time**, the **order of time**, and finally the **sum total of time** in regard to all possible objects."[39]

In accordance with this—faithfully interpreting Kant's thought—the schemata corresponding to the categories of modality refer to the *sum total of Time* and its action cannot be other than that of ordering and organizing the data of Inner Sense in general into a determinate form. But what is that way in which the categories of modality act upon Inner Sense, constructing in a temporal schema the profile of the possible (or the im-possible), the real actual (or the non-actual), the necessary (or the contingent) of the possible objects of representations? Let's remember, firstly, that the categories of modality do not have influence on the material constitution of objects themselves, but instead seem to take this process for granted and aim only at indicating how "the object itself (together with all its determinations)" is "related to the understanding and its empirical use, to the empirical power of judgment, and to reason (in its application to experience)."[40] Hence, their proper function, in their objective use, consists in determining whether that material synthesis constituting the representations is realized in accordance with the conditions of the possibility of Experience, and the degree of its possible realization, in order to "indicate the way in which in general" that concept in general (that of the object) "is combined with the cognitive power."[41] This is why their *schematism*—as a determination of the temporal structure of Inner Sense—does not refer directly to the *production* (Erzeugung) of Time, to its *action* (Erfüllung), or to its *ordering* (Zeitordnung), but to Time itself (or, more precisely, to the *sum total of Time* "as the correlate of the determination" of an object), in order to see "whether and how an object belongs to time"[42], viz., to Inner Sense as a formal receptacle of all possible representation for a consciousness. Thus, the *sum total of Time*—which encompasses all the constituent aspects of material synthesis—gathers up the various facets of that process; and it is to it, as a totality, that the categories of modality are applied in order to determine if and how the possible representations that have been formed therein correspond to possible, actual, or necessary objects, insofar as they have or have not agreed with the conditions (formal and material) of Experience.[43]

So, according to what has been said, an object is *possible* if its concept agrees with the *formal conditions* of Experience (regarding intuitions and concepts). But how do we determine that such agreement occurs? The concept of an object is in agreement with the *formal conditions* of Experience—and, therefore, is *possible*—as long as the process of its constitution is carried out in conformity with the strict laws that govern the synthesis of intuitions (in their merely formal guise). Such a law, relative to intuitive synthesis, is expressed in the *Principle* (Grundsatz) which Kant calls the "*Axioms of Intuition*."

According to this Principle, as we must remember, all appearances—in order to be apprehended, i.e., to be received in empirical consciousness—must submit to the synthesis of a diversity "through which the representations of a determinate space or time are generated,"[44] and through which they are integrated as objects into that consciousness "through the composition of that which is homogeneous and the consciousness of the synthetic unity of this manifold (of the homogeneous)."[45] Now, "the consciousness of the synthetic unity of the homogeneous manifold in intuition in general, insofar as the representation of an object is possible only in this way, is the concept of a quantity (quanti),"[46] whereby all appearances, as possible objects, become determined as *magnitudes*—and, even more precisely, as *extensive magnitudes*—"since, as intuitions in space or time they must be represented through the same synthesis as that through which space and time in general are determined."[47] Regarding this *synthesis*—i.e., of extensive magnitudes—it has a clear and manifest temporal meaning[48] and expresses the operation by which the various *Parts* of the appearance are *successively* added to one another as its apprehension is established and it is integrated, as representation, into Inner Sense. In such a way, as Kant expresses verbatim, "since the mere intuition in all appearances is either space or time, every appearance as intuition is an extensive magnitude, as it can only be cognized through successive synthesis (from part to part) in apprehension."[49]

Now, what the *schema* of possibility does, by referring to the process of the constitution of appearances in their merely formal character—viz., to the integration of their pure spatiotemporal structure and their construction as extensive magnitudes[50]—is prescribe the rule that orders the temporal flow of Inner Sense in general when that aspect of the constitutive process is achieved. Hence, only insofar as the appearances are *successively* apprehended, viz., insofar as their various Parts are *successively* added one to another in Inner Sense, can they be (possible) objects of an Experience. For this reason, the *schema* of possibility expresses nothing other than the *rule* of that *successive synthesis* which makes possible the constitution of objects and whose violation automatically decrees their im-possibility. Thus, e.g., the *production* of a magnitude requires that one Part be added successively to another, whereas if, for example, at the same instant of Time one tried to add or synthesize one Part with another opposed to it, the appearance would be destroyed in its quantitative aspect, and would be formally impossible. In this regard, referring the *schema of possibility* to the way concepts are formed in the Understanding, prescribing the postulates of the empirical use of the Understanding (that *possible* means simply what is in accordance with the formal conditions of Experience), and, finally expressing that only what conforms to the conditions of *successive synthesis* by which extensive magnitudes are integrated can be a (possible) object, that *schema*—to summarize and synthesize all these conditions—reads literally: "The schema of possibility is the agreement of the synthesis of various representations with the conditions of time in general (e.g., since opposites cannot exist in one thing at the same time, they can only exist one after another), thus the determination of the representation of a thing to some time."[51] Or, in other words: only insofar as appearances are objectified as extensive magnitudes—and conform to the axioms of Time itself (among which successivity is fundamentally included)[52]—can they be counted among the possibilities, viz., be possible objects.[53] Once the axioms of Time are violated (and the temporal flow of consciousness contradicts them) their formations (concepts) will be im-possible and, therefore, their objective correlates will also be "*Nothing*." "On this successive synthesis of the productive imagination"—

Kant could then say, referring to what he also calls *figurative synthesis*—"is grounded the mathematics of extension (geometry) with its axioms," those which "express the conditions of sensible intuition a priori, under which alone the schema of a pure concept of outer appearance can come about."[54] Among those axioms of geometry—which is supremely revealing for our purposes—Kant cites the one that reads: "two straight lines do not enclose a space."[55] Referring to the same example, and attempting to show the ontological roots of its *im-possibility*, he can then say in the *Postulates of Empirical Thinking*: "the impossibility rests not on the concept in itself, but on its construction in space, i.e., on the conditions of space and its determinations; but these in turn have their objective reality, i.e., they pertain to possible things, because they contain in themselves a priori the form of experience in general."[56]

It is therefore irrefutably demonstrated that the *possibility of an object*—e.g., the one constructed in accordance with the axioms of geometry insofar as these express the conditions of sensible intuition—has its ontological roots in the conditions of the possibility of Experience itself (since these are at the same time the very conditions of the objects of Experience). But it is also demonstrated above that those conditions of the possibility of Experience, as such, are referred to Time (to its laws and axioms) because this is the horizon that gathers, as Inner Sense, all the possible aspects of the process of the objectification of appearances. In such a way, the schematism constitutes the expression of the temporal lawfulness that consciousness must necessarily assume in its process of objectification, while Inner Sense in general is determined "in accordance with conditions of its form (time) in regard to all representations, insofar as these are to be connected together a priori in one concept in accord with the unity of apperception."[57]

Just as the axioms of geometry, or numerical formulas, express the temporal lawfulness of consciousness in the constitutive processes of extensive magnitudes—and in this sense, that lawfulness refers only to the *formal conditions* of Experience—the *Anticipations of Perception* and the *Analogies of Experience* (as well as the *schemata* corresponding to *Actuality* and *Necessity*) express the temporal lawfulness of consciousness in the respective constitutive process of such aspects.[58] In our endeavor—since it was what we were primarily interested in emphasizing—we have only referred to the aspect of *the possible* and *the im-possible*, but with what has been said the path is cleared for bringing to light those other aspects (the *actual* and the *necessary*) in their corresponding temporal meaning.

But what has been emphasized in relation to *the possible* and *the im-possible* has made it possible to highlight a fundamental thesis for our purposes. In effect: *the possible* and *the im-possible* have, as could be seen, a *temporal meaning*. Possible—as the respective *schema* tells us—is that object whose corresponding synthesis is in accord with the "conditions of Time in general"; viz., that whose meaning conforms to that of Time. Only what conforms to this Time belongs—as a possible Something—to possible Experience, and only this Experience—insofar as it is possible— bears witness to what "is" (be it possible, actual, or necessary). All that is not possible, that is, all that is not given or offered in Experience, is *im-possible*, viz., *Nothing*. Hence, only what conforms to Time and its laws, "is." *Nothing* is that which contradicts Time.

But what "Time"? Where did the structure of this "Time" come from, which, as a horizon of meaning, serves to determine *the possible* and *the im-possible*, Being and Nothingness? This is what we must ask if we want to have a fundamental ["radical"] understanding of that Nothing as *nihil negativum*.

§17 The Ontological-temporal Structure of the Possible and the Im-possible

The possible and the im-possible have been brought back into the sphere of Experience and its conditions of possibility. But Experience, and its conditions of possibility, is in any case a sphere of ontological objectification. Its possible correlates, whatever their modality, exhibit an entitative structure to which a Being can or should be imputed. All Experience, in effect, refers to appearances and, as such, they are appearances of Being. *The im-possible* also, in this way, corresponds with an objectification of Being.

But isn't the *im-possible* barred from being something which Being can possess? By contradicting or not complying with—by definition—the formal conditions of Experience ... is it not, eo ipso, excluded from that ontological sphere? So it seems. *The im-possible*, by definition, is an "*empty object without concept*,"[59] which means that, lacking the intelligible structure conferred by the concept, it becomes an unintelligible, un-thinkable, a-logical object, viz., something that is simply *there*, without λόγος. But what is this "empty object," this simple and bare emergence devoid of λόγος? Perhaps it is a Non-Being? If Being is just what is thinkable, that is, what is intelligible through concepts due to its logical structure, then *the im-possible* is that Non-Being lacking the innervation of λόγος.

But against this perspective—where *the im-possible* manifests itself as an object "without concept"—a different, apparently contradictory one, stands out. Indeed, how do we know something in relation to this "empty object," or in what way do we manage to conceive it as such, and even represent to ourselves something "im-possible"? For this isn't it necessary that we apprehend it through λόγος, a thought, or a concept? In this way, it is a fact that we can think, represent to ourselves, and even express something *im-possible* (e.g., a rectilinear figure with two sides). If *the im-possible* were completely devoid of the innervation of λόγος, then we could not think about it, represent it to ourselves, or even express anything about it.

What's more: within the Kantian doctrine itself—rigorously interpreted—that first perspective appears to be denied. Indeed, the objectification of something as *im-possible* is established thanks to a category of modality (that of *impossibility*) and it has a clear and definite ontological meaning, just like that of *non-existence* and *contingency*, which together with it complete the corresponding triad of this group.[60] And just as it would be wrong to think that *the contingent* expresses an absolute lack of Being (when, in truth, it is only the manifestation of an ontological modality), *the im-possible* is also only a deficient modality of Being, viz., the expression of the failure or privation of *the possible*. As such, if Being is what is thinkable or intelligible through concepts, *the im-possible* seems to perfectly meet such a condition.

But what, then, is the meaning of the definition of *the im-possible* as an empty object "without concept"? Is this not all a vulgar sophistry or a mere word game? Is it not totally contradictory that it appears first as an object "without concept" and then, immediately after, it is asserted that it is an object thought by means of a concept that negates Being or expresses its deficiency? And so ... what is *the im-possible*, that objective-something, which on the one hand seems excluded from the field of Experience and appears to lack all intelligible structure, but on the other hand testifies to a distinct ontological meaning opposed to that of the objects of what is characterized as *possible*?

If we fully and rigorously review the Kantian doctrine, we have to see that the objective structure of *the im-possible* does not express that it is something non-ontological—that is: something that is completely excluded from this sphere—but, as the product of a categorial "objectification" that is not realized in accordance with the *conditions of the possibility* of Experience, is contradictory and opposed to Being. That is, it is the bearer of a distinct and contrary structure to that of an object constituted in accordance with the laws that govern the sphere of the objectification of the phenomena of Experience as such. Now, as such, Experience is a sphere of ontological objectification where the possible correlates are constituted under the modalities of the *possible*, the *actual*, or the *necessary*, insofar as they agree with the conditions of its possibility. *The im-possible* therefore signifies a something or a phenomenon that presents itself or appears within the sphere of the objectification of Experience but which, by not agreeing with the conditions of possibility that are required for the constitution of something *possible* (or possibly as *actual* or *necessary*), assumes the form of an entity, something or phenomenon, whose structure reveals an ontological deficiency and refuses to be taken as a correlate of Experience as such. Insofar as *the im-possible* acknowledges this failure of its objectification with respect to the conditions of the possibility of Experience, and insofar as it is considered as the quintessential ontological sphere that which is *im-possible* is a putative *Non-Being*.

But it is supremely important to observe that *the im-possible* is an *object*, even if an "*empty object*."[61] This means that, in some way, its process of objectification has been carried out from the very moment in which it is capable of assuming that form or determination in its entitative structure. Or, in other words: to be an *object*, *the im-possible* requires the innervation of a "λόγος," even if different or opposed to that which innervates the sphere of Being and through which the corresponding objects are characterized as *possible*, *actual*, or *necessary*. Hence, as long as the λόγος of Being constitutes the intelligible structure of the objects of Experience, *the im-possible* can be characterized as an object "without concept."

And now we know exactly what this means. That the object (*the im-possible*) is something "without concept" does not just mean that it lacks a logical-intelligible structure, but that it conforms with a mode of "objectification" where the conditions demanded by Experience in relation to the correlates determined as *possible* (*actual* or *necessary*) are not met. But, as we have said, the best proof that *the im-possible* has an objective structure innervated by a "λόγος" is that we can perfectly well think it or represent it to ourselves as such. In fact, when trying to perform such an act (thinking or representing something im-possible to ourselves), the impossibility lies not in the inability to have such a representation (as attested to, for instance, by the example of the two-sided rectilinear figure or of a thought which contradicts itself), but rather that "the concept cancels itself out"[62] and is therefore a failed concept: contra-dictory, il-logical, or a-logical. But one wonders: contra-dictory, il-logical, or a-logical with respect to what? Now we can clearly see: with respect to the λόγος that innervates the objectifications of Being, as *possible* (or *actual* or *necessary*).

But now we must ask: from where does this twofold possibility originate in the structure of λόγος? Where is the support for the fact that this λόγος belongs to Being and that it can potentially contradict it? But above all: whence the presumed agreement between λόγος and Being—which Kant affirms as an understandable assumption in itself—and what is that based upon? Only by shedding light on such questions will we be on the path to illuminating the structure of "λόγος" when it fulfills the function of innervating *the im-possible*.

As highlighted in previous paragraphs, the synthesis effected by means of the intelligible structure of concepts is established in accordance with the laws of Inner Sense, and, therefore, as long as it exhibits and is exhausted in a temporal configuration, those concepts acquire their meaning from this horizon.[63] An objectification relative to Being—like, e.g., that of something possible—is one whose intelligible structure agrees with the laws or axioms of Time, insofar as Time constitutes the fundamental root of the conditions of the possibility of Experience, consequently exhibiting a coherent temporal meaning in relation to those axioms and laws. In this respect, only what is in agreement with the conditions of the possibility of Experience, and therefore with the structure of Temporality that confers meaning on them, belongs to the sphere of Being. Something is *possible*—viz., pertains to Being—insofar as the constitution of its objective structure is realized in accordance with the conditions of the possibility of Experience and obeys the norms established by the corresponding schematism in its temporal construction. Thus, e.g., a magnitude (Grösse) is *possible* insofar as it complies with the synthesis of successive addition that its temporal meaning prescribes. So, the *schema of possibility*—when referring to the way that the material structure of objects is constituted in Experience—does not express anything other than the rule of *successive synthesis* that governs the temporal construction of the constitution of objects as magnitudes (Grösse) in connection with "the conditions of Time in general,"[64] and whose violation, by disagreeing with the axioms that express these conditions of Time in general, automatically decrees the *im-possibility* of that constitution. *Im-possible* is, therefore, that which does not comply, in its constitutive process, with such temporal laws prescribed by the schematism and which, therefore, is incapable of being incorporated into the positive sphere of Experience as pertaining to Being. *The im-possible*, in this sense, is something opposed to Being—viz., a Non-Being or a "Nothing"—insofar as it denies or does not comply with the "conditions of Time in general" when being constituted, and therefore it is the opposite of possibility.

Now, what is this saying? What the above clearly expresses is that Time, insofar as it functions as a horizon that confers meaning onto *possibility* and *impossibility*, reveals itself *eo ipso* as the authentic horizon of Being and Non-Being. Non-Being, the "Nothing," the im-possible, is that which does not conform to or denies, in the process of its constitution, the temporal structure of the schemata corresponding to Being. In such a way, the meaning of the "λόγος" that innervates the *im-possible* expresses a contradiction with the laws of Time: it is a "λόγος" that is contradictory and opposed, in its temporal structure, to the λόγος that informs Inner Sense. But this contradiction does not signify the absolute absence of Time—nor of Being—but instead a transgression of its laws or axioms. And so, everything that transgresses Time or Being exists under the form of that negative agent that exercises or operates the transgression. That is, it has a certain "objectivity" insofar as it is the *object* of our consciousness, as can be clearly seen in the example of a contradictory or impossible representation. In such a way, e.g., we can establish the Principle of Contradiction as long as we think or represent that something is *im-possible* by being *contra-dictory*. Doing so—something perfectly feasible—means to think something in contradiction with the laws or axioms of Time, or, as Kant says, with the "conditions of Time in general." So, by realizing such an act in our consciousness—viz., by "objectifying" the im-possible—it is Time which enables us to discern, as a horizon of meaning, whether what is thought or represented is contradictory or not. Time is thus revealed to be the horizon of meaning of Being and Non-Being, of the possible and the im-possible.

But this Time, which constitutes the meaning of Being and decrees the possibility or impossibility of Experience ... in view of what has it been established? Where is its own structure drawn from? What source gives it its own "sense" (meaning) and, therefore, that prerogative of being and acting as a *horizon of meaning* with respect to Being and Non-Being? When trying to shed light on this question, we inevitably stumble upon the presence of the *circle* that has been pointed to so many times throughout this study. Indeed, by directing our attention to the structure of the temporal flow that functions as a *horizon of meaning* for Being (or for Non-Being), it becomes clear that it is constructed and exhibits a "meaning" that arises or originates from a prior *understanding of Being*. Or in other words: the essence of that temporal flow that serves or acts as a horizon of meaning for Being (or Non-being) is established by having as a presupposition the natural understanding of Being. However, achieved on this basis, that Time subsequently acts as a *horizon of meaning* in relation to the same ontological foundation from which it originates. Indeed, if we review the meaning of *permanence*,[65] or even the meaning of the *schematism* characteristic of the categories of modality, we can easily see that both *the permanent*, as well as any of the temporal determinations that give a temporal meaning to *the possible*, *the actual*, or *the necessary*, presuppose that the Time that functions there as a horizon has an *ontological* structure and a "Being" determined as *the present* (Anwesen). *The permanent*, in effect, is *the present* of Time, viz., a temporal substratum that remains unchanged (as *present*) throughout the course or flow of Time. Likewise, if *the possible* is conceived as the determination of the representation of a thing at a given Time, *the actual* as what is circumscribed in a determinate Time, and *the necessary* as what occurs at all Times, the question is whether that Time—which thus acts as a horizon of meaning—has, in turn, a "Being" determined as *present*, and if it is precisely on the basis of this *presence* of Time that those temporal characteristics acquire "sense." At a given Time—that is, what characterizes *the possible* as such—means, strictly, at any *present* Time; *the actual* is that whose existence is circumscribed in a determinate *present*; and *the necessary* is that which is *present* at all times.

Now, undoubtedly, this *present* of Time has a temporal meaning. But what is it that confers consistency or meaning on that temporal *present*? *The present* is that which is presented, what exhibits or manifests a *Presence* (Anwesenheit). Now—asked in relation to Kant's own doctrine—what is that which exhibits a *Presence*? Responding precisely, we must say that *Presence* has only that which is presented in Experience and, thus, has a Being. If Experience is the sphere of Being, and all that does not conform to its conditions of possibility "is" not, *Presence*—the present—is only that which conforms to its conditions of possibility. Time, in order to have a consistency, in order to be the Time that "is," must conform to the very conditions of the possibility of Experience. A Time that is not self-complying with its own axioms would be a non-existent, unreal, or fictitious Time. But to the extent that Time conforms with its own laws and self-constitutes the *Presence* of the present, that Presence falls within the sphere of Experience and, as such, reveals a "Being." That "Being" of Time—the Presence—is the *instant* or the *now*. The *instant* or *now* is, in such a way, the *ontological-temporal* concretization of the primordial representation of Time established from the natural *understanding of Being*. It suddenly becomes clear in such a way that if *the possible* (*the actual* or *the necessary*) has a temporal meaning, this meaning has its origin and significance only in the presupposition that this Time perfectly corresponds with Being understood from Experience. Being and λόγος (Time) mutually presuppose one another and a reciprocal illumination obtains between them. So, to repeat, that *present* (in Experience) is only what conforms to its conditions of possibility, and these in turn have a temporal meaning.

From this mutual and reciprocal illumination between Being and Time, the ontological-temporal meaning of *the possible* or *im-possible* is established (as well as that of the other categories of modality) and the meaning of the Postulates of Empirical Thinking is expressly fixed in its relation to the schematism. *Possible*—temporally—is that which conforms to the laws that govern the conditions of Experience, viz., that which conforms to the boundaries of ontological Time, which constructs the schematism of concepts in their constitutive function. *Im-possible*—temporally—is that which does not conform to such laws, transgresses them, or is contrary to it. A substance or a geometrical figure is *im-possible* because both equally transgress the laws of the ontological Time that gives them meaning. But this *meaning* conferred by Time is only this way—as it is so demanded and revealed by the configuration of its own structure—because that Time (and its "meaning") has been constructed from Experience as the sphere within which Being is manifested. As Kant says: "Time is therefore merely a subjective condition of our (human) intuition (which is always sensible, i.e., insofar as we are affected by objects), and in itself, outside the subject, is nothing."[66] Or, what is the same: only to the extent that Time is presented in Experience does it have a "Being." Considered outside of it, "then time is nothing."[67] Time only "is," viz., "is only of objective validity in regard to appearances"—and is therefore displayed as *meaning* with respect to them—because intuition (i.e., the ground of the possibility of Experience as the sphere of Being) "is the real condition under which time belongs to the representation of objects."[68] The agreement and mutual implication between Being and Time (λόγος) is thus presented in all its nakedness as a fundamental presupposition of the Kantian doctrine.

But faced with this perspective—where Being and Time imply one another—we have highlighted the possibility that, from the radical "experience" of *Nothingness* (as occurs in some situations we have described), a "Temporality" of a different nature is manifested. However, a notable effort must be made to distinguish such "Temporality" from the other sort which carries or exhibits an *ontological* nature, especially when it acts as the *meaning* of *Non-Being*. As such, this latter Temporality comes from the contradiction of Being's own Temporality—and in this way it is the product of its negation or of the transgression of the ontological laws established by its axioms—but, deep down, it continues being (since *negation* also takes an *ontological* stance) a Temporality that exhibits such a nature. This is why the *schema* of *im-possibility*, as such, serves to give *meaning* to *Non-Being*, but can in no way be used to interpret *Nothingness*.

From where, then, is the structure of that "Temporality" that manifests itself in the "experience" of Nothingness to be drawn? Such a question—as it is easy to see—is clearly displayed in the very statement of the problem. Indeed, just as ontological Temporality acquires its "sense" (meaning) from the prior natural *understanding of Being*, the "Temporality" of Nothingness must originate from the understanding of this Nothingness as manifested in its own "experience." If Being is understood as *Presence*—and correlatively ontological Temporality is structured via *nows* or *instants*—it is a matter of seeing that, on the contrary, the "Temporality" of Nothingness must exhibit a completely distinct structure. The "Time" of Nothingness "is" a Time without Presences—since in it nothing is presented or the Nothing "is presented"—and, in this sense, what is revealed is an *Absence*. Now, this *Absence* must be understood and interpreted correctly to avoid mistakes and ambiguities.

Indeed, what "is" that *Absence* through which the Nothing is revealed and manifested? Such *Absence* is not the mere (negated) *Presence* of Being (or of entities), since then it would be a product of a correlative ontological stance that would cross out the appearance of phenomena. In this sense, *Absence* does not mean merely *dis-appearance*, but rather *openness* [*la patencia*]. *Absence, strictly speaking, is the openness of Nothingness*. In this sense, it does not simply imply the dis-appearance of ontological Time, but rather the revelation or manifestation of a sui generis "Temporality." In the openness of Nothingness, Time does not cease, but rather "there is" Time, just as "there is" Nothing. And now, this "Time" that is thus manifested has a radically different structure from that of ontological Time. If this emerges and is understood from its insertion into the *world*—which is basically another way of expressing its insertion into the ontological sphere of Experience—it is a matter of seeing that, producing a total uprooting from that horizon in the "experience" of Nothingness, "Temporality" then exhibits a radical absence of such nexuses of worldly insertion, eo ipso losing its *meaningfulness*. Such "Temporality"—as we have shown elsewhere[69]—does not serve as a horizon of instrumental reference for use or orientation amongst worldly entities, at the same time absolutely lacking individualized *instants* or *nows* that fix its course, direction, etc. What is then opened up [*se patentiza*] is *Nothingness*, and in it, at the same time, an "empty" "Time" as the face of that *Nothingness*. The "*there is*"—which is then said to refer to the non-cessation of "Time"—expresses a naked and radical *Absence*. This "there is" is an *opening up*, but what it opens up is manifested and discovered as *Absence*. The *Absence* testifies that "there is" Nothing. This "*being*" [*haber*]—in which what "there is" refuses all ontic or ontological qualification—is a *having*. The *Absence* manifests the *having* of Nothingness in the one who is immersed in it and has "experienced" it. "Experience" here means—and thus is written in quotation marks—the *dis-solution of the world*.

She who "experiences" the openness of Nothingness, and grasps from it the "Temporality" revealed there, then has herself as *ab-solute*.

But, if what is thus shown is not a mere descriptive invention, or a simple plea intended to satisfy a totally subjective lived experience, there must exist testimonials, proofs, or at least some indications, throughout the extensive repertoire of concepts and experiences collected in the heritage of philosophy. Can it be shown that some previous idea or notion proves it? In this sense, even in the very intellection of *the im-possible* (though with neither complete clarity nor rigor), it is possible to see how—through a certain aporia—a glimpse of the described situation appears. The Kantian philosophy itself confronts it, although the presupposition revealed between Being and Time prevents it from resolving it satisfactorily. With all possible solutions in the ontological sphere obstructed, Kant is obligated to raise the question of *the im-possible* within the terrain of Reason and thus converts the *nihil negativum*, endowed with transcendentality, into a *noumenon*. With this, although he succumbs in the face of a certain ambiguity and even exposes himself to the danger of a contradiction with his own statements about the *nihil negativum*, he glimpses the terrain of the issue we have raised: the "Temporality" proper to the Nothing. *The im-possible*—losing and refusing all ontological meaning and therefore exceeding all meaning derived from the Temporality proper to Being (Experience)—gleams before us, in its intellection as *noumenon*, as the sphere of a sui generis "Temporality."

Indeed, if we run through the problems presented by the categories of modality, we are suddenly surprised by a strange fact that does not fit and is not satisfactorily resolved within the systematic guidelines of Kant's own doctrine. Thus, for instance, while among all the categories of this group there exists a certain *ontological* continuum, upon arriving at *the im-possible* (as an expression of a concept of the Understanding), this continuum seems to suddenly rupture, causing a break with the other remaining categories. Thus, in effect, what is not *necessary* is *contingent*, but what is *contingent* is *actual* and the *actual* is **ontological**[70]; likewise, what is not *actual* is *possible*, but *the possible* remains a modal category of Being. But what happens, instead, with what is not *possible*, viz., with *the im-possible*? Is it also **ontological** or is there a rupture here? Indeed, this seems to be the case despite the proper and declared *categorial* character [*textura*] that Kant assigns to such a term.

Therefore, if in this sense we revise what Kant himself expresses, a certain ambiguity prevails on this point. Through it, if we understand what it reveals, it is possible to see through the announced problematic in relation to the "Time" of the Nothing.

Indeed, when faced with the problem of whether the field of *possibility* is greater than that of *actuality*, and that of actuality greater than *necessity*—with the sole purpose, as he says, of leaving no "gap in what according to common opinion belongs among the concepts of the understanding"[71]—Kant comes to the conclusion that the fields of *possibility* and *actuality*, despite all appearances, are coincident. "It certainly looks as if one could increase the number of that which is possible beyond that of the actual, since something must be added to the former to constitute the latter." But, he adds meaningfully, "I do not acknowledge this addition to the possible. For that which would have to be added to the possible would be *impossible*."[72] Or, what is the same: *the possible* being the only thing capable of occurring within the field of Experience, *the im-possible*, as such, does not exist: it is a failed concept, without any function or ontological order. Within the field of Experience—viz., of Being—*the im-possible* has no place or relevance.

Then what happens with that *im-possible*? Is it perhaps abandoned as something useless due to its notorious lack of *ontological* significance? Absolutely not. If we pursue what is said about it—and here is what is decisive—we will notice that, a few lines after the previous statement, Kant states the following with patent equivocation: "That which is possible only under conditions that are themselves merely possible is not possible *in all respects*."[73] That is to say, outside of Experience—i.e., in the field of Reason—*the im-possible* seems to have a foundation. Such an assertion—which as noted, actually denies the previous point and unlimitedly extends the field of *possibility* over that of *actuality*—also has crucial importance for envisioning the true meaning of the Kantian doctrine.

Indeed, what "is" this *Reason* that seems to exceed the field of Experience and Being? Is it simply the ground soil of *Non-Being*? Is *the im-possible*, which takes effect in it, a mere *Non-Being* as an expression of an ontological negation of Being? Or does the face of an authentic *Nothing* shine through in it as that which is not only opposed and contradictory with respect to Being, but as essential and positive *negativity*? Does that *im-possible* not manifest—just by exceeding the ontological sphere—a *negativity* that does not simply negate this sphere but transcends and affirms its own rights against it?

But, along with the previous interrogations, others can be formulated of no less importance for our interests. Indeed, when dealing with the problem of the Temporality of noumena—where *im-possibility* now seems to lie—we saw that Kant emphatically affirms that Reason "is not in Time."[74] Does this mean that it is *a-temporal*? Is *the im-possible*, which manifests itself in it, therefore also something *a-temporal*? Or could it be that in Reason—by abolishing the borders of Experience and therefore the limitations of the natural *understanding of Being*—a sui generis "Temporality" is established? Is it possible, perhaps, to bear witness to such a "Temporality," experienced in the uprooting of Being and therefore of the phenomenal world that encircles Experience? If so, then it would be necessary to admit that this Reason possesses a distinct "λόγος," and perhaps one radically opposed to the λόγος of Experience. Or is the λόγος that innervates Being and the Being that is understood in terms of this λόγος the only horizon of Truth that man possesses?

At a certain moment, when he wants to refer to a purely intelligible "Being" (Wesen)—viz., thinkable only through pure Reason and totally uprooted from the conditions that establish the limitations of the sensible world or of Experience (Sinnenwelt)—with obscure and at once precise language, Kant calls such a "Being" (Wesen) an *ens extramundanum*.[75] Isn't this indicating the circumstance of the breakdown or rupture of the horizon of the surrounding world as the background of ontological comprehension? There is always the possibility—Kant notes, referring to this entity—that such an "intelligible Being" (Verstandeswesen) is "impossible in itself,"[76] but this cannot be in any way inferred from all that belongs to the world of the senses or by means of the exclusive support of the conditions of Experience.[77] On the contrary, what matters—as he says verbatim—is to avoid, based on the deeply rooted validity of the already noted ontological presupposition, declaring "the intelligible, even though it is not to be used by us in explaining appearances, to be impossible."[78] He adds: "Reason goes its way in its empirical use, and a special way in a transcendental use."[79] That is: there is a whole region, sphere or ambit, whose validity for man is not exhausted or coincidental with the kingdom of the "λόγος" that innervates Being. *The im-possible*, insofar as it fails as a category and loses meaning as an ontological concept, inaugurates *eo ipso* the kingdom of *transcendental possibility*.⁸⁰ In the dimension of pure Reason—the link with the phenomenal world and therefore with the conditions that limit the mere possibility of Experience is abolished—*the im-possible* (empirical) becomes *the possible* (transcendental). This *transcendental possibility* (*ens extramundanum*) is synonymous with something *im-possible* (*nihil negativum*) whose negativity does not simply express a mere ontological negation (Non-Being)—since then it would be something that would remain subject to the sensible world— but shows or exhibits the positive negativity of Reason. In this sense, that which is manifested—the transcendentally possible—exhibits a "possibility" that overcomes or transcends mere ontological possibility and whose "Being" is, for this very reason, *transcendent* in relation to the phenomenal world. But with this—as Kant rightly says—the point is not simply to demonstrate the unconditionally necessary existence of an entity, nor to found the possibility of a merely intelligible condition of the phenomena of the sensible world (Sinnenwelt), but only to (in the same way that Reason is limited so that it does not pretend to seek reasons for explanation in the sensible world, since of its own dimension and nature it exceeds it) "limit the law of the *merely empirical* use of the understanding, so that it does not decide (simply through this use) the possibility of things in general, nor declare the intelligible, even though it is not to be used by us in explaining appearances, *to be impossible*."⁸¹ Next to the λόγος of Experience—incardinated in the phenomenal world and whose ontological meaning is undeniable—is exhibited a "λόγος" of pure Reason, distinct and radically opposed in its function and order with respect to the former. Through this "λόγος"—while the face of the intelligible is revealed in its positive negativity—the laws of the sensible world are not transgressed, but rather transcended. Between the thesis asserting that *the im-possible* lacks ontological meaning, and that which ascribes to it a *positive negativity* as *transcendentally possible*, "there is no true contradiction" and, thus, "they can both be true."⁸² Furthermore: that which is revealed in both cases "is" Truth. The pure negativity of the intelligible—alien and transcendent in relation to the mere negation that expresses *the im-possible* as Non-Being—displays itself as having full rights. That *pure negativity* which Pure Reason manifests is the testimony that the Nothing—as distinct and opposed to Non-Being—is evident in it.⁸³

From such a perspective, it is now clear why the merely ontological Temporality—as a horizon of meaning for Being and Non-Being—is exceeded and transcended by the "Temporality" of Nothingness. Since the absolute negativity of Reason constitutes a dimension which on principle rejects ontological lawfulness, the "meaning" of its particular "Temporality" must be sought from an "understanding" rooted in the dimension that the Nothing itself inaugurates as *ens extramundanum*. In such a manner, the realm of Pure Reason is not *a-temporal*, but instead reveals a "Temporality" of a different nature from that which gives and acquires meaning from the phenomenal world. If this phenomenal Temporality sprouts and originates from the horizon of Being that serves as its *foundation*, the "foundation" of the former "Temporality" must be thought from the openness of the Nothing as an expression of the absolute negativity of Reason.

The intellection of *the im-possible* (*nihil negativum* as *ens extramundanum*)— and of its radical oppositions to and contrasts with the merely *ontological* conception—gives rise to such problems. Only to the extent that the radical contradictions and aporias that such a doctrine leads to (as Kant maintains) are noted, does this perspective experience the rejection that occurs to Thought. *Onto-logical* Thought notes its failure. This failure is not the result of a simple weakness, nor of a poorly chosen or poorly developed path. The failure reveals the essential impossibility of *onto-logical* Thought to face—from the assumptions that sustain and nourish it—a problem that exceeds it and negates its own basis. But when Thought fails, and when the reason for its failure is illuminated, the one who has thought is assisted by the intellection of what he cannot apprehend or express through its help. Only in such a way, insofar as the openness of *absolute im-possibility* is noted—distinct from and radically opposed in its properties to *ontological im-possibility*—Nothingness is also presented and with it the "Temporality" that gives it "meaning" in the realm of absolute negativity or the radical absence of Being. Then this *Nothingness* can no longer be seen as a Non-Being—as a mere negation of Being—but as the essential *otherness* of Being. But isn't "*the other*" only thinkable and apprehensible from "*the self-same*"? Or can Thought even break the bounds of identity that sustain it as *onto-logical* Thought? What is said here can bear witness to such an attempt. The reader, then, must judge for herself. For this, they are asked not simply for their formal benevolence, but for an explicit awareness of the *onto-logical* difficulties that must be overcome when entering a terrain where they have to abandon their own ways of thinking, and even their habitual modes of expression, since what is attempting to appear is found located *beyond* the reach of these and refuses on principle to be apprehended through their cooperation.

Notes

Introduction

1. [As noted in the Translator's Introduction, this term appears prominently in, and is perhaps borrowed from, José Ortega y Gasset].
2. *Science of Logic*, pp. 11–12.
3. *Op. cit.*, ibid.
4. From "Letter on Humanism" (*Pathmarks*, p. 246).
5. *Op. cit.*, p. 258. And as he states in *Off the Beaten Track*, "The oblivion of being is oblivion to the difference between being and the being." ("Anaximander's Saying," p. 242).
6. "Metaphysics, however, speaks continually, and in the most various ways, of Being. Metaphysics gives, and seems to confirm, the appearance that it asks and answers the question concerning Being. In fact, metaphysics never answers the question concerning the truth of Being, for it never asks this question. Metaphysics does not ask this question because it thinks Being only by representing beings as beings. It means beings as a whole, although it speaks of Being. It names Being and means beings as beings. From its beginning to its completion, the propositions of metaphysics have been strangely involved in a persistent confusion of beings and Being." Martin Heidegger, "Introduction to 'What Is Metaphysics?,'" from *Pathmarks*, p. 281.
7. Cf. Heidegger, *Being and Time*, § 38, pp. 175ff.; *Kant and the Problem of Metaphysics*, § 43, p. 165; and *Letter on Humanism*, p. 257.
8. In this respect, compare Heidegger's example of a poem by Knut Hamsun ("Nach Jahr und Tag") cited in *Introduction to Metaphysics*, p. 30.
9. "The difficulty lies less in the discovery, in thought, of being's word than in preserving the purity of the discovered word in authentic thinking." ("Anaximander's Saying," p. 276).
10. Cf. Heidegger's "The Nature of Language" (p. 63) and "Words" (p. 141), both included in the volume *On the Way to Language*; see, additionally, "Why Poets?" (*Off the Beaten Track*, p. 286).
11. [These would be the more literal translations of *Eigentlichkeit* and *Uneigentlichkeit*, which some English translators of Heidegger do use (cf.,

for instance, Haugeland 2013). The more traditional English translation is "authenticity" and "inauthenticity"].

12 Cf. *Being and Time* § 34 and especially § 35 (pp. 167ff.). Additionally, *On the Way to Language*, pp. 146–7.
13 " ... if indeed the truth of being entails that being never prevails in its essence without beings, that a being never is without being." ("Postscript to 'What Is Metaphysics?,'" p. 233).
14 *Being and Time*, § 34, p. 166. [English translation from Stambaugh 2010].
15 Ludwig Wittgenstein, *Tractatus Logico-Philosophicus*, Preface. He repeats this in § 7 of the same work.

   As it is well known, Wittgenstein himself, in a way, modified his initial views in later works. In this respect, cf. *Philosophical Investigations* (§ 5, § 107). Since it is not a matter here of attempting an exposition of his doctrine, but of making a simple reference to a point of view that appears insufficient to us, what has been pointed to is sufficient.
16 Cf. Wittgenstein, *Tractatus Logico-Philosophicus*, § 6.522ff.
17 [Here, I take Mayz Vallenilla to be offering a Heideggerian turn of phrase, referring to the "clearing" in which beings are enabled to show themselves].
18 An illustrative example of such a procedure is found indicated, in a way, by Hegel, who refers to the attempts to formulate ontological determinations of the concept of Being (and, therefore, of Nothing) from the analysis of the representation or concept of *beginning*. Although Hegel does not directly allude to our problem, his analyses and critiques may serve what we wish to suggest. Indeed, referring to the representation or concept of *beginning*, he says: "We have, therefore, only to see what there is in this representation." And he adds: "As yet there is nothing, and something is supposed to become. The beginning is not pure nothing but a nothing, rather, from which something is to proceed; also being, therefore, is already contained in the beginning. Therefore, the beginning contains both, being and nothing; it is the unity of being and nothing, or is non-being which is at the same time being, and being which is at the same time non-being" (*Science of Logic*, p. 51). But, when rejecting the attempt that tries to think Being from such a representation and analysis of the concept of *beginning*, he adds: "But the beginning ought not itself to be already a first *and* an other, for anything which is in itself a first *and* an other implies that an advance has already been made. Consequently, that which constitutes the beginning, the beginning itself, is to be taken as something unanalyzable, taken in its simple, unfilled immediacy; and therefore *as being*, as complete emptiness" (*Op. cit.*, p. 52).

19 Cf. *Being and Time*, § 5.
20 Cf. *Ontología del Conocimiento*, chapter IX. It seems unnecessary to us to repeat here what has been extensively developed in the cited work. The interested reader can find in it a detailed treatment of this fundamental problem.
21 [The word "illumination" will appear unusual to many readers. Here it may be important to remind ourselves that the Heideggerian roots of Mayz Vallenilla's approach are in turn grounded in a reading of the Greek *aletheia* (truth) as "unconcealment" or a "clearing" (*Lichtung*; cf. *BT* 133). Both terms are directly related to the notion of *bringing phenomena to light*, which is to allow them to show themselves to us, and hence *shine* or *glimmer* in the light, or even *radiate* (cf. Heidegger's *On Time and Being*, p. 66, tr. Stambaugh, 1972)].
22 Referring to the Greek conception of Time—which, through Aristotle, has determined essentially all subsequent doctrines—Heidegger says the following: "they take time itself as one entity among other entities, and try to grasp it in the structure of its Being, though that way of understanding Being which they have taken as their horizon is one which is itself naively and inexplicitly oriented towards time" (*Being and Time*, § 6, p. 26). For more details, cf. *Ontología del Conocimiento*, chapter IX.
23 [Here, for the first time, Mayz Vallenilla uses the term *temporariedad* as opposed to *temporalidad*. For him, this appears to mark the distinction between Heidegger's terms *Temporalität* and *Zeitlichkeit*, respectively. *Temporalität*, for Heidegger, refers to the temporality of Being in general, while *Zeitlichkeit* refers to the temporality of Dasein (for an overview, see Blattner 2021). In some Spanish translations of Heidegger, *Zeitlichkeit* is translated as *temporeidad*. Since it is not done so here, I presume that Mayz Vallenilla intends *Zeitlichkeit* by *temporalidad*. While MV will mainly employ the latter term, I will note in brackets when he switches to *temporariedad*].
24 Cf. Chapter IV, § 17 of this work.
25 It is easy to see that the relation of these notions responds, above all, to the tradition of the school of Leibniz and Wolff present in Baumgarten's *Metaphysics*. As it is possible to verify in Volume XVII of Kant's *Complete Works*, published by the Prussian Academy of Sciences (Berlin and Leipzig, 1916, Verlag Walter de Gruyter), the fourfold notion of Nothing that appears in the *Critique of Pure Reason* is constructed from Kant's explanations of and comments on Baumgarten's *Metaphysics*. This will be specified, in due course, throughout our investigation.

Through Baumgarten, and hence the school of Leibniz and Wolff, Kant picks up the rich tradition that has accompanied these notions from almost the very beginning of philosophy. The issue here, however, is not to delve into such historical links. The systematic examination of these notions may shed some light on what is thus scarcely suggested.

Chapter 1

1. [MV writes that Kant "le adscribe a la noción de Nada es la de ser semejante a un *noúmeno*" (51). This may suggest that the "notion of Nothingness" is *like* or that it *resembles* a noumenon. However, as you will see a few lines below, MV specifically asserts that this notion *is* of the noumenon].
2. B348. [MV will often use the word "texture" (*la textura*) in a way that resembles the word "character" or "feature," as in "Nothingness exhibits the *character* of an 'empty concept without object,'" This is not without precedent, as Ortega y Gasset also sometimes uses *la textura* in this way as well; see, for example, Ortega's *Kant, Hegel, Dilthey* (p. 76)].
3. It should be noted that in the first edition of the *Critique of Pure Reason*, Kant assigned *objective reality* to noumena (cf. especially A249–50), while in the passage that replaces the one quoted in the second edition (cf. B305ff.) he emphatically denies noumena such a condition. The reason for this radical divergence in point of view—as will be understood later—lies in the introduction and exclusive acceptance of the concept of noumenon in the n*egative sense* (cf. B309, B311).
4. Cf. B298.
5. [Kant refers to the *ens rationis* as an Erdichtung or "fiction" at B348. Guyer and Wood, however, translate Erdichtung as "invention"].
6. "But if we understand by that an **object of a non-sensible intuition,** then we assume a special kind of intuition, namely intellectual intuition, which, however, is not our own, and the possibility of which we cannot understand, and this would be the noumenon in a **positive** sense." B307.
7. "The concept of a noumenon is therefore merely a **boundary concept,** in order to limit the pretension of sensibility, and therefore only of negative use," B311. [MV uses the term *concepto-límite*, but English readers should keep in mind that Kant himself draws a distinction between "limits" and "boundaries" (*Schranken*

and *Grenzen*, respectively), and in this passage uses *Grenz* (cf. *Prolegomena*, AA 4: 352)].

8   "Now the doctrine of sensibility is at the same time the doctrine of the noumenon in the negative sense," B307. [MV does not mean here that the literal or objective reality of noumena is established; see his claim at the end of the paragraph to this effect].

9   B310.

10 B346 [capitalization added by MV].

11 B309.

12 B307.

13 [That is, for the purpose of maintaining this definition of the Nothing as well as its function in constituting phenomena].

14 [MV appears to be referring to Heidegger's "ontological difference," as applied to "Nothingness" and "noumena" instead of "Being" and "beings"].

15 Let this be an opportune place to fully transcribe the text of this first notion of Nothingness: "1. To the concepts of all, many, and one there is opposed the concept of that which cancels everything out, i.e., **none,** and thus the object of a concept to which no intuition that can be given corresponds is = nothing, i.e., a concept without an object, like the *noumena*, which cannot be counted among the possibilities although they must not on that ground be asserted to be impossible (*ens rationis*), or like something such as certain new fundamental forces, which one thinks, without contradiction, to be sure, but also without any example from experience even being thought, and which must therefore not be counted among the possibilities." B347.

16 B147–8. The informed reader will excuse us for not embarking upon an elucidation of the problem presented by mathematical knowledge, since this would totally deviate us from our purposes. It should be pointed out, however, that mathematical knowledge, when proceeding via the *construction* of concepts, does not imply a contradiction with what is being suggested. Cf. B298–9.

17 B347. It is to observe the difficulty of expression that was presented to Kant in this case. As can be seen in the quoted passage (cf. the German text in footnote 31), the correlate of the concept *None* cannot, strictly speaking, be a true *object* (Gegenstand). On the contrary, without the existence of the corresponding intuition, such a concept turns out to be strictly "a concept without object" (ein Begriff ohne Gegenstand). For this reason, we have enclosed the term "*object*" in quotation marks.

18 Cf. B308.

19 B347.

20 B310–11.
21 On this point, in addition to B72, B139, B145, B312, B344, A286, compare Kant's famous letter to Marcus Herz from February 21, 1772 (Königlich Preussischen Akademie der Wissenschaften edition, vol. X, pp. 129ff).
22 It should be understood that what we wish to show is not the nonexistence of Nothingness as *ens rationis*—that is to say, of a Nothing with a structure like that of the *noumenon*—, but that our purpose lies in trying to take advantage of the very possibilities offered by Kantian thought for introducing us to the discussion of a problem and raise the central question at hand. If we provisionally exclude the acceptance of Nothing as noumenon—which should not be done within a literal interpretation of Kantian thought—it is for the simple reason that this would lead us to the logical negation of a temporal structure in Nothingness, as it happens—in a strict Kantian sense—with respect to the *noumenon*. Cf. B308. The hypothesis of Nothingness as *noumenon* and its possible temporal meaning will be discussed more later.
23 "No one can define the concept of magnitude in general except by something like this: That it is the determination of a thing through which it can be thought how many units are posited in it. Only this how-many-times is grounded on successive repetition, thus on time and the synthesis (of the homogeneous) in it." B300.
24 [Mayz Vallenilla's capitalization, although Kant also bolds this word in the original text].
25 "The pure **schema of magnitude** (*quantitatis*), however, as a concept of the understanding, is **number,** which is a representation that summarizes the successive addition of one (homogeneous) unit to another. Thus number is nothing other than the unity of the synthesis of the manifold of a homogeneous intuition in general, because I generate time itself in the apprehension of the intuition." B182.
26 In this respect cf. *Ontología del Conocimiento*, chapters 8–9.
27 "*Versuch, den Begriff der negativen Grössen in die Weltweisheit einzuführen*" [I use the standard English translation of Kant's title, though MV's Spanish translation of it ("*Intento de introducir en la sabiduría del universo el concepto de las magnitudes negativas*") indicates Kant's use of terms that in English might be translated as "world wisdom" instead of "philosophy," specifically by indicating the *universality* of this wisdom (*sabiduría del universo* ...)].
28 This same concept is later picked up in the *Critique of Pure Reason* when referring to the Amphiboly of the Concepts of Reflection. Cf. B321, B329, and B338.
29 Cf. "Negative Magnitudes," AA 2: 171, as well as *CPR* B321.

30 Kant's words are clear and explicit: "The second opposition, namely real opposition, is that where two predicates of a thing are opposed to each other, but not through the law of contradiction. Here, too, one thing cancels that which is posited by the other; but the consequence is *something* (*cogitabile*). The motive force of a body in one direction and an equal tendency of the same body in the opposite direction do not contradict each other; as predicates, they are simultaneously possible in one body. The consequence of such an opposition is rest, which is something (*repraesentabile*). It is, nonetheless, a true opposition. For that which is posited by the one tendency, construed as existing on its own, is cancelled by the other tendency, and the two tendencies are true predicates of one and the self-same thing, and they belong to it simultaneously. The consequence of the opposition is also nothing, but nothing in another sense to that in which it occurs in a contradiction (*nihil privativum, repraesentabile*). We shall, in future, call this nothing: zero = 0. Its meaning is the same as that of negation (*negatio*), lack, absence—notions which are in general use among philosophers—albeit with a more precise determination which will be specified later on." ("Negative Magnitudes," AA 2: 171–2).

31 "A negation, in so far as it is the consequence of a real opposition, will be designated a *deprivation* (*privatio*). But any negation, in so far as it does not arise from this type of repugnancy, will be called a *lack* (*defectus, absentia*)" (*Op. cit.*, 2: 177–8).

32 "Where this temporal unity cannot be encountered, thus in the case of the noumenon, there the entire use, indeed even all significance of the categories completely ceases" (B308).

The text that we have transcribed could give rise to some confusion if it were understood that Kant excludes or completely ceases the "use" of the *categories* (and therefore of the understanding and its concepts) in relation to the noumena. To avoid this confusion, it is necessary to carefully distinguish and keep separate the concepts of understanding (in their pure intelligible use) from the *categorial* function of those same concepts, when they act as conditions of the possibility of Experience. Kant himself does not always do so, and hence the confusion that sometimes arises (cf. e.g., B304).

The word "*use*" (Gebrauch) utilized by Kant in the quoted text—and which he had already applied in the title of paragraphs 17 and 22 of the Transcendental Deduction of the Categories—cannot be interpreted to mean that concepts of understanding do not work, or are not used, in the case of noumena. The noumena are products or entities generated in the understanding (*Verstandeswesen*, Kant himself calls them), and as such they have their original source there, being therefore the concepts of the understanding (*Verstandesbegriff*) which, through a merely intelligible use, without limiting their application to the matter provided by sensible intuition, they bring about the emergence of a purely noumenal, that is to say intelligible, structure.

What Kant tries to express is that, in the case of the noumena, the pure concepts of understanding do not have an *objective* application, are limited to phenomena, and therefore, do not assume the particular function of authentic *categories*, whose "use" is none other than to serve as conditions of possibility for the knowledge of objects of experience, that is, of *phenomena*. "The merely transcendental use of the categories"—says Kant at B304—"is thus in fact no use at all … "

For a full confirmation of what we are saying, we ask you to refer to paragraph 23 of the Transcendental Deduction (B148–50), in which the problem raised here is explicitly addressed.

33   "Pure reason, as a merely intelligible faculty, is not subject to the form of Time, and hence not subject to the conditions of the temporal sequence," B579. ["Time" capitalized by MV].

34   Cf. B307 and also (with the pertinent reservations) A249–51.

35   "Wherever our representations may arise, whether through the influence of external things or as the effect of inner causes, whether they have originated *a priori* or empirically as appearances—as modifications of the mind they nevertheless belong to inner sense, and as such all of our cognitions are in the end subjected to the formal condition of inner sense, namely time, as that in which they must all be ordered, connected, and brought into relations. This is a general remark on which one must ground everything that follows," A98–9.

36   Cf. A107; B139–40.

37   "The consciousness of oneself in accordance with the determinations of our state in internal perception is merely empirical, forever variable; it can provide no standing or abiding self in this stream of inner appearances, and is customarily called **inner sense** or **empirical apperception**," A107.

38   "For the standing and lasting I (of pure apperception) constitutes the correlate of all of our representations, so far as it is merely possible to become conscious of them, and all consciousness belongs to an all-embracing pure apperception just as all sensible intuition as representation belongs to a

pure inner intuition, namely that of time," A123–4. [Translator: "Standing and lasting" can also be accurately rendered "standing and permanent," which is what I will use in the following pages].

39 "That which should **necessarily** be represented as numerically identical … " A107.
40 A109. [Mayz Vallenilla translates Kant's *Gemüts* as "espíritu" rather than "mind," but for consistency with the standard English translations, we will continue to use "mind"].
41 A108.
42 "It, reason, is present to all the actions of human beings in all conditions of time, and is one and the same, but it is not itself in time, and never enters into any new state in which it previously was not," B584.
43 "For the standing and lasting I (of pure apperception) constitutes the correlate of all of our representations … " A123.
44 [Here, as I mentioned in the Translator's Introduction, the reader should compare the similar remarks made by Heidegger in *Kant and the Problem of Metaphysics* (e.g., at *KPM*, p. 112)].
45 These quotations are taken from two different places in the *Critique of Pure Reason*. The first two statements are found in the chapter on schematism (B183), where he says verbatim: "Time itself does not elapse, but the existence of that which is changeable elapses in it. To time, therefore, which is itself unchangeable and lasting, there corresponds in appearance that which is unchangeable in existence, i.e., substance, and in it alone can the succession and simultaneity of appearances be determined in regard to time." The other statement is found in the proof of the First Analogy [MV mistakenly writes "Second Analogy"], where he says verbatim: "The time, therefore, in which all change of appearances is to be thought, lasts and does not change; since it is that in which succession or simultaneity can be represented only as determinations of it," B224–5.
46 The reader will excuse us if this idea is only provisionally outlined. Its explicit development in the present context would greatly divert us from our purposes.
47 As will be seen in due course, Time is not at all what is called a *property*, Time acquires the appearance of a *property* when it is *entified*, considering it one entity among other entities. Then it comes to be considered "substance" or "accident" in relation to the sphere of entities in which it is inserted. But, precisely, as we are seeing, there are sufficient reasons to be cautious of this way of conceiving it.

Chapter 2

1. B348.
2. "The *nihil privativum* (No. 2) and the *ens imaginarium* (No. 3), on the contrary, are empty *data* for concepts." B349.
3. *Metaphysics*, 1004 a10–17; 1022 b22ff.
4. B347. [MV's capitalizations].
5. B182–3. Cf. likewise B211.
6. [In this sentence, MV uses a passage from B182 *nearly* word-for-word, for which reason I substitute the verbatim quote here, with MV's capitalization of "inner sense"].
7. B183.
8. "Now that in the empirical intuition which corresponds to the sensation is reality (*realitas phaenomenon*)," B209.
9. B348.
10. B210. [MV's italics].
11. B214. [MV's italics].
12. B214.
13. Hegel, *Science of Logic*, Introduction.
14. Let's remember what Hegel says when he tries to define Nothingness: "*Nothing, pure nothingness*; it is simple equality with itself, complete emptiness, complete absence of determination and content; lack of all distinction within" (*Science of Logic*, p. 59). With the intention of pointing to the assumptions on which this notion rests, we will return to this point in due course. For now it should be noted that, despite his brilliant dialectical attempt, Hegel could not be rid of the ontologizing presuppositions we have pointed out. This is palpably revealed in his famous statement: "*Pure being and pure nothing are therefore the same*" (ed. cit., p. 59).
15. "But the real, which corresponds to sensations in general, in opposition to the negation = 0, only represents something whose concept in itself contains a being … " (B217).
16. Cf. the previous paragraph, as well as B214.
17. [MV, like Heidegger, often uses the expressive metaphors of light and darkness when referring to *phenomena* or that which, as Heidegger would say, "shows itself in itself." This, as Heidegger notes, has its root in the Greek notion of truth (*aletheia*) as uncovering or bringing something to light].
18. B214. Parenthetical remark added.

19 Ibid.
20 [There is a notable affinity here between MV's phenomenological description of the nothing of sleep and Heidegger's notion of *death* as the "possibility" of all "impossibility" for Dasein. Death, clearly, represents a more total nothingness, which is in line with MV's discussion of the *nihil privativum* as a relatively narrow and limited concept of nothingness].
21 The term "*aseity*" has been used, throughout the tradition, with a different meaning than the one we assign to this new word: *abseity*. Therefore, we ask the reader not to confuse them and understand the meaning of the latter within the strict context of meaning in which we use it. [The "tradition" he refers to includes, probably most importantly, St. Thomas Aquinas's *Summa Theologica*. But Schopenhauer turns this somewhat on its head when he attributes aseity not to God but to the will (*World as Will and Representation*, Vol. 2, pp. 333, 364)].
22 "Anxiety makes manifest the nothing." Heidegger, "What Is Metaphysics?," from *Pathmarks*, p. 88.
23 Ibid., p. 93.
24 Ibid., p. 92.
25 Ibid., p. 92.
26 Cf. B185.
27 B182.
28 B210.
29 Cf. the previous paragraph.
30 B214.
31 We believe it necessary to point out an apparent contradiction into which Kant falls. Indeed, as it is possible to notice, Kant denies on the one hand the possibility that an *empty* Time can be given (B214), but on the other he expressly affirms that the opposition between *reality* and *negation* lies in the difference between the same Time as a "filled" or "empty" Time (B182). But is there a real contradiction between these two statements? Indeed, this would occur if it were admitted that *negation*, as such, means the total abolition of *reality*, absolute zero or total Nothingness, which would correspond, in the strict sense, to an "emptiness of sensation." "Emptiness" means, in the Kantian sense, a *privation*, or rather a *diminution* of the *positive degrees* of sensation. *Negation* does not imply, therefore, the total "emptiness" of sensations, but the privation of their *positive* degree. An "empty" instant, for Kant, is thoroughly *non-existent*. Time is made up of a *series of moments* more or less full of *reality*, but never absolutely

devoid of it. Time is, in the strict sense, the *pure image* of intensive *magnitudes* and these are always and necessarily magnitudes of the real.

32 We will not attempt here to describe in detail the original form of presentation that Time assumes as an intraworldly entity and the process required for its progressive *de-worlding*. In this sense, I refer the reader to my book *Ontología del Conocimiento*, Chapter IX, § 42, as well as *Being and Time*, § 81. [MV uses the phrase "before the eyes" ("ante los ojos") for the German "Vorhande," but we will retain the more standard English translation of Vorhande as "present at hand"].

33 Regarding the *irreversibility* of Time, a caveat should be made in relation to the laws of Thermodynamics. But, in the current context, it is not a question we are interested in for provoking such a discussion. Let us say the following, anyway: to arrive at the affirmation of the *reversibility* of Time (as occurs in certain laws of Thermodynamics) one must *assume*, at least as a possibility, its *irreversible direction*. It is this historically verifiable fact that we are basically interested in pointing out, since it confirms what we say.

But whether Time is viewed as *reversible* or as *irreversible*—and this is essential for understanding what we want to hold—such characteristics are, in a strict sense, "instrumental," that is, they are properties that are ascribed to Time in order to facilitate, through their assistance, the handling of physical phenomena. The *reversibility* or *irreversibility* of the *direction* of Time assumes, therefore, the prior character of *use* that is assigned to it. This clearly demonstrates that both marks spring from the ground where the natural *understanding of Being* dominates.

34 "The property of magnitudes"—Kant says in this respect—"on account of which no Part of them is the smallest (no Part is simple) is called their *continuity* [MV's italics]. Space and Time are *quanta continua*, because no Part of them can be given except as enclosed between boundaries (points and instants), thus only in such a way that this Part is again a Space or a Time. Space therefore consists only of spaces, Time of times. Points and instants are only boundaries, i.e., mere places of their limitation; but places always presuppose those intuitions that limit or determine them, and from mere places, as components that could be given prior to Space or Time, neither Space nor Time can be composed." B211.

35 Aristotle, *Physics*, Δ 11, 219b1. It will be easily understood that we cannot enter into a detailed analysis of the ontological structure implied by such a notion of time—nor can we develop the subsequent step, which would be the reinterpretation of Being from its horizon—lest we deviate excessively from the central problem with which we wish to deal in the present context.

Not with respect to Aristotle—on whose conception of Time I recommend reading chapter I of Gunther Eigler's magnificent work entitled "*Metaphysische Voraussetzungen in Husserls Zeitanalysen*" (Verlag Anton Hain, 1961)—but in relation to Kant, only the following should be pointed out: the parallelism and mutual illumination that exists between this notion of Time and the conception of Being (the Being of "natural understanding") that serves as a supporting structure of the *real*—to *reality* as such—is perfectly verifiable within the Kantian doctrine. Without going into a dry and tiring analysis, let's just say the following: just as the *present-instant*—*the now-present*—is the only thing to which an authentic existence can be imputed, *the real*, on the ontological plane, is the *now-filled*, by a sensation that is present in an *instant*. The *reality, the real*, is the *instant* of Time "filled" by a sensation. That this sensation fills only an *instant* is shown by the very definition of *degree*. The *degree* of sensation, and therefore of *reality*, designates a quantity whose apprehension is instantaneous (B210).

The same parallelism is repeated with respect to the indicated character of *continuity*. Just as the uninterrupted sequence of *nows* (instants) is *continuous*, the ontological structure of *reality* reflects a parallel character. "All appearances whatsoever are accordingly continuous magnitudes" (B212).

And no less than the two previous characters, the *infinity* of Time is also reflected in the parallel ontological features exhibited by *reality* (B214).

36 This phenomenon of the fading or loss of the world is not to be understood in an identical sense to that implied, for example, by the *de-worlding* required for the transformation of *worldly Time* (Zuhandene) into *vulgar Time* (Vorhandene). Cf. *Being and Time*, § 81. In the fading of the world, which occurs in nihilation or in deep sleep, it is a more radical event. Instead of the passage or progressive transformation of some structures into others, what occurs is the total loss, dissolution, or nullification of these. It is very important to take such nuance into account in order to understand the meaning of the phenomena that we intend to point out.

37 As a simple allusion—and taking into account the warning that we have made in the previous observation—the connection that these phenomena seem to keep with the de-realizing and spectralizing effect is characteristic of the ἐποχή. Likewise, the so-called *neutrality modification* (cf. Edmund Husserl, *Ideas: General Introduction to Pure Phenomenology*, § 109 and 117) would seem to be connected in a certain way with the phenomenon of *anxiety*. But here we cannot—lest we deviate excessively from the central theme at hand—address these questions, which require the finest and most delicate descriptive qualification to avoid gross confusion.

38 [The use of "quantum" for "amount," "magnitude," or "quantity," echoes Kant. Cf., for example, B183].
39 Altazor, Canto V.
40 Aware of the almost insurmountable difficulties that language presents due to its *ontological* origin, our reader will know how to excuse the deficient and equivocal use of these expressions. Although the verb "to be" [Transl. "*haber*"]—like the majority of Castilian verbs—has a clear ontological resonance, we believe that once this circumstance is noticed, the reader will know how to make the de-ontologizing effort that is required here to understand the true meaning of the expressions used. The Nothing (and Time viewed from it) "are" not. But "*there is Nothing*" and "*there is Time*," as evidenced by the *understanding* of both data.
41 This proposition must be understood in a similar way as that proposed by Heidegger with regard to Being and entities. It is not that chronological and entitative Time ceases or begins with the fact that a human being "present to hand" [Transl. "*ante los ojos*"] "in time" exists or not. Time continues to pass, just as it already was, regardless of whether there are humans or not. (Cf. *Being and Time*, § 81, p. 425). Now, just as "*there is Being*" only as long as Dasein *is* and there exists an "*understanding of Being*" (cf. *Being and Time*, § 43; c, p. 212), Nothing and Time *are*, or *they are given*, only as long as there is an Existence and a corresponding "*understanding*" of them. And whether it can be affirmed that Time—as an entity—is finite or not, really exists or not in its entitative course, depends only on this.

Chapter 3

1 B348.
2 B347. [The brackets and italics are added by MZ].
3 "Now that in the empirical intuition which corresponds to the sensation is reality (*realitas phaenomenon*)," B209.
4 Cf. B34ff.
5 " … like space and time (for these cannot be perceived in themselves)," B207.
6 "Thus, if it were to be supposed that space and time are in themselves objective and conditions of the possibility of things in themselves …," B64.
7 "Space is not an object of intuitions (an object or its determination), but the intuition itself, which precedes all objects and in which if the latter are posited, the appearance of them is possible" (*Reflexion* 4673, AA 17: 638–9).
8 Ibid.

9   "It (Time) precedes all real things and hence can itself also be cognized *a priori* as the condition of objects" (ibid., AA 17: 637). [Parentheses added by MV].

10 "It (Time) is therefore to be regarded really not as object but as the way of representing myself as object," B54. [Parentheses added by MV].

11 Cf. B266.

12 This statement should not be surprising. It is hinted at several times in *CPR* (cf. A118–20, B151, B741), and clearly expounded in the *Anthropology*. In a text that fully confirms the interpretation that has been provided of Space and Time as entities that do not require the presence of the real in order to exist, Kant writes the following: "The power of imagination (*facultas imaginandi*), as a faculty of intuition without the presence of the object, is either *productive*, that is, a faculty of the original presentation of the object (*exhibitio originaria*), which thus precedes experience; or *reproductive*, a faculty of the derivative presentation of the object (*exhibitio derivativa*), which brings back to the mind an empirical intuition that it had previously.—Pure intuitions of space and time belong to the productive faculty; all others presuppose empirical intuition, which, when it is connected with the concept of the object and thus becomes empirical cognition, is called *experience*" (*Anthropology*, AA 7: 167).

Such a text fully agrees with another from *CPR* that reads as follows: "**Imagination** is the faculty for representing an object even **without its presence** in intuition. Now since all of our intuition is sensible, the imagination, on account of the subjective condition under which alone it can give a corresponding intnuition to the concepts of understanding, belongs to **sensibility**," B151.

13 "The pure image of all magnitudes (*quantorum*) for outer sense is space; for all objects of the senses in general, it is time. The pure **schema of magnitude** (*quantitatis*), however, as a concept of the understanding, is **number,** which is a representation that summarizes the successive addition of one (homogeneous) unit to another," B182.

14 B348.

15 "Now this representation of a general procedure of the imagination for providing a concept with its image is what I call the schema for this concept," B179–80.

16 " … the schema is to be distinguished from an image," B179.

17 "The schema of a pure concept of the understanding, on the contrary, is something that can never be brought to an image at all …, " B181.

18 [This paragraph appears to draw on Kant's description of the faculty of imagination from the previously cited *Anthropology* passage, AA 7: 167. In

this passage Kant refers to the *exhibitio originaria* as the *original presentation* (*ursprünglichen Darstellung*) of the object, and the *exhibitio derivativa* as the *derivative presentation* (*abgeleitete Darstellung*) of the object. Following Kant, I will typically use "presentation" (*Darstellung*) to translate MV's use of the term *aspecto* (which, as he notes in parentheses, derives from the Latin "aspectus," meaning *appearance* or *presence*)].

19 [Here we can compare "prefiguring" with the German *Vorbildung*. Heidegger, in *KPM*, makes use of a passage in Kant's *Reflexionen* where it is said that "Space and Time are the forms of the pre-forming [*Vorbildung*] in intuition" (*KPM* 142-3, fn. 199). Heidegger notes that Erich Adickes, with reference to Benno Erdmann's reading, mistakenly reads *Vorbildung* as *Verbindung* ("connection"). Cf. also Kant's mention of a *Vorbildungs-kraft* ("anticipatory power") in the *Pölitz* lectures on metaphysics, AA 28: 231].

20 "The pure image of all magnitudes (*quantorum*) for outer sense is space; for all objects of the senses in general, it is time," B182.

21 "But since every appearance contains a manifold, thus different perceptions by themselves are encountered dispersed and separate in the mind, a combination of them, which they cannot have in sense itself, is therefore necessary. There is thus an active faculty of the synthesis of this manifold in us, which we call imagination, and whose action exercised immediately upon perceptions I call apprehension," A120.

22 A120.
23 A121.
24 A122.
25 A122.
26 Cf. A122.
27 A118, A123.
28 A123.
29 A123. [Italics added by MV].
30 A118. The reader will excuse us for not going into detail concerning this most important point, which would require a great digression in relation to our theme. Indeed, it is extremely difficult (if not impossible) to present Kant's thought (all the more in this regard), without bringing up a multitude of extremely important questions, and in the absence of which his ideas seem confused and obscure. However, even running this risk, there is no other recourse (on pain of making the exposition extremely long) than to attempt a mere gesture at it and to trust that the reader will be able to correct the faults

by means of a study of the indicated problems. To this end, in addition to the indicated text, cf. A124, A125; B151, B152.
31   A118, [MV's italics].
32   A124.
33   Cf. B176ff.
34   [MV here uses the term *fenómenos*, but we should note that the Spanish translations of Kant's original German usually do not distinguish clearly between *phenomena* and *appearances*, translating the latter [Erscheinungen] as "fenómenos" just like the former [Phaenomena]. But Kant is clear that "phenomena" refers to the determined objects of knowledge, while "appearances" refers to the *un*determined objects of empirical intuition. Cf. A20/B34, A248–9].
35   "Now it is clear that there must be a third thing, which must stand in homogeneity with the category on the one hand and the appearance on the other, and makes possible the application of the former to the latter. This mediating representation must be pure (without anything empirical) and yet **intellectual** on the one hand and **sensible** on the other. Such a representation is the **transcendental schema**," B177.
36   B179–80, [MV's italics].
37   B180.
38   B185.
39   We have had the opportunity to address extensively the problem of the *transcendental schematism* in various courses taught at the Universidad Central de Venezuela from 1953–5. Perhaps on another occasion we can publish the results achieved there, which would greatly illuminate what can hardly be outlined here.
40   "In the synthesis of the appearances the manifold representations always follow one another. Now by this means no object at all is represented; since through this sequence, which is common to all apprehensions, nothing is distinguished from anything else," B243.
41   B240.
42   "Now connection is not the work of mere sense and intuition, but is here rather the product of a synthetic faculty of the imagination, which determines inner sense with regard to temporal relations," B233.
43   B184–5.
44   B177–8.
45   B180.

46 B179.
47 B181. Strictly speaking, it should be noted that the present determination is used by Kant to refer to the *schema* of a pure concept of the Understanding. If we apply it to the *schematism* it is because in the present context it is about the function or product of this *schema*, that is, precisely of the *schematism*.
48 B50 [MV's italics]. Note that Space does not lose its significance and undeniable function for this reason. On the contrary, as Kant correctly says, because Time "cannot be a determination of outer appearances," since it belongs neither to the shape, nor to the position, etc. (B49–50), it is only possible for us to "represent" ourselves externally to Time with the help of Space. For this reason, it is clear that the explicit function of each one of the intuitive sources is indispensable.

But, in this respect, a problem can be formulated. Indeed, when representing ourselves, for example, by a Time-line (*spatial* representation of Time), this line (in turn), in order to be apprehended as our representation (temporal image), must necessarily be reduced to Time (*temporal* representation of Space).

It therefore turns out that the original data of Time undergo a dual process: being in principle temporal, they are spatialized, and then this spatial manifold becomes temporalized again. The possibility of directly apprehending Time and expressing these original data without the aid of a spatial representation (temporalized again) has been attempted by Bergson, Husserl, and Heidegger.

It is not a question of asking here if this is possible—or if it is legitimate—but, rather, if the general problem admits of the support that the Kantian assumptions give to it. In this regard, it is not only possible to question the assumptions inherent in *ontological Time*, but, even more radically, in *non-ontological Time* (Temporality of Nothingness). This is precisely what we have proposed to undertake throughout this work.
49 B347.
50 B347.
51 "These principles have the peculiarity that they do not concern the appearances and the synthesis of their empirical intuition, but merely their **existence** and their **relation** to one another with regard to this their existence," B220.
52 " … and as a principle it will not be valid of the objects (of the appearances) **constitutively** but merely **regulatively**" B222.
53 B219.
54 B183–4.

55 "Time is not something that would subsist for itself or attach to things as an objective determination, and thus remain if one abstracted from all subjective conditions of the intuition of them ... " B49.
56 "Now time cannot be perceived by itself," B225; cf. also B219 and B226.
57 This representation of Time is absolutely necessary, since, without it, there wouldn't be the possibility of determining the apodictic principles, relations, and axioms that regulate it.
58 B225–6.
59 B225.
60 B227.
61 B229.
62 B228.
63 B183.
64 B347. [MV's italics].
65 Kant has interrogated this phenomenon when he expresses: "Time itself does not elapse, but the existence of that which is changeable elapses in it. To time, therefore, which is itself unchangeable and lasting ... " B183.
66 B243.
67 Indeed, the concept of *eternity* has been traditionally represented under the image of a *static now* (nunc stans). (Cf., among others, Plato's *Timaeus*, 37 d; Aristotle's *Physics*, 8, 263 a 3). It is possible to find a parallel representation in the thought of Plotinus (*Enneads*, III) and in each of the great Christian theologians (St. Augustine, St. Thomas, etc.).

We cannot stop here to judge or criticize the assumptions contained in this, much less try to find out how this image of the *nunc stans*—which in all those thinkers corresponds to the determination of an *ontological Time*—brings about a determination of the Time of Nothingness. Is it a mere contradiction or due to a failure of our analysis? On the contrary. Perhaps, for the reasons that we indicate at the end of the present paragraph as well as in the next, it is possible to understand the reasons that lead to such an identification and, therefore, to confusing the structure of the corresponding temporality.
68 B225.
69 B183.
70 B231.
71 B231.
72 Cf. the previous chapter, as well as B214.
73 B229.

74 B225.
75 B231–2. Note that the first italics in the translation is ours.
76 Such a statement does not in the least contradict Kant's doctrine of the ideality of Time and Space. We ask the reader to confront the decisive passages that attest to this. The ideality of Time refers to its a priori subjective condition, but leaves its ontological structure intact. In this respect, cf. B53–4, where Kant says verbatim: "Time is certainly something real, namely the real form of inner intuition."
77 B347.
78 Cf. Chapter II, paragraphs 8 and 9.
79 In Kant's own definition of *infinity*—if examined fully—it is possible to see that, in it, Time is taken as a horizon "present at hand." Indeed, here is what he says verbatim in reference to a similar point: "The infinitude of time signifies nothing more than that every determinate magnitude of time is only possible through limitations of a single time grounding it. The original representation, time, must therefore be given as unlimited," B48.
80 B231.
81 Cf. *Being and Time*, § 81.
82 It should be noted that the comparison that Kant makes between *Time* and a *straight line* that can be extended to infinity (B50)—which he repeats in B154 and B292—is not just casual, but conforms to fundamental ontological reasons. What we are interested in highlighting is the following: that *Time* can and should be represented as a *line* (i.e., in something *spatial*) clearly demonstrates the process of its "objectification" as that of a "present at hand" entity. Not surprisingly, Kant will later demonstrate the empirical reality of phenomena—refuting Idealism—relying entirely on the fact that my own consciousness (as Inner Sense, i.e., as Time) presupposes and demonstrates the existence of objects outside me (B274 and following) and that it is these, at the same time, that guarantee as a *foundation* the determination of my existence in Time and, therefore, the existence of Time itself. The *nervus probandi* of this Refutation of Idealism is just the best evidence that can be adduced to illustrate our assertion.
83 For more details, cf. *Ontología del Conocimiento*, Chapter IX.
84 Hence Kant identifies, at a certain point, the *nihil privativum* with the *ens imaginarium* (B349). This is also why we have followed this path that identifies them and shows that the notion of "Nothing," in both cases, has a similar structure.
85 B229.
86 Cf. B195–7.
87 B214.

Chapter 4

1. B348.
2. B348.
3. "One sees that the thought-entity (No. 1) is distinguished from the non-entity (No. 4) by the fact that the former may not be counted among the possibilities because it is a mere invention (although not self-contradictory), whereas the latter is opposed to possibility because even its concept cancels itself out," B348–9.
4. Recall that Kant defines the *nihil privativum* under the following formula: *Empty object of a concept*, B348.
5. [Mayz Vallenilla uses the term "nudo objeto" here, which may be a typo. "Nulo" is more appropriate, as it indicates that the object in question is, paradoxically, void or non-existent].
6. B348.
7. Aristotle, *Metaphysics*, book Γ 3, 1005b18ff. [English translation from *The Complete Works of Aristotle*, ed. Jonathan Barnes 1991. Oxford University Press. MV's italics].
8. In order to avoid unfounded objections, we would like to point out that we are aware of the objections that this statement may raise, and even of the textual citations that could be produced to refute it. One of them, we suppose, could be extracted from book Θ, 4, lines 12ff., where Aristotle separates *the impossible* from *the false*. But there are other texts—cf., for instance, book Δ, 12, 1019b, lines 24ff.—in which our opinion seems to be confirmed. "*The impossible*"—Aristotle asserts—"*is that of which the contrary is of necessity true.*" If the apparent contradiction between the two previous statements is fully understood—and this requires taking into account the ways in which the examples adduced by Aristotle himself are used for illustrating them—it will be possible to confirm that our interpretation turns out right.
9. " ... a concept without an object, like the *noumena*, which cannot be counted among the possibilities ... " B347; cf. also B348.
10. B307.
11. B302. It is noteworthy that in his own marginal notes (*Nachträge* CXXI), Kant substituted the expression "transcendental possibility" for that of "real possibility" (der realen Möglichkeit).
12. "In a word, all of these concepts could not be **vouched for** and their **real** possibility thereby established, if all sensible intuition (the only one we have) were taken away, and there then remained only **logical** possibility, i.e., that the

concept (thought) is possible is not the issue; the issue is rather whether it relates to an object and therefore signifies anything," B302–3 footnote.
13 B191.
14 For more details, cf. especially Definitions 19 and 23, as well as *Common Notion IX* of the *Elements*. It should be observed that in *Definition* 19, when enumerating the rectilinear figures, Euclid begins by naming the *trilaterals*. *Euclid's Elements of Geometry*. 2008. Edited/translated by Richard Fitzpatrick. https://farside.ph.utexas.edu/books/Euclid/Elements.pdf
15 In general, as is known, the *Principle of Non-contradiction* is applied to the relation between two judgments. The case dealt with by the example we are studying, on the contrary, is that of a contradiction existing internally to a single judgment. In this sense, he refers to what Pfänder calls in his "Logic" the "*Special Principle of Contradiction*," whose symbolic formula would be SP ↔ P. Cf. *Op. cit.*, Part Three, Chap. II, 2. Alexander Pfänder. 2009. *Logic*. Translated by Donald Ferrari. Ontos-Verlag, Frankfurt.
16 B268. Cf. likewise Euclid's "*Elements*," *Notion IX*.
17 B268.
18 B265.
19 *Kant's gesammelte Schriften*, ed. cit. Bd. XVII, *Reflexionen zur Metaphysik*, 4480, p. 567, cf. also 3991, p. 379. [My translation of the passage from the Spanish].
20 Cf. *Op. cit.*, Bd. XVII, 4657, p. 627.
21 B267–8.
22 B266.
23 B288. Cf. also B266.
24 B286.
25 B266.
26 Cf. B266.
27 B196.
28 Cf. B741ff.
29 B272 (parenthetical remark is our addition).
30 B197.
31 Regarding the fundamental significance of this twofold nuance, cf. the following paragraph.
32 Cf. above, § 14.
33 B195.
34 B196.

35 B151, B154.
36 B177.
37 B178.
38 B181.
39 B184–5.
40 B266.
41 Cf. B287. Parenthetical remark added by MV.
42 Cf. B184.
43 "If the concept of a thing is already entirely complete, I can still ask about this object whether it is merely possible, or also actual, or, if it is the latter, whether it is also necessary?" B266.
44 B202–3.
45 Ibid.
46 B203. (We must note that we are here following the version of this sentence proposed by Vaihinger.)
47 B203. It's worth recalling—because it is here that it finds its precise application—the statement that expresses the Fundamental Principle of Experience: "The conditions of the **possibility of experience** in general are at the same time conditions of the **possibility of the objects of experience**," B197.
48 Cf. Chapter I, and 3, where precisely this aspect was pointed out.
49 B203–4.
50 In this sense, both the *Axioms of Intuition* as well as the other *Principles* (Grundsätze) are simply explanations of the *schematism*. The connection between the *schemata* and the *Principles* (Grundsätze) has been something we have tried to demonstrate throughout this work.
51 B184.
52 B47–9.
53 It is a matter of seeing that the *schema of possibility*, referring in general to all objects that are given as *extensive magnitudes*, encompasses both geometrical (spatial) objects, as well as numbers and arithmetic formulas. In this regard, although in the latter case the aspect of *successivity* in the synthesis of their representation is of itself quite clear, it is not uncommon to find resistance to admitting that Space (and all its possible representations) has, ultimately, a temporal meaning by means of its synthesis. In this respect, in addition to what Kant expresses in the passages referring to the *schematism of magnitudes* (B182), and in the *Axioms of Intuition* (B203–4), what he says with respect to this problem can be compared with the *System of Cosmological Ideas*. There he states: "Yet the synthesis of the manifold parts of space, through which we apprehend

it, is nevertheless successive, and thus occurs in time and contains a series," (B439). For more details, compare what we have already said in Ch. III, § 12-B, especially in footnote 161.
54 B204.
55 Ibid.
56 B268.
57 Cf. B181.
58 "The schema of actuality is existence at a determinate time." "The schema of necessity is the existence of an object at all times," B184.
59 B348.
60 B106.
61 B348.
62 B349.
63 Recall what Kant says: "Thus the schemata of the concepts of pure understanding are the true and sole conditions for providing them with a relation to objects, thus with **significance**," B185.
64 "The schema of possibility is the agreement of the synthesis of various representations with the conditions of time in general," B184.
65 Cf. Ch. III, § 13 of our study.
66 B51.
67 "If we abstract from our way of internally intuiting ourselves and by means of this intuition also dealing with all outer intuitions in the power of representation, and thus take objects as they may be in themselves, then time is nothing," B51.
68 B52.
69 Cf. Chapter II, § 9.
70 [In this paragraph, MV italicizes *and* adds space between each letter in the word "ontological." I use bolded letters to indicate the emphasis].
71 B285.
72 B284 [MV's italics and brackets].
73 B284 [MV's italics]; cf. also B590.
74 "It, reason, is present to all the actions of human beings in all conditions of time, and is one and the same, but it is not itself in time … " B584.
75 " … but here the necessary being would have to be thought of as entirely outside the series of the world of sense (as an *ens extramundanum*) and merely intelligible … " B589.
76 Cf. B590–1.

77   A clear manifestation of a certain consciousness of the limitations of the presupposition mentioned here—and, therefore, of its possible consequences for the construction of Temporality—can be found in Kant's own doubtful statements. It is evident, however, that he does not look to solve this problem in a positive sense—as we intend to do—although his statements sketch the path we try to follow. In effect, by posing the indicated problem—of whether the possible is wider than the real—and by declaring negatively (as he does in the first instance) that he is unaware of this addition, "for that which would have to be added to the possible would be impossible" (B284), Kant expressly leaves open the possibility of denying that presupposition—the limitation of the possible to Experience—by declaring the following: "Whether other perceptions than those which in general belong to our entire possible experience and therefore an entirely different field of matter can obtain cannot be decided by the understanding, which has to do only with the synthesis of that which is given" (B283). "Otherwise the poverty of our usual inferences through which we bring forth a great realm of possibility, of which everything actual (every object of experience) is only a small part, is very obvious" (*ibidem*). Because of this—as he concludes—the problem of *the possible*—viz., of that which is *im-possible* within Experience—must be examined from another point of view (that of Reason, as the sphere where the presupposition of Experience is broken) "when one wants to know whether the possibility of things extends further than experience can reach" (B284). Isn't it expressed clearly that Experience—and therefore its respective Temporality—thereby ceases to have an exclusive function to judge about *possibility*? What's more—as Kant himself says—if there can be "a different field of matter," even the Understanding limited to Experience cannot decide this. Is this not insinuating—by leaving open the presumed existence of "other perceptions than those which in general belong to our entire possible experience"—that it is a *non-ontological* correlate endowed with a *negativity* like that exhibited by the openness of the Nothing in its own "experience"?
78   B590.
79   B591.
80   This may be an opportune occasion to clarify a confusion that may arise in readers if one recalls that Kant—in his observations about the various modalities of Nothingness—points out that the notion of the Nothing as a *noumenon* must be distinguished from that corresponding to the *nihil negativum* (B348). Has our attempt not confused them by omitting this advice? If our procedure is fully understood, it must be seen that what is now called here *nihil negativum*

has transcended even the sphere of the simply *ontological im-possible*. If it is true that there is a difference between this and the *noumenon*, it is a matter of seeing that, in the terrain where the question is now raised—made possible as we have seen when the *ontological presupposition* was abolished by the work of Kant's own indications—that opposition is, de facto, overcome. *The im-possible*—as a *transcendental possibility*—remains *eo ipso* converted into a *noumenon*. *The im-possible* is no longer (as it was as an *ontological im-possibility*) a *non-thing* (Unding), but a *noumenon* (Gedankending). The possibility of such a transformation does not imply an error in his conception, but the logical consequence of rupturing the *ontological presupposition* in Kant's conception of *the im-possible*. His own doctrine, by showing the limitations of such a *presupposition* and by indicating the possibility of breaking it, indicates the path that our reflections have followed.

The im-possible thus achieves a third connotation: that of Nothingness as such. Faced with mere *logical* im-possibility (§ 15) and the *ontological* im-possibility of Non-Being (§ 16), *the im-possible*, as *nihil negativum*, now shows the truly positive *negativity* as authentic and radical *Nothingness*. It should therefore be observed that, when we refer to *Non-Being—nihil negativum* in the *ontological* sense—we have written the term "Nothing" in quotation marks.

81 B590. The parenthetical remark is our addition. [MV's italics].
82 B590.
83 Cf. Chap. I, § 4.

Index of Names and Subjects

abseity
  and aseity 49
  as "presence" of negative "contents" 56
  as revelation of Nothingness 49
absence
  as degree of sensation 41
  and Nothingness 119
  and the Temporality of Nothingness 119
Analogies of Experience
  as expression of the temporal lawfulness of consciousness 110
  the function of 77
anti-category
  the concept of None as 25–8, 30–1
  as exhibition of negativity 12
Anticipations of Perception
  as expression of the temporal lawfulness of consciousness 110
anxiety
  and nihilation 50
  and the "presence" of Nothingness 50, 56–8
appearance/phenomenon
  and Being 15, 47–8, 111
  the concept of negative "phenomenon" 25
  as correlate of an ontological representation 23–5
  and Nothingness 15, 25, 47–8, 51
  phenomenal reality as quantum 41
  the principle of the affinity of appearances and its relation to Imagination and Apperception 70
apperception
  and Imagination 69–70
  Inner Sense as empirical apperception vs. transcendental apperception 33
  the temporal structure of transcendental apperception 33–5

transcendental apperception and noumenon 36
transcendental apperception and transcendental unity 33–4
Aristotle 13, 39, 55, 80, 96
association and imagination 69
Augustine 80
Axioms of Intuition and their function within experience 108

Baumgarten 17
Being (see also Nothingness, Non-Being)
  and the categories 2–3
  the circle between Being and Time 13, 54, 59, 82, 84, 96, 116
  and existence 4, 6, 87
  forgetfulness of Being 4–6
  as highest genus of entities 4
  and the im-possible 111, 123 n.80
  and its metaphysical notion 2–3
  and language 3–5, 7
  and Logos 16, 96, 113, 122
  Nothingness as the essential otherness of Being 14, 124
  Nothingness as negation of Being in its possibility 98
  Nothingness as negation of the Being of entities 5, 46
  Nothingness as such as the Nothing of Being as such 5
  and phenomena 15, 111
  possible-being and real-being 64
  as such 4–19
  and Temporality [*Temporalidad, Zeitlichkeit*] 53, 82, 84–5, 88, 122, 124
  the Temporality [*Temporariedad, Temporalität*] of Being 14
  and Thinking 45, 124–5
  time as meaning of Being 12, 115–24
  and the understanding of it 2–3, 16, 87

Index of Names and Subjects

the understanding of Being qua Being 87
the understanding of Being qua degree of reality 53
the understanding of Being and the *ens extramundanum* 122
the understanding of Being and the im-possible 123 n.80
the understanding of Being and inauthentic Existence 87
Bergson 75 n.48

The Categories
the categories of modality and their function within experience 103–6
the categories of modality and the *nihil negativum* 94
the categories of modality and Nothingness 94–6
the categories of modality and their ontological continuum 120
the categories of modality and their ontological origin 95
the "categories" of Nothingness (see Anti-category) 89
the categories of quality and absolute negation 43–4
the categories of quality and Nothingness 39
the categories of quality and privation 39–40
the categories of quantity and Nothingness 24–5
the categories of relation and their determining function of temporal ordering 76–81
the category of negation and the absence of real objects 41
the category of reality and the appearance of the real object 41
the function of the categories within experience 31
the function of Time in categorial synthesis 29, 106–7
and language 1–7
as manifestations of Absolute Spirit 2
Nothingness as expression of the ontological categories 23–4
and ontological presuppositions 2
and schemata 17, 107
the use of the categories and noumena 31
circle
between Being and Time 13–18, 54, 82–4, 116
between Being and Time, consequences for the meaning of "possible" and "impossible" 96, 116
between Nothingness and Time 13, 15, 54–9, 123
concepts (see also Categories)
the emptiness of the object as annihilation of the possibility of 92, 101
the function of schemata in relation to 71, 73, 76
and images 74
Nothingness as object of a self-contradictory concept 97, 101
as rules 74, 76
and schemata 72, 76
the temporal meaning of 114
of the understanding and noumena 31
of the understanding and their ordering function in experience 73
of the understanding and their purely intelligible function 31 n.32
continuity of Time 55
contradiction
and the laws of Time 114
and Logos 113–14
the Principle of Non-contradiction and the im-possible 92, 96, 99ff, 114
the Principle of Non-contradiction and judgment 100
the Principle of Non-contradiction and logical or ontological possibility 99, 102
the Principle of Non-contradiction and the *nihil negativum* 92
the Principle of Non-contradiction and Nothingness 92, 97
the Principle of Non-contradiction and the possible 92, 96, 116

degree
as intensive magnitude 52
and its temporal apprehension 52–3
and negation 41–2

and qualities 43
and reality 41–2
and sensation 41, 43, 52
and the structure of Temporality 53
the understanding of Being as a degree of reality 53–4
direction of time 55–7
the disappearance of direction in the course of time 85–6

Eigler 55 n.35
ens extramundanum
and Experience 122
and the im-possible 96
as "Intelligible Being" 122
as *nihil negativum* 123
and the Temporality of Nothingness 124
as the transcendentally possible 123
and the understanding of Being 122
ens imaginarium
and the categories 17
as empty intuition without object 61
the ideal character of 65
as impeding the understanding of the authentic Temporality of Nothingness 88–9
as mere form of intuition without substance 79
as merely formal object 41
and the *nihil negativum* 92
and the *nihil privativum* 88–9
as Non-Being 82
Nothingness as 17, 61–89
as originating from the Imagination 64
as pure intuition 63
as pure Time or Space 61
as Something deprived of substance 84
the temporal structure of 76–89
ens rationis
and the categories 17
and the *nihil negativum* 91–2
Nothingness as 21–38
entity
and Being 4–14
and Nothingness 18–19
Nothingness as the negation of 5, 46
and the Word 6–8

eternity
symbolized by the "static now" (nunc stans) 80, 85
Euclid 100–1
existence
authenticity and inauthenticity as modes of existence 7
as condition of Time 58
inauthentic existence and the conception of Time 87
inauthentic existence and its understanding of Being 87
the states of thrownness and falling, and forgetfulness of Being or Nothingness 6
Experience
the conditions of the possibility of Experience and ontological possibility 110
the conditions of the possibility of Experience and their relation to Time 110
and the *ens extramundanum* 122
the formal conditions of, and possibility 102, 105
and the im-possible 113, 122
the Logos of Being as intelligible structure of Experience 113
the Logos of Experience and the Logos of Reason 122–5
the material conditions of, and reality 105
and matter 122 n.77
and the negativity of Nothingness 122
and Nothingness 111
and perception 122 n.77
and presence 117
the Principle of the possibility of, and objective reality 94, 101
as sphere of ontological objectification 111
and Time 117, 122

fiction and Nothingness 21–2
finitude
of existence 51, 58, 86–8
of Time 58–9, 86–8
and the Word 8–10

form as negative 24
freedom and its autonomy in the practical "I" 33

Hamsun 7 n.8
Hegel 2–3, 11 n.18, 45, 46 n.13–14
Heidegger 4–7, 12, 13 n.22, 37, 50, 58 n.41, 75 n.48, 87
Herz 28 n.21
Huidobro 57
Hume 32
Husserl 55 n.35, 56 n.37, 75 n.48

image (see also "imagination")
  and concept 74
  the diverse modalities of 66
  as generated by the faculty of Imagination 66, 70
  and object 67
  and presentation 66, 72, 74–5
  pure and empirical 67
  as pure image 75
  as pure temporal presentation 76
  and schema 64–6, 71–4
  Temporality of the ens imaginarium as pure de-substantialized image 81–2
  time and space as pure images 64, 66, 75
imagination
  and apperception 70
  and association 69
  the function of imagination within Experience 68
  as fundamental faculty of the human soul 71
  as an intermediate faculty between sensibility and understanding 70
  and Nothingness 64–74
  as place of origin of the ens imaginarium 64
  productive and reproductive imagination 64 n.12, 69
  as the productive faculty of images 66, 70
  and schemata 64
  and the schematism 65, 74
  and sensibility 68–9
  and Temporality 62
  and understanding 73–8

impossibility (see also "impossible")
  absolute impossibility and ontological impossibility 124
  logical impossibility and ontological impossibility 123 n.80
  ontological impossibility and the principle of the possibility of Experience 94–5
  ontological impossibility and space 101, 110
  and schematism 110
  the schema of im-possibility 115
  the schema of im-possibility as inadequate for interpreting Nothingness 118–19
the impossible
  as contradictory structure of Logos 96–7, 113–14
  as deficient modality of Being 112
  as empty object without concept 111–2
  and the *ens extramundanum* 96, 122–4
  and Experience 113, 122
  and the intelligible 122
  and its objective structure 112
  and its ontological-categorial character 120
  and its representation 112
  and Logos 96, 112–23
  and negativity 121–2
  and the *nihil negativum* 123 n.80
  as non-being 113
  as Nothingness 91–125, 115, 119–20, 123 n.80
  as noumenon 120, 123 n.80
  as an object unthinkable-because-untrue 96
  as objectification of Being 111–2
  and the principle of non-contradiction 92–101
  as privation of the possible 112
  and Reason 121, 123–5
  as structure of the object 92
  the temporal structure of the impossible 96, 109, 115
  as transcendental possibility 123
  and the understanding of Being 123 n.80
  as unthinkable or a-logical object 112

infinitude
    of time 55, 86
    of time as negation of its original finitude 87
    of time and Nothingness 86

instant (see also "now")
    "filled" by a sensation, as reality 53 n.31
    as limit of Time 55 n.34
    as ontological-temporal concretization of the representation of Time 117
    the series of instants of ontological Time as always marked by a reality 53
    the Time of Nothingness as not having individualized instants 56-7

The Intellect (see also Understanding, Reason, The Categories)
    and the hypothesis of the *intellectus archetypus* 28
    the *intellectus echtypus* 28

The intelligible
    and the im-possible 122
    the negativity of the intelligible 123

intuition
    the axioms of intuition and the possible 108
    the axioms of intuition and its temporal meaning 108
    empty or pure form of intuition as Nothing 64-5, 75
    ens imaginarium as empty intuition without object 61, 64
    and imagination 69
    intellectual intuition in the *intellectus archetypus* 28
    and Nothingness 21
    and the noumenon 21
    and schemata 71
    and Time 117
    Time and Space as pure intuitions 62-5

irreversibility of Time 55

judgment and the Principle of Non-contradiction 100 n.15

knowledge
    and objective reality 25
    and thought 22

language (see also The Word)
    and the categories 1-4
    the "failure" of language 125
    metaphysical language and the forgetfulness of Being 5-6
    and negation 11
    and Nothingness 10-1
    ontological language and its difficulties qua expressive instrument 49, 58 n.40
    and Thought 12

Leibniz 17 n.25

Locke 32

logic as ontology 45

Logos
    and Being 16
    of Being as intelligible structure of the objects of Experience 113
    of Being and the possible 113-25
    and conceptual contradiction 113-14
    and the im-possible 96-7, 113-25
    and its apophantic or phenomenological function 16
    and Nothingness 16
    as positive negativity of Reason 16
    of Reason and Experience 122-5
    and Time 115-25, 117-18
    and Truth 122
    the twofold possibility in the structure of 114

magnitude (see also "quantity")
    intensive magnitude and degree 52
    and its concept in general 29
    and its temporal meaning 29, 114
    positive and negative 29-30
    Time as pure image of intensive magnitudes 53 n.31

material/matter
    and Experience 122 n.77
    and negation 41
    and reality 41
    sensation as matter of the phenomenal object 62
    "transcendental matter" of dream phenomena as absolute negativity 49

meaningfulness
　the loss of meaningfulness in the instrumental character of Time 56–7, 85, 119
　the loss of meaningfulness and Nothingness 56–7
modality (see also The Categories)
　the categories of modality and their determination of Time 107
　the categories of modality and their function within Experience 103–11
　the categories of modality and Nothingness 95
　the categories of modality and their ontological continuum 120

the necessary and its temporal structure 116–17
negation (see also "negativity")
　as absence of sensation 41
　absolute negation and the ontological categories of quality 44
　absolute negation and its aporia 44
　as category of Nothingness 44
　as expression of the Non-Being of something in the substance 88–9
　and its schematism 51–4
　and language 11
　and matter 41
　and the nihil privativum 41–53
　and nihilation 50
　and Non-Being 11
　and the "Not" 50
　ontological negation and the absolute negativity of Nothingness 46, 51
　ontological negation and Nothingness 5, 11, 14, 46, 50
　as ontological positing 11, 46–7, 118
　as ontological privation, not an authentic Nothing 88–9
　as presence of negative qualities 47
　as a priori condition of the possibility for Experience 42, 44, 47
　as quality 46
　of Something as Nothing 40
　and the structure of time 53 n.31
　as zero or absence of degree of sensation 41, 53 n.31

negativity (see also "negation")
　as absence or lack of intuition 28
　as absolute emptiness of sensation 48
　of the categories of quality 53
　and dream phenomena 49
　and the im-possible 121–4
　and the intelligible 123
　and its temporal meaning 51, 54
　and the *nihil negativum* 51, 122 n.77
　and Nothingness 15, 45–6, 49, 50–1, 54, 85, 89, 122 n.77, 123
　and Reason 123–4
nihil negativum (see also Nothingness)
　and the categories of modality 95
　as empty object without concept 91, 101
　as *ens extramundanum* 123–4
　and the ens imaginarium 92–3
　and the ens rationis 91–2
　and the im-possible 123 n.80
　and its ontological structure 94–5
　and logical or ontological possibility 99
　and negativity 51, 123–4
　and the nihil privativum 92
　as Non-Being 123 n.80, 124
　as Nothingness 17, 91, 94, 111
　as noumenon 120
　as opposed to possibility 91–2
　and the Principle of Non-contradiction 92–102
　as the transcendentally possible 123
nihil privativum (see also Nothingness)
　and the degree of sensation 42
　and the ens imaginarium 88
　and its phenomenal structure 42–5
　and negation 42, 51
　and the *nihil negativum* 91–2
　as non-existent object 41
　as Nothing 17, 39, 47
　and privation 39
　as Something 43–4
nihilation
　and anxiety 50
　and the fading of the real world 56, 85
　and negation 50
　and Nothingness 49–50, 85, 88
　the structure of Time experienced in 56

Non-Being (see also Nothingness, Being)
   as ens imaginarium 82
   as the im-possible 111, 115
   and negation 11
   as *nihil negativum* 123 n.80
   and Nothingness 46–7, 123–4
   and ontological Temporality 118
   as privation of Being 54
None
   as anti-category 25–31
   and its relation to negative magnitudes 30
   and its relation to Nothingness 24–30
   the quantitative categorial concept of None 24
The "Not" and negation, nihilation, and anxiety 50–1
Nothingness/Nothing
   as abseity 49
   and absence 119
   and anxiety 49–51
   as boundary concept 21
   and The Categories 2, 23
   and the categories of modality 95
   and the categories of quantity 25–31, 29
   and the categories of quality 39–51
   the circle between Nothingness and Time 15, 54, 59, 124
   and the concept of None 24–30
   and deep sleep 48–9, 88
   as dissolution of the world 119
   as empty concept 21, 23
   as empty intuition 65, 75
   as empty object of a concept 42
   empty Time as aspect of 119
   and the *ens extramundanum* 96
   and the ens imaginarium 61–89
   and entity 4–5, 46, 50–1
   as the essential otherness of Being 15, 50, 124
   and Existence 49–51, 58, 86
   and Experience 110–1, 122 n.77
   as expression of an absurdity or contradiction 97
   as exteriorization of the impossibility of Thought 97–8
   as fiction 21
   and finitude 51, 58–9, 86
   and the finitude of Time 58–9
   and Imagination 65–89
   as the im-possible 91–124, 114, 117, 118, 122–3
   and the infinitude of Time 86–7
   and intuition 21–30
   and its "categories" 89
   and its ontological representation 5, 24, 46
   and its qualities 46–7
   as lack of an object 21, 23, 40
   and language 10
   and Logos 16
   and the loss of meaningfulness 56, 119
   as negating Form 24
   as negation 5, 11, 14–15, 40, 46, 50–1, 89, 98
   as negation of Being in its possibility 98
   as negative determination of a quantity 29
   and negativity 14–18, 26, 30, 38, 43, 46–56, 85, 89, 122 n.77, 123
   and the negativity of Reason 124
   and nihilation 49–51, 88
   and the *nihil negativum* 91–125
   and the nihil privativum 39–59
   and Non-Being 5, 50, 123–4
   the non-cessation of Time in experience of 119
   as the Nothing of Being qua Being 5
   and the noumenon 21, 25, 36
   and object 40
   as object of a self-contradictory concept 91, 98, 101
   and objective reality 21, 28
   and the ontological difference 5, 18
   as "phenomenon" 15, 25, 47–8, 51
   and possibility 21
   and the Principle of Non-contradiction 92–102
   and privation 42, 88–9
   as privation of positive qualities 46
   as problematic and limiting concept 28
   as pure image 75
   and the schema of im-possibility 118
   and schematism 65, 76
   and Something 24, 40, 44, 50

Index of Names and Subjects

the Temporality of Nothingness 1, 14–15, 18, 25, 37–8, 58–9, 79, 85, 88, 118
the Temporality of Nothingness as ens imaginarium 76, 79
the Temporality of Nothingness or Non-Being 115
the Temporality of Nothingness as Nothingness of Being as such 14
the Temporality of Nothingness qua noumenon 26–7, 36–7
the Temporality of Nothingness and its ontological basis 81
the Temporality of Nothingness qua purely negative schematism 18
as testimony to the finitude of Existence 51
as thing in itself 22
and thought 12, 45, 97
and Time 13, 110–1, 118–20
and the understanding of Being 3, 45–6
the understanding of Nothingness 6, 15, 46
and the understanding of Time 54, 85, 88, 118
as Zero 30
noumenon (see also ens rationis)
as boundary concept 21–3
and the categories 31
as the im-possible 122 n.77
and inner sense 32–3, 37
and intuition 21, 98
and its objective reality 21, 23
and its temporal structure 27, 31, 36–7, 120
and its twofold modality 22
as *nihil negativum* 120
as Nothingness 21, 26–8, 36
and the object 22
and possibilities 98
and the Principle of Non-contradiction 97–8
as pure form without content 23
and Pure Reason 37
as representation 23, 31
and schematism 26–7
now (see also "instant")
the disappearance of 85–6
and "instant" 55

static now (nunc stans) as symbol of eternity 80 n.67
Time as static now 80, 84–5
Time as uninterrupted series of *nows* 87
number
and its temporal meaning 29
as schema of the categories of quantity 29, 52–3

object
the emptiness of the object as cancellation of the possibility of the concept 92, 101
the im-possible as object 92, 111
the Logos of Being as intelligible structure of the objects of Experience 113
the modes of being an object (possible, actual, necessary) and the conditions of Experience 103–4
the *nihil negativum* as object 91, 101
not every "Something" is an object 63
Nothingness as lack of an object 40
the noumenon as no object 22
the object in general as empty "X" 40, 44–5
the object in general and its possibility for appearing as Something or Nothing 40
the object in general as Something 45
as phenomenal correlate of a cognition 22
qua positive "Something" 26
Pure Space and Time as non-objects 61, 62, 67, 68
ontological difference 3–6
and language 5–10
and metaphysics 3
and Nothingness 18
and Time 13–18

perception
the anticipations of perception as expression of the temporal lawfulness of consciousness 110
and Experience 122 n.77
permanence
and its temporal meaning 84, 116
and presence 116
as schema of substance 77

Pfänder 100 n.15
Plato 80 n.67
Plotinus 80 n.67
point as limit of Space 55 n.34
possibility (see also "the possible")
   analytic vs. synthetic 102
   the im-possible as transcendental possibility 122–3
   and its schema 109
   the *nihil negativum* and logical or ontological possibility 99–101
   Nothingness qua noumenon, cannot be counted among the possibilities 21
   and objective reality 104
   ontological possibility and the conditions of the possibility of Experience 110
   ontological possibility and the synthesis of Experience 102–3, 105–6
   the Principle of Non-contradiction and logical or ontological possibility 99, 102
   and reality/actuality 122 n.77
   and Reason 123–4
   and Temporality 95–6
the possible (see also "possibility")
   and the axioms of intuition 108
   and Experience 102, 104, 121–2
   and the intelligible 98
   and its temporal structure 108, 114
   and the Logos of Being 113–14
   possible-being and real-being 64
   and the Principle of Non-contradiction 92–102
   the privation of the possible as the im-possible 112
   the transcendentally possible as *ens extramundanum* 123
   the transcendentally possible as *nihil negativum* 123
The Postulates of Empirical Thinking (see also "modality") and their ontological origin 95
presence
   as the absolute presence of transcendental apperception and *supratemporality* 34
   as the "Being" of Time 116–19
   as degree of sensation 41
   and experience 117
   and permanence 116
privation
   and the categories of quality 39
   and Nothingness 42, 46–54
   as qualitative modification of Something 40
   as quantitative degree of sensation 40
   relation between the Kantian and Aristotelian conception of privation 39
   and schematism 40

quality (see also The Categories)
   the categories of quality and absolute negativity 53–4
   and the data of sensations 43
   negation as negative quality 44
   Nothingness as privation of positive qualities 46
   positive and negative 47–54
   the qualities of Nothingness 46
   the unity of positive qualities as constitutive of Something 43
quantity (see also "magnitude," The Categories)
   the categories of quantity and their temporal structure 29
   extensive magnitudes and the schema of possibility 109
   Nothingness qua negative determination of a quantity 25, 29
   positive magnitudes 25

the real/actual (see also "reality," "objective reality")
   the actual and its temporal structure 116–17
   and Experience 105
   possible-being and real-being 64
reality/actuality (see also "objective reality")
   and its schema 41, 52
   the negation of reality as Nothing 40
   negative "objective reality" 29
   objective reality and knowledge 25–6
   objective reality and Nothingness 21, 28

objective reality and noumena 21, 23
objective reality and possibility 104
objective reality and the principle of
    the possibility of Experience 94,
    101
phenomenal reality as quantum 41
and possibility 122 n.77
as a priori condition of the possibility
    of Experience 42
as *realitas phaenomenon* 42
and sensation 41–2
as Something 40
and Time 53, 55
and the understanding of Being 53–4
Reason
    and the im-possible 121–4
    and Logos 122–3
    and negativity 123–4
    and Non-Being 121
    and the noumenon 37
    and possibility 122 n.77
    Pure Reason and Time 31, 33–4
    the Temporality of Reason 122–4
relation (see also The Categories)
    the categories of relation and their
        determinative function of temporal
        ordering 76–81
    the categories of relation and their
        schemata 77
representation
    and inner sense 32
    the noumenon as representation 31

schemata (see also "schematism,"
    Temporality, Time)
    of the categories of relation 77
    and images 64–6, 71, 74, 76
    and Imagination 62, 64
    and their nature 71
    as a priori determinations of Time
        73–4, 107
    the schema of magnitude 29
    the schema of possibility and extensive
        magnitudes 109
    the schema of reality 41
    and their function within Experience
        67–81
    and their function in relation to
        intuition and concepts 71, 76, 106

schematism (see also "schemata,"
    Temporality, Time)
    and the categories 106
    and the categories of modality 95,
        107–8, 116, 120
    and the categories of quality 52
    as expression of the temporal
        lawfulness of consciousness 110
    and images 65–81
    and Imagination 65–70
    and im-possibility 115
    and inner sense 107
    and its function within Experience
        71, 74
    and negation 52, 54
    and negativity 52, 54
    and Nothingness 18, 26–7, 65–6, 76,
        79, 95
    and the ontological categories 17
    and possibility 109, 114–15
    and the primacy of ontological
        presuppositions 53–4
    and privation 40
    and Time 17, 74, 107, 110
sensation
    and deep sleep 48–9
    and degree 41, 43, 53, 54
    the degrees of sensation and quality 43
    the emptiness of sensations and its
        apprehension 48
    and inner sense 41, 53
    and its diminution as gradated reality
        54
    and its function as content of Time
        52–3
    and negation 40–2
    and negativity 48
    and privation 39
    as *realitas phaenomenon* 62
    and reality 41
Sense, Inner (see also Time)
    and the categories 106
    as Empirical Apperception, and its
        distinction from Transcendental
        Apperception 33–7
    the Logos of inner sense and its
        temporal structure 115
    and noumena 32
    and privation 40

as pure succession of consecutive *nows* 78
and representations 32
and schematism 73, 107
and sensations 41, 53
as Time 32
sleep
  dreamlike experiences and language 49
  and the experience of "emptiness" 48–9
  and the fading of the real world 56–7, 85
  and Nothingness 48–50, 85, 88
  and sensations 48–9
  and the structure of Time 56–8, 85–6
Something
  and negation 43
  as not always an object 63
  Nothingness as negation of Something 40–8
  object in general as Something 40, 45
  the ontological representation of Nothingness as ingredient of Something 24
  as opposed to Nothing 24–36
  as positive Something 26, 43
  privation qua qualitative modification of Something 40
  as reality 40–7
Space
  as absolute 63
  empty space and its empirical im-possibility 53
  the ens imaginarium as pure Space 61
  and its temporal meaning 109 n.53
  as mere possibility 65
  and ontological im-possibility 100, 110
  the ontological structure of, as pure intuition 63
  as pure form of the phenomenal object 62
  as pure image 64–70
  as pure intuition 62–3
  pure space exists "objectively" 62
  pure space as no object 61, 62–3, 67–8
  the temporalization of 75
  and Time, as quanta continua 55
subjectivity 32–3
substance
  and change 78–9, 82–4
  and its schema 77, 84
  the lack of substance in the ens imaginarium 76, 81, 84
  and negation 89
  as permanent substratum 78–9
  as the real in appearances 78
  Time and its determination as substance 83–7
succession/successivity
  as ingredient of Being or Nothingness 81–2, 88
  as ordering aspect of appearances 72–80
synthesis
  figurative or *synthesis speciosa* 106
  knowledge as synthesis of form and matter 25

Temporality [*Temporariedad, Temporalität*] (see also Temporality [*Temporalidad, Zeitlichkeit*])
  of Being 14
  of Nothingness qua Nothing of Being as such 14
  of Nothingness qua purely negative schematism 18
Temporality [*Temporalidad, Zeitlichkeit*] (see also Temporality [*Temporariedad, Temporalität*])
  and the actual and necessary 110, 116–17
  and the analogies of experience 110–1
  and the anticipations of perception 110–1
  and appearances/phenomena 75
  and Being 53–4, 81, 122
  and the categories of relation 76–81
  and the conditions of the possibility of Experience 110, 114
  and degree 53–4
  and the ens imaginarium 76, 79, 84, 88
  everyday and vulgar Temporality 37
  and Experience 117, 121–2
  and finitude 58–9, 86–8
  and Imagination 62
  and the im-possible 95–6, 109–24
  non-presentative Temporality 85
  and Nothingness 14, 18, 25, 37, 51, 57, 75–6, 79, 85, 88, 115, 118, 124

and noumena 27, 31
ontological Temporality 13, 17, 53–4
original Temporality 37
and permanence 82–5
and the possible 95–6, 109–23
and the pure "I" 35–8
and Reason 31, 34, 121–5
and schematism 110
and substance 82
Temporality without direction 85, 119
Temporality without "*nows*" 85, 119
and Transcendental Apperception 33–8
transcendental Temporality 37
and the World 56, 119
thing in itself and Nothingness 22
Thought
  and knowledge 22
  and language 11
  and Nothingness 12, 45–6, 97–8
  ontological 11–2, 45–6, 124–5
Time
  and the axioms of intuition 108
  and its "Being" as presence 116–19
  and the categories 29, 106
  and the categories of modality 107–23
  and the conditions of the possibility of Experience 110
  and continuity 55, 58
  and deep sleep 56–8, 85
  and the direction of its course 55–7
  "empty" Time as impossible to conceive 53, 83
  and the ens imaginarium 61, 80–9
  and Existence 58
  and Experience 117–23
  and the fading of the world 56, 85
  as horizon of possibility and impossibility 115–24
  and ideal entities 36–7
  as *intraworldly* entity 55, 87
  and intuition 118
  and irreversibility 55
  and its determination as substance 83–4
  and its finitude 58–9, 86
  and its infinitude 55, 58, 86
  and its instrumental character 56
  and its onto-logical structure 54, 83–4, 116, 118–24

  and its preeminent function in schematism 74–5
  and its preeminent function with respect to Space 74–5
  and its quantification 55
  and its spatialization 75 n.48, 87 n.82
  and its structure as pure successivity 79–80, 81–8
  and its understanding from the point of view of Being 12–13, 53–6, 83–4, 87–9, 115–18
  and its understanding from the point of view of Nothingness 54–9, 85–9, 118–24
  and Logos 115–23, 117, 118
  as the meaning of Being 12, 116
  as the meaning of phenomena 118
  as the meaning of Space 109 n.53
  as mere possibility 65
  as neither an entity nor property of entities 37
  as neither subsisting for itself nor pertaining to things in themselves 77–8
  as no object 61–2, 67–8, 77
  as not itself elapsing 80–1
  and Nothingness 12–13, 56, 111, 118–20
  and the ontological difference 13–18
  and the ordering of appearances 72–6
  and permanence 35–6
  and the Principle of Non-contradiction 115–16
  and privation 39–40
  Pure and "empty" Time 84
  as pure form of the phenomenal object 62–80
  as pure image 53 n.31, 64, 66, 75
  as pure image of intensive magnitudes 53 n.31
  as pure intuition 63–8, 86
  and Pure Reason 31, 34
  and real entities 37
  real and everyday 56
  and reality 53, 55
  and schemata 73–81, 107–11, 115–18
  and transcendental unity 33
  as uninterrupted series of *nows* 55, 78–80, 87
  worldly and vulgar 56 n.36

Understanding (see also The Categories, "concepts") and Imagination 73–8
Unity of Apperception (empirical) as temporal continuum 33
Unity of Apperception (transcendental) and its atemporal character 33

Vaihinger 108 n.46

Wittgenstein 8
Wolff 17 n.25
The Word (see also language)
    and Being 4–9
    and the entity 6–8
    and finitude 8–11
    and the forgetfulness of Being 4–6
    and meaningfulness 7–8
    and Nothingness 5, 7, 10–1
    and the ontological difference 5–10
    and the World 7–8
world
    the fading of 56, 85, 119
    the fading of, and the structure of Time 56 n.36, 119–22
    and The Word 7–8

www.ingramcontent.com/pod-product-compliance
Lightning Source LLC
Chambersburg PA
CBHW052115300426
44116CB00010B/1675